Inheritance Claims and Challenges

CALLOW PUBLISHING

Inheritance Claims and Challenges

A Guide to Claims under the Inheritance Act

with

a Short Introduction to Challenging Testamentary Dispositions

by
Nazreen Pearce

London
Callow Publishing
2004

ISBN 1 898899 71 1

Printed and Bound in Great Britain by MPG Books Ltd, Bodmin, Cornwall.

Published by Callow Publishing Limited,
4 Shillingford Street,
London N1 2DP
www.callowpublishing.com

Foreword

It is trite that the one certainty in life is death. It is equally certain that the one class of litigation most likely to be even more acrimoniously contested than a boundary dispute is the dispute over the disposition of a deceased person's estate. All the more essential it is, therefore, that practitioners have at hand a concise yet complete work to which they may turn to find ready answers to the seemingly intractable problems presented by their clients so bristling with righteous indignation.

Nazreen Pearce had provided the solution. Drawing upon her considerable experience from practice at the Bar, as a District Judge in the Principal Registry and now as a Circuit Judge, she has in this one volume comprehensively dealt with all issues practitioners would ordinarily expect to confront – and many more besides. The Judge's approach is robustly practical. The text is characteristically cogent and authoritatively stated. Casting a quick eye down the Contents enables the point to be identified swiftly. The precedents give helpful guidance. What more could a busy practitioner want?

This is an admirable work which I shall use and which I warmly commend.

Sir Alan Ward
Lord Justice of Appeal

Preface

The Inheritance (Provision for Family and Dependants) Act 1975 has been the subject of interpretation in recent years, in response not only to the continuing high divorce rate, but also as a consequence of social changes, such as the greater number of couples cohabiting without marrying, increasing awareness and acceptance of same-sex couples, and the impact of the European Convention on Human Rights and Fundamental Freedoms. The law has developed considerably in the last decade and is likely to continue to evolve along with changes in family law generally and, more particularly, in the provisions relating to adoption and to financial provision pursuant to the divorce jurisdiction and under the Children Act 1989, and developments under the Human Fertilisation and Embryology Act 1990.

The more immediate changes which will undoubtedly occur very shortly are those relating to transsexuals and same-sex couples, when the Gender Recognition Bill and the Civil Partnership Bill become law. The provisions of both Bills have been dealt with only briefly in this book, as there are bound to be amendments to the Bills as they progress through Parliament. Practitioners are advised to refer to the statutes when the proposed legislation becomes law.

This work also includes a "bird's eye view" of challenges which can be made to testamentary provisions. It is hoped that this will be useful to draw to the attention of claimants and practitioners that, alongside any possible claim under the 1975 Act, it may also be possible to challenge the validity of a testamentary provision by reference to the formal statutory requirements, by bringing a probate claim or a civil claim against the estate of the deceased, for example, by applying the doctrine of proprietary estoppel. Claims of this type may be becoming more common. As this book goes to press, there are news reports of a challenge to the will of a wealthy man who died unexpectedly; it is said that his will, which favours his second wife over the children of his first marriage, was made under duress.

The purpose of this work is to provide a user-friendly, straightforward guide to the law, practice and procedure relating to inheritance claims and challenging testamentary dispositions, but it is not intended to be an academic study or an exhaustive commentary on the law on these subjects. In particular, where a summary of case law is provided it is merely to illustrate the point raised and it is advised that in all instances the full report should be studied.

The law set out is as at March 2004.

I would like to thank Keith Biggs, District Probate Registrar at Winchester, who provided useful suggestions which have been included in the text.

Finally, I would like to express my appreciation to Lord Justice Alan Ward for writing the Foreword.

Nazreen Pearce
June 2004

Contents

PART I: A GUIDE TO INHERITANCE CLAIMS

PART II: A SHORT INTRODUCTION TO CHALLENGING TESTAMENTARY DISPOSITIONS

Table of Cases

Table of Legislation

PART I

A GUIDE TO INHERITANCE CLAIMS

Chapter 1

Introduction

Background

It has long been a characteristic of English law that, provided a person has testamentary capacity and complies with the formalities relating to the making of a valid will, he may dispose of his entire estate on death as he chooses, and his estate will devolve in accordance with the terms of the will. If a person dies without having made a will, or leaving a will which is not valid, the law relating to intestacy operates and the estate devolves in accordance with that law. If the will does not dispose of the entirety of the estate, then the property devolves in part in accordance with the terms of the will, and the remainder passes under the law of intestacy.

Statutes have, however, made inroads into this freedom. The first statutory provision to do so was the Inheritance (Family Provision) Act 1938 ("the 1938 Act"). It applied to the estates of persons dying after 13 July 1939 who were domiciled in England and Wales. The 1938 Act introduced into English law the concept of reasonable testamentary provision and provided for the maintenance of dependants out of the deceased's estate. The Intestates' Estates Act 1952 amended the 1938 Act. The most important change was the extension of the 1938 Act to cases where the deceased was intestate. It also permitted the court to award to a surviving spouse the whole of the income of the net estate; increased the amount of the lump sum order which could be made; provided for the extension of the six months' time limit in certain circumstances; and made provisions for the protection of personal representatives.

The Matrimonial Causes Act 1965, sections 26 to 28, made provisions for a former spouse to apply for an order for maintenance from the deceased's estate on the ground that the deceased had not made reasonable provision for the survivor's maintenance after the deceased's death. The Family Provision Act 1966 further amended the 1938 Act, most importantly by extending the jurisdiction to hear such claims to the county courts where the value of the net estate did not exceed £5,000.

The Inheritance (Provision for Family and Dependants) Act 1975

The Inheritance (Provision for Family and Dependants) Act 1975 ("the 1975 Act"), which came into force on 1 April 1976, repealed the previous enactments and made comprehensive provisions for the court to make orders out of the estate of a deceased in favour of the dependants of the deceased as categorised in the Act. Section 15 of the Act was extended by the Matrimonial and Family Proceedings Act 1984 to give the court power, when dealing with a claim under the 1984 Act for financial relief after an overseas divorce, annulment of marriage or legal separation order, to give a direction disentitling the parties from making any claims for an order under the 1975 Act.

The Law Reform (Succession) Act 1995 amended the 1975 Act by extending the classes of person who can apply for financial provision, to include any person (not the spouse or a former spouse of the deceased) who, during the two years immediately preceding the death of the deceased, had been living with the deceased in the same household as the deceased as the husband or wife of the deceased.

Further amendments are proposed as the government considers extending the rights enjoyed by married couples to same-sex couples. The Relationships (Civil Registration) Bill (Bill 36 2001–2002) and the Civil Partnership Bill (HL Bill 41 2001–2002) (both of which have been dropped) contained proposals for changes to provide for a system of partnership registration for same-sex, and opposite-sex, cohabitants, to give both partners in such relationships the rights and duties set out in the Bills. Both Bills provided that a registered partner should have rights to inherit some or all of the partner's estate and to apply to the court under the 1975 Act if no financial provision, or inadequate financial provision, had been made for that partner either by will or by the operation of the rules on intestate succession. Under the Relationship (Civil Registration) Bill, a partner would have been treated as the spouse of the deceased partner and thus entitled to such financial provision as would be reasonable in all the circumstances of the case for a husband or wife to receive, whether or not that financial provision was required for his or her maintenance. Under the Civil Partnership Bill, a partner would have been entitled only to such provision as would be reasonable in all the circumstances for that person's maintenance.

In the Queen's Speech in November 2003, the government indicated its commitment to providing same-sex couples equal rights with married couples. The government has now published the Civil Partnership Bill (HL 53 2004). It contains proposals to enable same-sex couples to make formal commitments to each other by registering as civil partners of each other. The provisions contained in the Bill would give same-sex couples who enter into civil partnerships the same rights as those enjoyed by married heterosexual couples, including the right to claim maintenance, the ability to succeed to tenancy rights and testamentary and inheritance rights. It envisages the amendment of sections 1, 2, 3, 6, 14, 15, 16, 17, 18 and 19 of the 1975 Act, so as to apply the existing law relating to married couples, to same-sex couples who have entered into civil partnerships. The precise nature of the rights to which they will be entitled generally, and more specifically under the 1975 Act, remains to be seen when the proposed legislation receives Royal Assent.

The 1975 Act, as amended, governs claims by specified dependants of a deceased person, against the estate of the deceased who died domiciled in England and Wales, on the ground that the disposition of the deceased's estate effected by his will or the law of intestacy, or the combination of his will and that law, is not such as to make reasonable financial provision for the claimant (see Chapter 4). Thus a claim arises only if it can be established that:

(a) the deceased died domiciled in England and Wales;
(b) the claimant is one of the restricted classes of person, set out in section 1(1) of the 1975 Act as amended, who has a right to make a claim (see Chapter 3); and
(c) the deceased failed to make reasonable financial provision for the claimant.

In the definition of "financial provision", the Act makes a distinction between a surviving spouse and other claimants. In the case of a surviving spouse, it means such financial provision as it would be reasonable in all the circumstances of the case for the surviving spouse to receive, whether or not that provision is required for his or her maintenance. In respect of all other claimants, it means such financial provision as it would be reasonable for the claimant to receive for his maintenance (section 1(2); see page 57).

If the court finds that the deceased has not made reasonable financial provision for the claimant, then, in determining whether and in what manner the court should exercise its powers under the Act, it is required to have regard to the matters set out in section 3 as amended (see Chapter 5). The orders which the court may make are set out in section 2 of the Act. The court also has powers to vary, discharge or suspend orders made for periodical payments under section 2(1)(a) and a limited power to vary a lump sum order. Secured periodical payments orders made under the Matrimonial Causes Act 1973 and maintenance agreements may also be varied or discharged. See Chapter 6.

The orders made by the court under the Act may be met only out of the net estate of the deceased as defined by section 25(1) of the Act. Sections 8 and 9 make further provisions for other property to be regarded as part of the net estate of the deceased. A claim under section 9, however, must be made within six months from the date on which representation with respect to the deceased's estate was first taken out; the time limit cannot be extended. The court also has powers in relation to transactions entered into by the deceased with the intention of defeating a claim for financial provision under the Act (sections 10 and 11; see Chapter 8).

Save with the leave of the court, a claim for an order under section 2 of the Act cannot be made after the end of six months from the date on which representation with respect to the estate of the deceased is first taken out (section 4; see Chapter 2).

Finally, a claim under the 1975 Act is personal to the claimant, so that if the claimant dies during the course of the proceedings the claim comes to an end and is not enforceable by the personal representatives of the claimant. Only where an order has been made upon a claim is there an enforceable cause of action which can continue to subsist for the benefit of one estate against the other (*Whyte v Ticehurst* [1986] Fam 64, [1986] 2 All ER 158, [1986] 2 WLR 700; and *Re R* (1986) 14 Fam Law 58).

Domicile

Establishing the deceased's domicile does not usually give rise to any difficulty, particularly if the deceased was born in and lived all or the best part of his life in England and Wales. It is none the less important to bear in mind that domicile is the first prerequisite to any claim under the 1975 Act and to the court's assuming jurisdiction. If the deceased died domiciled elsewhere there is no jurisdiction to entertain a claim under the 1975 Act.

Section 27(2) provides that the Act does not extend to Scotland and Northern Ireland.

Domicile is a concept of law which is relevant in many situations where it is necessary to establish which legal system should be applied, particularly those which relate to matters of personal status. There are three types of domicile, namely domicile of origin; domicile of choice; and domicile of dependency.

Domicile of origin

A person acquires a domicile of origin at birth from his parents. A domicile of origin is capable of persisting during the lifetime of the person. The domicile of origin of a legitimate child born during the lifetime of his father is that of the child's father. If the father dies before the child's birth the child acquires the domicile of his mother. An illegitimate child acquires the domicile of his mother at birth. A child's domicile thereafter will change if and when the parent(s) change their domicile. A foundling's domicile of origin is that of the country where he is found.

Domicile of choice

A domicile of choice is acquired when a person leaves his domicile of origin and lives in a country of his choice with the intention of permanently or indefinitely living there. The test is whether the person intended to make his home in the new country until the end of his days and until something happens to change his mind (*IRC v Bullock* [1976] 1 WLR 1178, [1976] 3

All ER 353, [1976] STC 409).

> "Domicile of choice is a conclusion or inference which the law derives from the fact of a man fixing voluntarily his sole or chief residence in a particular place with the intention of continuing to reside there for an unlimited time. This is a description of the circumstances which create or constitute a domicil and not a definition of the term. There must be a residence freely chosen, and not prescribed or dictated by any external necessity, such as the duties of office, the demands of creditors, or the relief from illness; and it must be residence fixed not for a limited period or particular purpose, but general and indefinite in its future contemplation. It is true that residence originally temporary, or intended for a limited period, may afterwards become general and unlimited, and in such a case so soon as the change of purpose, or *animus manendi*, can be inferred the fact of domicil is established." (per Lord Westbury in *Udny v Udny* (1869) 1 LR Sc & Div 441.)

If that person subsequently abandons that domicile and fails to acquire another domicile of choice he reverts to his domicile of origin. Once a child attains the age of sixteen he is able to acquire a domicile of choice independently of his parents.

Domicile of dependency

A child under sixteen or a person who is mentally disabled has a domicile of dependency, which is that of his parents. Where the parents are married and living together the domicile is that of the father. Where the parents are separated, the child's domicile is that of the parent with whom he has his home to the exclusion of the other; for example, if the child lives with his mother he takes his mother's domicile (section 4, Domicile and Matrimonial Proceedings Act 1973).

Evidence of domicile

It is for the claimant to establish that the deceased died domiciled in England and Wales. The evidence generally relied on includes the length of time a person remained in a country; whether he had family ties there; whether he purchased property or acquired a business there; any change of nationality or citizenship; and his involvement with the community:

> "There is no end to the evidence that may be adduced; for the whole of a man's life and all that he has said and done, however trivial, may be prayed upon in aid in determining what his intention was at any given moment of time." (*Re Flynn* [1968] 1 WLR 103, [1968] 1 All ER 49).

The standard of proof required is on the balance of probabilities, but since it is a serious matter, the court is unlikely to infer it from slight indications or casual words.

Statements or declarations made on the application for a grant of representation or by the deceased during his lifetime are not conclusive. In

Re Evans (Deceased), National Provincial Bank v Evans [1947] 1 Ch 695, [1948] LJR 498, the deceased had been born in Wales. He eventually settled in Belgium, but in 1940, during the war, he moved to the south of France and wrote a statement in which he confirmed that he was domiciled in Belgium. The document was accepted as providing evidence that the deceased had not abandoned his domicile of choice in Belgium.

In *Re Liddell-Grainger's Will Trusts* [1936] 3 All ER 173, an English man had moved to Scotland. He lived there for almost four decades before his death. In his will he asserted that he had not abandoned his domicile of origin. It was, however, contended that the statement in the will had been made to avoid the effect of the law in Scotland, which restricted a testator's right to dispose of property. The court held that the deceased's actions during his life and his continued residence in Scotland were strong evidence of his having acquired a domicile of choice in Scotland.

In *Mastaka v Midland Bank Executors and Trustees Co Ltd* [1941] Ch 192, [1941] 1 All ER 236, the deceased testatrix had married a Russian in England. As the law then stood the testatrix, on marriage, acquired the domicile of her husband. His whereabouts at the time of the deceased's death were not known. There was no direct evidence either that he was dead or that he had acquired a domicile of choice in England. In the absence of evidence to the contrary, the deceased was held not to be domiciled in England and Wales.

In *Bheekhun v Williams* [1999] 2 FLR 229, a couple from Mauritius set up home in England. They retained their British nationality when Mauritius became independent. The husband had business interests and property in both England and Mauritius. The couple separated and the wife obtained a decree *nisi*, but before decree absolute and the resolution of her claim for financial relief the husband died leaving his entire estate to his niece. It was contended by the personal representatives that the deceased had retained his domicile of origin and had not acquired a domicile of choice in England. It was held that evidence of the deceased's actions during his lifetime, and taking into consideration his British nationality, the length of his residency in England, and statements that he had made during the divorce proceedings, clearly indicated that the deceased had considered England his domicile of choice.

Residence by itself, even if it is for a long period, without evidence of the necessary intent to abandon the domicile of origin and to remain in the country of choice, does not lead to the acquisition of a domicile of choice. Reference should be made to works on the conflict of laws for the law relating to domicile and on the distinction between habitual residence and domicile. Case law under the Child Abduction and Custody Act 1985, where the issue is frequently raised, may also be relevant.

Where there is or may be any doubt about the deceased's domicile, the evidence upon which it is intended to rely to establish domicile should be stated in the affidavit in support of the claim.

Chapter 2

Time Limits

Introduction

Time limits have always applied to claims for financial provision from a deceased's estate, ever since the right to make such claims was introduced by the Inheritance (Family Provision) Act 1938. The 1938 Act limited the time within which an application could be made to six months from the issue of a grant of representation, with a provision for time to be extended with leave of the court. The Intestates' Estates Act 1952 introduced a provision for the court to extend the time limit of six months in specified circumstances.

The Family Provision Act 1966 repealed the earlier provisions and gave the court a general discretion to extend the limitation period. This provision is now incorporated in the Inheritance (Provision for Family and Dependants) Act 1975, section 4 of which provides that:

> "an application for an order under section 2 of the Act shall not, except with the permission of the court, be made after the end of the period of six months from the date on which representation with respect to the estate of the deceased is first taken out."

It is thus essential that a claim for an order under section 2 of the Act is issued within the prescribed time limit.

Commencement of the Period of Six Months

Section 23 of the 1975 Act provides that, in considering when representation with respect to the estate of a deceased person was taken out, a grant limited to settled land or trust property is to be left out of account; and a grant limited to real estate or to personal estate is to be left out of account unless a grant limited to the remainder of the estate has previously been made or is made at the same time. The Act makes no other provision for determining the date for the commencement of the six months' limitation period, nor does it make any reference to grants which are limited for a particular purpose. Thus, the effects of these grants for the purposes of the time limit under the 1975 Act are unclear. They are dealt with briefly below.

Grant ad colligenda bona

A grant of letters of administration *ad colligenda bona* is applied for when it is necessary to prevent loss to the estate because there is no one authorised to administer it. The grant is limited to the purposes of collecting and getting in and receiving the deceased's estate and doing such acts as may be necessary to preserve the estate, until further representation is granted. The grant ceases when the object for which it was granted has been achieved or a full grant has been issued.

It is submitted that, by reason of its limited nature, a grant *ad colligenda bona* does not operate to start time running in respect of claims under the 1975 Act.

Grant pending determination of a claim

Under the Supreme Court Act 1981, section 117, a limited grant of letters of administration pending determination of a probate claim commenced in the Chancery Division may be issued as a matter of urgency when there is a dispute which gives rise to a probate claim, for example, to determine the validity of a testator's will. In such cases the administrator has all the rights and duties of a general administrator except that he is subject to the immediate control of the court and must act under its direction. The object of this grant is to enable the administrator to collect and safeguard assets pending the outcome of the claim. Once the claim has been determined, the grant terminates and the person entitled as a result of the probate claim may take out a grant of probate or administration.

In this case too it is unlikely that time will begin to run in respect of any claim under the Act, but it would be prudent, if it is intended to make a claim under the 1975 Act, to notify the executors and the beneficiaries of that intention. In some cases it may be desirable to have all issues relating to the deceased's will and estate to be determined by the same tribunal. If a probate claim is pending, the court's direction should be sought. (See also page 12 on claims made before a grant is issued.)

Grant ad litem

A grant *ad litem* enables proceedings to be begun or continued on behalf of the deceased's estate or against it. It is limited to bringing or defending a claim, or otherwise being a party to a claim. Once the proceedings are over, application may be made for a general grant, and on the issue of a general grant the limited grant terminates.

In *Re Johnson (Paul Anthony) (Deceased)* [1987] CLY 3882, a grant limited to solicitors for the purposes of issuing a claim for negligence in respect of the deceased's estate was held not to be the first taking out of representation. On the basis of the decision in *Re Johnson*, a general proposition is often made that a grant *ad litem* does not start time running in respect of claims under the 1975 Act. It is, however, submitted that the decision is not unequivocal, because such a grant may be issued to commence or defend proceedings brought under the 1975 Act itself, and in such circumstances the limitation period should start running as soon as the grant is issued.

On the other hand, such a grant does not allow the administrator to distribute the estate. The administrator may not have full knowledge of the extent and nature of the estate or the identity of the beneficiaries entitled, and therefore time ought not to run. It is submitted that in such cases the practitioner will need to consider the nature of the proceedings in respect of which the grant was issued, and make a decision whether time may begin to run.

If the circumstances are unclear, it may be wise to err on the side of caution; it is suggested that, to avoid any risk, proceedings under the Act should be commenced to protect the client, and, if necessary, adjourned generally or stayed until the outcome of any pending proceedings.

Grant in common form

Where a grant in common form is followed by a grant in solemn form in respect of the same will, time begins to run from the date on which the grant in common form was granted (*Re Miller, Miller v De Courcey* [1969] 1 WLR 583, [1968] 3 All ER 844).

Successive grants

Where letters of administration are replaced by a grant of probate, for example, because a will is subsequently found, time begins to run from the grant of probate (*Re Bidie, Bidie v General Accident Fire and Life Assurance Corporation* [1949] Ch 121, [1948] 2 All ER 995). In *Re Bidie,* the deceased made a will on 10 February 1937. He died on 16 January 1945. The will was not found. On 13 April 1945, letters of administration were issued to his widow and one of their children. The will was later found and probate was granted on 7 September 1946. On 8 January 1947 the widow applied for financial provision under the 1938 Act. Her claim was allowed to proceed as it had been made within six months of the grant of probate.

Similarly, where the grant of probate is revoked and replaced by letters of administration, time begins to run from the grant of letters of administration, because, for the purposes of section 4 of the 1975 Act, time begins to run from the date on which "effective" or "valid" representation was "first taken out" (see *Re Freeman, Weston v Freeman* [1984] 1 WLR 1419, [1984] 3 All ER 906, for the absurd situation which would have prevailed if the court had taken a different view).

De bonis non grant

A grant of letters of administration *de bonis non* is made following the death of the sole or last personal representative who obtained a grant in relation to the estate of the deceased but died before completing its administration. The grant relates only to the estate remaining unadministered. It is a second effective and valid grant, but it does not relate to the whole estate. Time therefore runs from the date of the original grant. (See also *Cessate grant,* below.)

Cessate grant
A *cessate* grant issues when the first grant was conditional or limited and the condition or limitation has been fulfilled, or the grantee dies without fulfilling the purpose for which the grant was made. Unlike a *de bonis non grant*, a *cessate* grant operates in respect of the whole estate. In this case, time begins to run from the original grant, because the second grant is a re-grant.

Standing Search for Grant
To ensure that a claimant is notified of the issue of a grant of representation, facilities are available for a standing search to be made for an office copy of every grant of representation which tallies with the particulars given on the application, and which either was issued in the twelve months before receipt of the application or is issued within six months thereafter.

The application is made by completing Form 2 (see page 230) and sending it to, or lodging it at, any probate registry or sub-registry. The appropriate fee must accompany the application. Where the applicant wishes to extend the period of search, a written application for an extension should be lodged or sent by post to the registry at which the standing search was entered. A standing search which has been extended may be further extended by filing a further application for extension. See the Non-Contentious Probate Rules 1987, SI 1987 No 2024, rule 43, as amended.

It should also be noted that *Practice Direction (Names of Deceased: Death Certificates)* dated 12 January 1999 [1999] 1 WLR 259, [1999] 1 All ER 832, [1999] 1 FLR 503 directs that in all instances where the deceased died in the UK and the death has been recorded in the Register of Deaths:

(a) the names and dates of birth and death of the deceased as recorded in the register must be included in the oath lodged in support of an application made through a solicitor or probate practitioner for a grant of representation;
(b) the names and date of death of the deceased as recorded in the register must be included in the notice for a standing search or caveat;
(c) in any case where the name of the deceased or by which the deceased was known differs from that recorded in the register, the name must also be included in the oath or the notice, as the case may be.

Pursuant to the *President's Direction: Probate Records: Grants of Representation,* dated 3 November 1998, [1999] 1 FLR 102, [1998] Fam Law 780, as from November 1998, records of all grants of representation made in the Principal Registry of the Family Division and in district probate registries after that date, kept pursuant to section 111 of the Supreme Court Act 1981, are maintained in the form of computer records. Records from 1980 to 1988 are maintained on microfilm. The annual calendar books continue to be maintained for years prior to 1980. The information comprises:

(a) the full names of the deceased and any alias names;
(b) the last address of the deceased;
(c) the date of death and domicile of the deceased;
(d) the name(s) and address(es) of the executor(s) or administrator(s);
(e) the type of grant;
(f) the gross and net values of the estate or, in the case of an exempted estate, the limits within which the estate falls;
(g) the name and address of the extracting solicitor (if any) or the fact that the grant was obtained by way of personal application;
(h) the date of the grant and the issuing registry.

Claim Made Before Grant

There are two conflicting authorities on whether a claim for an order under section 2 of the 1975 Act can be issued before the grant of representation has been taken out. In *Re Searle, Searle v Siems* [1949] Ch 73, [1948] 2 All ER 426, the originating summons was issued before probate was granted. A grant of representation was obtained before the final hearing. It was argued that an application made before the grant had been taken out was a nullity. Roxburgh J rejected this submission because it would have been contrary to natural justice to prevent the applicant from making the claim. He also considered that the objection raised was one of procedure and could be dispensed with, particularly as it had not been made at any stage prior to the final hearing.

In *Re McBroom* [1992] FLR 376, the applicant, before a grant of representation had been issued, sought orders under section 9 of the 1975 Act against the deceased's severable share in property jointly owned. No attempt had been made to obtain a grant before the final hearing, nor was there any indication whether or not a grant of representation would be obtained before the final hearing. Eastham J struck out the claim on the basis that it was premature.

The right to make a claim arises, however, as a result of the provisions of section 1 of the Act. Section 1(1) provides that where a person dies domiciled in England and Wales and is survived by any of the persons referred to in the section, such a person may apply to the court for an order under section 2 on the grounds set out in the section. The right to make a claim therefore accrues against the estate on the death of the testator, not on the grant of representation.

In setting the time limit within which such a claim may be made, section 4 provides that the claim cannot, except with the permission of the court, be made after the end of six months from the date on which representation with respect to the estate of the deceased is first taken out. It therefore fixes the moment from which time begins to run, not the point at which the right to make a claim accrues. There is no provision in the Act which prohibits the making of a claim until a grant of representation has been issued. Furthermore, if a claim for financial provision under the 1975 Act could not be made until a grant of representation has been taken out, the court would be deprived of its power to preserve property pending trial.

If it were the case that the claim does not accrue until the first effective grant of representation is issued, the consequence would be that, if the will is contested, the claim for financial provision could not be commenced until the probate claim has been concluded. The resultant delay in pursuing the claim for financial provision would lead to injustice and possibly more expense. There may also be situations where the person contesting the will could also have a claim under the Act. The two matters could be conveniently and expeditiously dealt with by the same court simultaneously if the claim under the Act does not have to await the result of the probate claim. If the decision in *Re McBroom* is to be followed, then where there is a contested probate claim which fails, it is inevitable that the claim for financial provision under the Act will be out of time because it is not until the probate claim has been determined that it will become clear whether the grant of representation issued, if any, is effective. It is inevitable that this claim will take longer than six months. If the challenge fails and the grant is found to be effective, then the claimant will be out of time. It is therefore submitted that, in the absence of any specific provision in the 1975 Act preventing the issue of proceedings until after the grant of representation has been issued, a claimant under the 1975 Act should be able to proceed as soon as practicable after the deceased's death.

Where there is no person willing or able to take out a grant of representation, application should be made to the court to appoint an appropriate person to act, or for the Official Solicitor to represent the estate of the deceased.

Applications in Respect of Joint Property

An application under section 9 of the Act, to treat the deceased's severable share of a joint tenancy as part of the net estate of the deceased (see page 114), must be made within the period of six months from the date on which representation with respect to the deceased's estate was first taken out. The court does not have the power to extend the time limit imposed by statute in cases under section 9.

Extension of Time

The powers of the court

In addition to setting the time limit for bringing a claim under the Act, section 4 confers on the court a general discretion to extend the time limit.

The Act does not, however, set out any criteria or principle which the court should apply when considering an application for an extension of time, nor does it in any way restrict the court's power. The court thus has unfettered discretion, and the circumstances in which the court may be asked to exercise its discretion are limitless.

In dealing with an application for an extension of time, guidance is often sought from case law following the 1938 Act under which the time limit of six months was first imposed. Regard should, however, be had to the fact that, as respects the estates of persons dying after 1952 and before 1967, when the Family Provision Act 1966 came into force, the court's discretion to extend the six months period was limited by the Intestates' Estates Act 1952. That Act provided that the period could be extended only in limited specified circumstances, and then only if it could be shown to the satisfaction of the court that the time limit would operate "unfairly". The pre-1966 case law is therefore of limited value to an application under section 4 of the Act. It should also be borne in mind that social conditions and attitudes have changed significantly and continue to do so.

The principles

The judgment of Megarry VC in the leading case of *Re Salmon (Deceased), Coard v National Westminster Bank* [1981] Ch 167, [1980] 3 All ER 532, [1980] 3 WLR 748, and the principles formulated by him, are generally relied on by courts when exercising the discretion under section 4. These principles are:

(a) The discretion is unfettered and one that is exercised judicially in accordance with what is just and proper.

(b) The onus lies on the applicant to establish sufficient grounds for taking the case out of the general rule and depriving those who are protected by it of its benefits. Furthermore, the time limit prescribed is a substantive provision laid down in the Act itself, and is not merely a procedural time limit imposed by rules of court which may be treated with indulgence appropriate to procedural rules. The burden on the applicant is thus not a triviality. The applicant must make out a substantial case for its being just and proper for the court to exercise its statutory discretion to extend the time.

(c) The court must consider how promptly and in what circumstances the applicant is seeking an extension of time. The whole of the circumstances must be looked at, including the reasons for the delay and how promptly the applicant gave a warning to the defendant of the proposed application.

(d) It is material whether or not negotiations have been commenced within the time limit; if they have, and time has run out while they are proceeding, this is likely to encourage the court to extend the time. Negotiations commenced after the time limit has expired might also aid the applicant, at any rate, if the defendants have not taken the point that time has expired.

(e) It is relevant to consider whether the estate has been distributed before the claim was notified.

(f) The court should also consider whether refusal to extend time would leave the applicant without redress against anybody.

In *Re Dennis (Deceased), Dennis v Lloyds Bank* [1981] 2 All ER 140, Browne-Wilkinson J, while applying the principles stated by Megarry VC, formulated two further factors which should be adopted when exercising the court's discretion. These are:

(g) The applicant must show that "he has an arguable case, a case fit to go to trial and that in approaching that matter the court's approach is rather the same as it adopts when considering proceedings for summary judgment" (see Civil Procedure Rules 1998, Part 24).

(h) Where, after a full understanding of the nature of the claim and the prospect of success, the applicant makes a conscious decision not to make a claim and then later changes his/her mind, the court ought not to permit the claim to be made irrespective of the length of time which has elapsed, save only that no distribution has taken place (*Escritt v Escritt* [1982] 3 FLR 280).

In *Re Dennis,* the applicant was the son of the deceased. He had received £90,000 by way of a gift, with other sums, during the deceased's lifetime. The deceased had left him a legacy, free of duty, of £10,000, and £30,000 in trust. Probate was granted on 17 January 1978. On 19 February 1980 the son applied for financial provision and for an extension of time. His claim was limited to such sums as would enable him to discharge the capital transfer tax on the £90,000 received during the deceased's lifetime. The court found the application totally unmeritorious.

The application of each of the above eight factors to the facts of individual cases, and the consideration of them by the courts, are reviewed below.

Unfettered discretion

The court's discretion under section 4 of the 1975 Act is wide, and the circumstances in which the court may be asked to exercise the discretion are limitless. When exercising its discretion, the court has regard to all the circumstances of the case, and considers whether it is reasonably clear that the extension of time is required in the interests of justice; the court will need to carry out a balancing exercise: *Re Ruttie (Deceased) Ruttie v Saul* [1970] 1 WLR 89, [1969] 3 All ER 1633). In *Re Ruttie*, the court, allowing an application for an extension of time, considered the hardship to the applicant if an extension was not granted, the fact that there had been no distribution of the estate and that the application was six weeks out of time, against the fact that there would be no prejudice whatsoever to the defendants except what was inevitably involved in any extension of time, that is, the loss of the advantage of a rigid time limit. The delay in making the application earlier was explained on three grounds, namely:

(a) there had been lengthy negotiations with a view to reaching a compromise, during which arose the question whether the doctrine of community of property under Polish law would be applicable;
(b) the applicant had been ill;
(c) in concentrating on the issue of community of property the solicitors had overlooked the time limit.

In *Re Adams, Adams and Adams v Schofield and Adams,* CAT July 22 1981, an appeal succeeded because the judge had placed too great an emphasis on the fact that the delay was wholly due to the negligence of the solicitors and that the applicant would have had a good claim against them; and had failed to give due weight to the other factors in favour of the applicant.

In exercising its discretion, the court will also be mindful of the human rights issues, particularly those under Article 6 (the right to a fair trial) of the European Convention on Human Rights and Fundamental Freedoms, and the provisions of CPR rule 1.1(2) (dealing with a case justly).

Establishing sufficient grounds

It would seem from the authorities that, to take the case out of the general rule, the applicant must not only establish sufficient reason for the delay in making the application, but must also show a good prospect of succeeding in the claim. The following cases further illustrate the court's approach to an application for leave to extend time.

In *Re Stone* (1969) 114 SJ 36, the Court of Appeal stated that the applicant must establish that there is a triable issue, and satisfy the court that in all the circumstances of the case the court ought to exercise its discretion.

In *Re Dennis (Deceased), Dennis v Lloyds Bank* (above), it was held that, in exercising its discretion, a factor to which the court was required to have regard, in addition to other matters, was whether the applicant was able to satisfy the court that he had an arguable case that he was entitled to reasonable financial provision out of the estate. The criterion to be applied in deciding whether the applicant had an arguable case was the same as that applied by the court in deciding whether a defendant should have leave to defend: see CPR Part 24, but note also that under this rule the test appears to be whether there is a "real prospect" of success, or "compelling" reasons. In *Re Dymott, Spooner v Carroll* CAT December 15 1980, the principle applied was whether there was any merit in the application, rather than whether the applicant had an arguable case.

In *Smith v Loosley* [1986] CAT June 18, the issue was decided on the basis of whether the applicant had an arguable case. The applicant was seven weeks out of time. She did not understand what a life interest meant and she had been involved in a dispute with one of the members of the extended family. The delay was not regarded as excessive. In addition, a warning letter had been sent by her solicitors to the executors a day before the time expired.

In *Polackova v Sobiewski* CAT October 28 1985, there had been inactivity for six months after the solicitors and the applicant discovered that probate had been granted, and the application was made three months out of time. No satisfactory explanation for the delay was given, but leave was granted on the basis that, at the date of the hearing, the applicant had an arguable case. It is difficult to reconcile this decision with the principles set out by Megarry VC in *Re Dennis* and the other authorities. It can be explained only on the basis that the court took the view that as the applicant was the former spouse of the deceased, the case must have some merit.

These authorities seem to suggest that the onus on the applicant has gradually shifted from having to "make a substantial case"; to having to show an "arguable case" or a "triable issue"(*Re Dennis* (above); to showing that the applicant's case has merit (*Re Dymott);* and, if *Palackova v Sobolewski* is to be regarded as good law, to a "triviality" and an inquiry which is superficial. It is submitted that *Polackova v Sobiewski* should not be regarded as setting a new standard, but as a case which turned on its own facts; and that the correct approach is to show that the applicant has a good arguable case on the merits which ought to be tried, or that the applicant has a "real prospect of success".

In *Re C (Deceased)* [1995] 2 FLR 24, leave was granted although there had been a delay of two years before the mother of the deceased's child sought to make a claim. The delay was not properly explained. There had not been any distribution of the estate. If leave was refused the child would have suffered as a result of her mother's default. The court considered the merits of the application and the prospects of success if the child's claim was allowed to be made. It was inevitable that there would be a substantial provision out of the estate in favour of the child for the child's ordinary maintenance requirements. Wilson J stated that in none of the reported cases to which he had been referred had the prospects of substantial success been so clear as in this case, and "in the end the task is to determine whether the net weight of the relevant factors is such as to justify permission outside the normal period".

Promptness in making the application

In considering an application for an extension of time, the court looks not only at the length of time that has elapsed, but at the whole of the circumstances. In *Re Salmon (Deceased), Coard v National Westminster Bank Ltd* (above, page 14), the reasons for the delay, as well as the promptness with which the applicant gave warning to the defendants of the proposed claim, were regarded as important considerations. In *Re Ruttie* (above, page 15), besides the delay of six weeks, the court took into account other considerations. In *Re Gonin (Deceased), Gonin v Garmeson* [1979] Ch 16, [1977] 3 WLR 379, [1977] 2 All ER 720, where the delay was of two years, the court refused the application because the applicant had been in control throughout and the delay had occurred as a result of the negligence of the applicant's solicitors and the advice they gave her. The applicant had a good case against her solicitors and the injustice to her could therefore be remedied by an action against them.

In *Re Bone (Deceased), Bone v Midland Bank* [1955] 1 WLR 703, [1955] 2 All ER 555, an issue had arisen as to the construction of the deceased's will. The widow's solicitors were informed that an application would be issued for the question to be determined by the court. The application was not made, so the widow issued an application under the 1938 Act. The application was two days out of time and leave was sought to extend time. Leave was granted because the executor's solicitors had led the widow to suppose that proceedings would be commenced; the delay was short; and refusal would have caused hardship.

In *Re Trott, Trott v Miles* [1958] 1 WLR 604, [1958] 2 All ER 296, the deceased had died on 8 October 1954. Probate was granted on 17 November 1954. The widow applied for financial provision for herself. On 13 April 1955 the widow gave birth to the deceased's daughter. The application on behalf of the daughter was not issued until 11 July 1955, almost two months out of time. Leave was granted, as it was plain that on the birth of the child another circumstance affecting the administration or distribution of the estate arose. No time had been wasted between the date of the child's birth and the date of the application; an application for the child to be represented by means of public funds had also been in progress.

In *Re McNare, McNare v McNare* [1964] 1 WLR 1255, [1964] 3 All ER 373, the deceased died in 1961. Probate was granted to his son on 8 May 1962. The deceased had left nothing to his widow, who was blind, crippled and seventy-one years of age, and who had not discovered the deceased's death until the end of October 1962. She had no information regarding the deceased's assets. Her sister, on her behalf, sought legal advice and as a result the son was contacted, but he refused to give any information. Solicitors were instructed on the widow's behalf and there then followed preliminary negotiations between them and the son's solicitors. There was deadlock. The widow then issued the application for financial provision and sought an extension of time. Leave was granted because:

(a) the applicant had not had any information about the deceased's estate;
(b) there were negotiations between solicitors;
(c) refusal to extend the time would have caused hardship and would have operated unfairly against the applicant.

In *Re Longley (Deceased), Longley and Longley v Longley* [1981] CLY 2885, the application for an extension of time was refused because there had been a delay of about fourteen months before making the application; distribution of the estate had taken place; there had been no negotiations for a settlement; and the applicant had a good case for negligence against her solicitors.

In *Escritt v Escritt* [1982] 3 FLR 280, despite the fact that the applicant had been properly advised, she had delayed for three years in bringing her claim, to avoid differences within the family. Leave to apply out of time was refused.

Negotiations
It seems clear from the authorities that where the delay has occurred because the parties were attempting to negotiate a settlement, the court will consider an application for an extension of time favourably. Cases where this view is demonstrated include *Re McNare, McNare v McNare* (above). See also *Re Ruttie* (above, page 15) where the negotiations with a view to compromising the claim had commenced before the grant of probate and had continued for the whole of the period of six months.

In *Re John, John v John* (1966) 111 SJ 115, the application was made by the widow of the deceased three years after probate was taken out because she had relied on promises made to her by the legatees which never materialised. Her application was granted.

Distribution of the estate
Section 20(1) of the 1975 Act stipulates that the provisions of the Act do not render the personal representative of the deceased person liable for having distributed any part of the estate of the deceased, after the end of the period of six months from the date on which representation with respect to the estate of the deceased is first taken out, on the ground that he ought to have taken into account the possibility that the court might permit the making of an application after the end of six months, or might exercise its powers under section 6 (provision for variation etc. of an order; see page 102). The section goes on to provide that this does not prejudice any power to recover, by reason of the making of an order under the Act, any part of the estate distributed. If, therefore, distribution has taken place, the prejudice to the beneficiaries will be that much greater by reason of the conversion of hope and expectation to reality when they received their shares:

> "For most people, there is a real difference between the bird in the hand and the bird in the bush. In addition, of course, the beneficiaries are more likely to have changed their position in reliance on the benefaction if they have actually received it than if it lies merely in prospect. If it is always prejudicial to claimants not to receive money that they are entitled to receive at the earliest moment, it is likely to be even more prejudicial to have taken away from them money that they have actually received and have begun to enjoy. The point is strengthened if they have changed their

> position in reliance on what they have received, as by making a purchase or gifts they would otherwise not have made." (*per* Megarry VC in *Re Salmon,* above, page 14).

Although Megarry VC referred to the fact that the court could go behind the fact of distribution, it is submitted that the applicant for an extension of time would be required to establish compelling reasons and exceptional circumstances to succeed. There have been no reported cases of leave being granted after distribution has taken place. In *Re Longley (Deceased), Longley and Longley v Longley* [1981] CLY 2885, distribution had taken place when the application was made. It was a factor which the court took into account when refusing leave.

Claims against third parties or solicitors

Although Megarry VC stated that the fact that the applicant had a possible claim against a third party was a relevant factor to consider, it appears, from the decision in *Re Adams, Adams and Adams v Schofield and Adams* (above, page 16), that the court will not refuse an application for an extension of time merely on the ground that the applicant has a claim against his lawyers. But in *Re Longley (Deceased), Longley and Longley v Longley* (above), the deceased had made a will appointing his mistress executor, and bequeathing to her his house, in which she was living with her daughter. The remainder of his estate devolved on his widow on a partial intestacy. The mistress wished to make a claim against the estate under the Act. She renounced probate in the widow's favour. Thereafter, although her solicitors were involved, the matter did not result in any settlement. The solicitors took no further action to pursue the claim on behalf of the mistress or her child. The mistress took further advice, but when she issued proceedings the claim was fourteen months out of time and the estate had been distributed. Her application for an extension of time was refused because of the delay; because distribution had taken place; and because she had a claim against her former solicitors. In exercising its discretion and carrying out the balancing exercise the court had regard to all the important issues involved. The decision in *Re Adams* was not followed and it seems therefore that where the application for an extension of time is opposed on the basis that the applicant has a possible claim against a third party, the applicant should not place too much reliance on the decision in *Re Adams* in support of the application.

Case law on the subject of possible claims against a third party in other actions which are barred because the limitation period has expired, for example, personal injury claims, should be considered. On the other hand, there may be exceptional circumstances justifying the court in taking a different view, as in *Re C* (above, page 17) where the claimant may have had a case against her mother but the court nevertheless granted leave.

Arguable/triable case
See above, pages 16–17.

Conscious decision not to make a claim
Escritt v Escritt (above, page 19) is an illustration of a case where the applicant had been properly advised but sought not to pursue her claim promptly and then changed her mind. Save for the fact that distribution had not taken place, none of the other factors referred to in *Re Salmon* were found to be present. In contrast, in *Re C* (above, page 17), the court took a different view on the particular circumstances of the case, especially because the applicant was a child and dependent on the decision on her mother.

Claimant under Disability
In the case of civil litigation, the Limitation Act 1980, section 28(1) extends the limitation period where the claimant is a person under disability. The 1975 Act does not make any special provision for a claimant who is physically or mentally disabled. The disabled claimant should not, however, be disadvantaged or prejudiced by the absence of any specific provisions since the court has an unfettered discretion under section 4 of the 1975 Act. In exercising its discretion, the court is obliged to have regard to all the circumstances, including human rights issues under the European Convention on Human Rights, and to consider whether it is reasonably clear that the extension of time is required in the interests of justice.

The constraints of time are often more pressing when the practitioner has to deal with a disabled client, particularly if the client is mentally handicapped, has a speech impediment or is deaf. In the case of a claimant who suffers from a mental handicap, consideration should be given to the appointment of a receiver or the intervention of the Court of Protection. In either case, delay is likely, and steps must be taken to safeguard the interest of the disabled claimant. The duty and burden on the solicitor is necessarily a heavy one. Time may have begun to run or may have expired before advice is sought. It is essential that a meticulous note is kept of every step taken in the proceedings to show that the matter was dealt with expeditiously and efficiently. If there is any likelihood of delay before a claim can be issued, contact with the personal representatives or their solicitors must be maintained to ensure that they are kept informed, and, if possible, to obtain an extension of time by agreement. In some cases it may be appropriate to apply for leave to issue the claim without the necessary supporting evidence, to protect the claim.

Where delay has occurred and it is necessary to apply for an extension of time the principles set out above should be taken into account when preparing the supporting evidence. In addition, the extent and nature of the claimant's disability and the reason for the delay in making the claim are relevant factors, particularly if the delay is attributable to the claimant's disability. The claimant, through his solicitor, must set out any other factor which establishes that it would be just and fair for the court to exercise its discretion in his favour. Any evidence to show that the matter was dealt with diligently, efficiently and expeditiously will be relevant.

The following are some of the cases where the court has waived the time limits, the applicant having been a person under disability:

In *Re McNare, McNare v McNare* (above, page 18) where the applicant was blind, crippled and seventy-one years of age and did not discover the death of the deceased until five months after the grant of probate had been issued to her son.

In *Re Wood (Deceased), Wood v Wood* [1982] LS Gaz R 774, the deceased had died intestate in April 1980. She was survived by a severely mentally handicapped child and the deceased's husband who was not the child's natural father. The estate was valued at £26,737. The husband inherited £25,000, the child the balance. The husband died in January 1981 leaving his entire estate to his son. The child's application, brought out of time, was allowed.

In *Re C* (above, page 17) a claim on behalf of a child was allowed despite the fact that it was two years out of time and notwithstanding the fact that the mother of the child, who could have made the claim on behalf of the child on time, could not give any reason for the delay.

Delay Caused by Application for Public Funding

Solicitors should be mindful of the fact that there is no guarantee that any delay in issuing a claim, resulting from the time taken by the Legal Services Commission to deal with an application for public funding, will be treated by the court sympathetically. It is the duty of the solicitor to ensure that the Legal Services Commission is made fully aware of the urgency when making the application, and subsequently by sending regular reminders to the Commission that time is running out. If it appears that the application will take some time to process, then it would be advisable to seek an emergency certificate, or one limited to issuing the proceedings.

It is also well worth notifying the personal representatives or their solicitors of the application for public funding, keeping them informed at all times of the progress of the application, and seeking an extension by agreement. If all else fails the solicitor should advise the client of the implications, with a view to ascertaining whether the client is able to meet the costs of issuing the claim out of his own resources. It is also possible to apply to the court for leave to issue the proceedings without the supporting evidence on the undertaking that the evidence will be filed upon the determination of the application for a public funding certificate.

Chapter 3

Claimants

Introduction

Section 1(1) of the Inheritance (Provision for Family and Dependants) Act 1975, as amended by the Law Reform (Succession) Act 1995, sets out the classes of person entitled to make an application for an order under section 2 for financial provision on the ground that the disposition of the deceased's estate effected by his will, or the law of intestacy, or the combination of his will and that law, is not such as to make reasonable financial provision for the applicant. These persons are:

(a) the wife or husband of the deceased;
(b) a former wife or husband of the deceased who has not remarried;
(c) any person (not being included in paragraph (a) or (b) above) who is a cohabitant of the deceased within the meaning of section 1(1A);
(d) a child of the deceased;
(e) any person (not being a child of the deceased) who, in the case of any marriage to which the deceased was at any time a party, was treated by the deceased as a child of the family in relation to that marriage;
(f) any person (not being a person included in the foregoing classes) who, immediately before the death of the deceased, was being maintained, either wholly or partly, by the deceased.

See the Civil Partnership Bill 2004, Schedule 4, for proposed amendments to this section.

The Wife or Husband of the Deceased

There is usually no dispute about the identity of the person who was the wife or husband of the deceased immediately before death, and in most cases the production of a valid marriage certificate suffices. The parties remain married unless the marriage has been dissolved by a decree absolute. The remarriage of the widow or widower of the deceased after the claim under the 1975 Act is issued but before the claim is finally determined does not affect the validity of the claim. It is, however, a factor which the court is entitled to consider when determining whether reasonable financial provision was made by the deceased and, if not, what orders the court should make having regard to all relevant circumstances of the case and the criteria set out in section 3 of the 1975 Act.

Separation by a decree of judicial separation

If the deceased and his or her wife or husband were separated by a decree of judicial separation and they remained separated at the date of the deceased's death, the survivor is considered the spouse of the deceased. If the decree was made within twelve months of the deceased's death the provisions of section 14 of the Act apply, subject to the conditions set out in that section (see page 28).

Void marriages, voidable marriages and non-marriage

A void marriage is one that is regarded, in any case in which the existence of the marriage is in issue, as never having taken place. It may be put in issue at any time, even after one or both parties to it has died.

Section 11 of the Matrimonial Causes Act 1973 provides that a marriage is void on the following grounds only:

"(a) that it is not a valid marriage [in that]:
  (i) the parties are within the prohibited degrees of relationship;
  (ii) either party is under the age of sixteen; or
  (iii) the parties have intermarried in disregard of certain requirements as to the formation of marriage;
(b) that at the time of the marriage either party was already lawfully married;
(c) that the parties are not respectively male and female;
(d) in the case of a polygamous marriage entered into outside England and Wales, that either party was at the time of the marriage domiciled in England and Wales.

For the purposes of paragraph (d) … a marriage is not polygamous if at its inception neither party has any spouse additional to the other."

Where a void marriage has been annulled, a party to it who has not remarried may claim as a former spouse. If the decree of nullity was granted within twelve months of the death of the deceased under the provisions of section 14, the claimant may be able to claim for financial provision as a spouse. See further page 28.

Section 12 provides that a marriage is voidable on the following grounds:

"(a) that the marriage has not been consummated owing to the incapacity of either party to consummate it;
(b) that the marriage has not been consummated owing to the wilful refusal of the respondent to consummate it;
(c) that either party to the marriage did not validly consent to it, whether in consequence of duress, mistake, unsoundness of mind or otherwise;
(d) that at the time of the marriage either party, though capable of giving a valid consent, was suffering (whether continuously or intermittently) from mental disorder within the meaning of the Mental Health Act 1983 of such a kind or to such an extent as to be unfitted for marriage;

(e) that at the time of the marriage the respondent was suffering from venereal disease in a communicable form;
(f) that at the time of the marriage the respondent was pregnant by some person other than the petitioner."

Marriage entered into in good faith
A voidable marriage is one that is regarded as valid and subsisting until annulled by a decree made by a court having jurisdiction over matrimonial causes. A voidable marriage can be annulled only at the suit of one of the parties to it in the lifetime of the parties; it cannot be challenged once either party to it has died (*Re Roberts, Roberts v Roberts* [1978] 1 WLR 653, [1978] 3 All ER 225 (CA)).

The "wife or husband of the deceased", for the purposes of section 1(1) of the 1975 Act, includes a person who, in good faith, entered into a void marriage with the deceased, unless either:
(a) the marriage of the deceased and the claimant was dissolved or annulled during the lifetime of the deceased and the dissolution or annulment is recognised in English law; or
(b) that person has, during the lifetime of the deceased, entered into a later marriage (section 25(4)).

A person falling within either of the above two categories is not able to make a claim as a spouse of the deceased. The issue of whether the marriage between the deceased and the claimant is void but was entered into in good faith is determined on the facts.

In *Ghandi v Patel* [2002] 1 FLR 603, the claimant had undergone, at an Indian restaurant in London, a Hindu ceremony of marriage with the deceased, whose marriage to his first wife was subsisting at the date of his marriage to the claimant. The marriage between the claimant and the deceased was conducted to comply with the rituals and requirements of the Hindu faith; no effort was made to comply with the requirements of English law to constitute a lawful marriage. Thereafter the claimant and the deceased had a stormy and troubled relationship and, following the birth of their second child, they lived separate lives. The claimant had, during the lifetime of the deceased, issued proceedings against the deceased seeking the transfer to her of one of the deceased's properties. In those proceedings she maintained that she was not married to the deceased. On his death, she applied for financial provision under the 1975 Act on the basis that, while she accepted that her marriage to the deceased was void by reason of the bigamy, she had nevertheless entered into the marriage with the deceased in good faith and was therefore entitled to claim as his spouse. On the facts the court held that the claimant had not established "good faith" within the meaning of section 25(4).

Marriage requires the participation of two people – a man and a woman; and the ceremony must purport to be a marriage of the kind contemplated by the Marriage Acts and must comply with the requirements of English Law or purport to do so.

Ghandi v Patel (above) is a recent example where a claimant in an Inheritance Act case sought to bring herself within the provisions of section 25(4) of the Act, but on the evidence it was held that the Hindu ceremony did not comply with the requirements of English law and did not purport to do so. The Hindu marriage did not give rise to a void marriage. It was no marriage at all. In any event, it was also held that, even if the ceremony had created a void marriage by reason of bigamy, the claimant had not entered into the marriage in good faith. Her claim therefore failed on both grounds.

Marriage with a person of the same sex or a transsexual

A marriage between two people of the same sex is not a marriage (see section 11(c), Matrimonial Causes Act 1973). A male-to-female transsexual and a man cannot claim a right to marry (*Sheffield and Horsham v United Kingdom* (1998) 27 EHRR 163, [1998] 2 FLR 928). Under the law as it stands, where a person's biological and sexual characteristics at birth were congruent, those characteristics determine the person's sex for the purposes of marriage. It is for the court to determine, by assessing the facts of the individual case, whether a person is male or female. In his dissenting judgment in *Bellinger v Bellinger* [2002] 2 WLR 394, [2001] 2 FLR 1048, Thorpe LJ considered that other factors, including psychological considerations, should be considered by the court; that the family justice system should be sufficiently flexible to accommodate social change; and that one of the objectives of statute law reform and of the family justice system in this field must be to ensure that the law reacts to and reflects social change in the construction of existing statutory provisions. On appeal ([2003] UKHL 21, [2003] 2 WLR 1174, [2003] 2 All ER 593, [2003] 1 FLR 1043]), the House of Lords confirmed that, in determining whether a person was male or female for the purposes of section 11(c) of the Matrimonial Causes Act 1973, the test set out in *Corbett v Corbett (Otherwise Ashley)* [1971] P 83, [1970] 2 All ER 33, still applied; and that any change in the law was a matter for Parliament, particularly as the Government had already announced its intention to introduce primary legislation on the subject. The House of Lords also held, however, that the non-recognition of gender change for the purpose of marriage was incompatible with Articles 8 and 12 of the European Convention on Human Rights, and made a declaration to that effect in respect of section 11(c) of the Matrimonial Causes Act 1973. See also *Goodwin v United Kingdom* (2002) 35 EHRR 18, [2002] 2 FLR 487 and *I v United Kingdom* [2002] 2 FLR 518, where the European Court of Human Rights held that to deny legal recognition to transsexuals was no longer sustainable and was a violation of their rights under Articles 8 and 12.

As a result, the Gender Recognition Bill was introduced into Parliament in November 2003. The Bill contemplates the establishment of a gender recognition panel, which would have authority to issue gender recognition certificates to transsexuals who no longer wish to be associated with their birth gender. The certificates would have the effect of giving recognition to the acquired gender. The applicant for such a certificate would be required to provide a declaration stating that he or she has lived in the new gender for a period of at least two years; that he/she intends to continue to live in the new gender until death; whether he/she is married; and any other information required by the panel or the Secretary of State. The application would have to be supported by medical evidence, namely from a general practitioner practising in gender dysphoria and one other medical practitioner, or a chartered psychologist practising in gender dysphoria and one other medical practitioner, confirming a diagnosis of gender dysphoria. Details of any sex change treatment undergone or contemplated by the applicant would have to be provided. An unmarried applicant will be issued a full gender recognition certificate, and a married applicant, an interim certificate. Schedule 2 to the Bill proposes the amendment of the Matrimonial Causes Act 1973, section 12, to add an additional ground of voidable marriage, namely where an interim gender certificate has been issued to either party to the marriage. Nullity proceedings would have to be commenced within six months of the issue of the certificate. In such cases, full recognition would be given only when the marriage is annulled, when the court would issue a full gender recognition certificate. Where the marriage ends for any other reason, or because of death, the holder of the interim certificate would have the right to apply for the certificate to be converted into a full certificate within six months of the event. For the final contents and effects of the legislation, practitioners should refer to the statute when it has received Royal Assent.

Same-sex couples
On same-sex couples, see the proposals set out in the Civil Partnership Bill 2004, mentioned on page 2.

Polygamous and potentially polygamous marriages
Where the deceased and the claimant entered into a polygamous marriage overseas under a law which permits polygamy, the marriage is recognised in England and Wales, and the claimant may pursue a claim under the 1975 Act as a spouse of the deceased. In *Re Sehota (Deceased), Kaur v Kaur* [1978] 1 WLR 1506, [1978] 3 All ER 385, the claimant and the deceased were married in India in 1937. The marriage was potentially polygamous under Indian Law. In 1948 the deceased married again. The deceased and his two wives subsequently acquired English domicile. In 1976 the husband died, leaving his entire estate to his second wife. The first wife applied for an order for financial provision as a wife of the deceased. She was adjudged

to be the wife of the deceased notwithstanding that the marriage was polygamous. It was held that section 1(1)(a) of the 1975 Act should be construed in the light of the Matrimonial Proceedings (Polygamous Marriages) Act 1972, section 1, under which matrimonial relief may be granted in cases where the marriage is polygamous.

Under the Matrimonial Causes Act 1973, section 11(d), a marriage celebrated after 31 July 1971 was void if it was a polygamous marriage entered into outside England and Wales and either party was, at the time of the marriage, domiciled in England and Wales. Thus, in *Hussain v Hussain* [1982] 3 All ER 369, a man domiciled in England and Wales married a woman domiciled in Pakistan, where the law permits a man to take more than one wife but does not extend the like right to women. It was held that since, under the law of domicile of both parties, neither could enter into a second marriage, the marriage was monogamous. Had the woman been domiciled in England and Wales and the man in Pakistan, the marriage would have been potentially polygamous as the man would have been permitted under the law of Pakistan to take a second wife.

The Private International Law (Miscellaneous Provisions) Act 1995, section 5, has, however, amended section 11 of the Matrimonial Causes Act 1973, to provide that a marriage entered into outside England and Wales between parties, neither of whom is already married, is not void under the law of England and Wales on the ground that it is entered into under a law which permits polygamy and that either party is domiciled in England and Wales. The effect is to render void only a marriage entered into in a foreign country by a person domiciled in England and Wales which is actually polygamous, not one which is potentially polygamous.

Claims within twelve months of dissolution or annulment of marriage

Section 14(1) of the 1975 Act applies in cases where, within twelve months from the date on which a decree of divorce or nullity has been made absolute or a decree of judicial separation has been granted, a party to the marriage dies and, at the date of death, either no application for financial relief under the Matrimonial Causes Act 1973 sections 23 and 24 has been made by the other party to that marriage, or such an application has been made but has not been finally determined. In such a case, if a claim under section 2 of the 1975 Act is made by the surviving spouse, the court has power, notwithstanding anything in sections 1 and 3 of the Act, if it thinks just to do so, to treat that party, for the purposes of the claim under the 1975 Act, as if the decree of divorce, nullity or judicial separation had not been made. In other words, the court may treat that person as the spouse of the deceased (section 14(1)). In the case of a decree of judicial separation, this provision is operative only if, at the date of the deceased's death, the decree was in force *and* the separation was continuing (section 14(2)).

The power conferred by section 14 is discretionary and will be exercised only if the court considers it just to do so.

Claim by a surviving husband
The 1975 Act makes no distinction between a claim by a surviving husband and a claim by a surviving wife. In the early cases, however, the courts appeared to be disinclined, save in exceptional circumstances, to grant relief where the claim was made by a surviving husband. This is illustrated by two cases in particular. In *Re Sylvester, Sylvester v Public Trustee* [1941] Ch 87, [1940] 4 All ER 269, the parties were married in 1931. The husband subsequently gave up his employment and thereafter did all the housework and nursed his wife during her illness. The wife had her own income. The husband had none. She died in 1940. She bequeathed to him an annuity of £525 per annum and gave her residuary estate to a number of charities. The husband made a claim against the estate for his maintenance under the 1938 Act. Farwell J, in allowing the husband's claim and awarding him three shillings a week, stated:

> "I do not consider that, in the ordinary way, applications by husbands for this sort of assistance should be readily entertained. *Prima facie* a husband should be able to maintain himself, and ought not to ask the court to give him, out of his wife's estate, more than she thought fit to provide for him. There are, of course, exceptional cases in which such an application may be justified, but personally I should not be very willing to assist husbands in cases of this sort, unless the circumstances were indeed exceptional."

In *Re Styler, Styler v Griffiths* [1942] Ch 387, [1942] 2 All ER 201, the deceased had made an agreement with her second husband that, on his making a will in her favour, she would make a will leaving the income of her estate to him for life. They both made wills in accordance with the agreement. Subsequently, the wife made another will leaving all her estate to her daughter by her first marriage. On the wife's death, the husband applied for reasonable provision. In refusing his application Morton J approved the judgement of Farwell J in *Re Sylvester* (above) and criticised his own decision in *Re Pointer* [1941] Ch 60. He stated:

> "Having now had more experience of administering the Act since I decided that case, I do not think that I should now make any provision, as I did there for a husband with a pension of £180 a year, an annual income of £124 from investments and £25 a year net from property, unless the circumstances were exceptional."

It is submitted that the court's approach today would be different, having regard to decisions concerning applications for financial relief under the Matrimonial Causes Act 1973, and more particularly to the decisions in *White v White* [2001] 1 AC 596, [2000] 2 FLR 981 (HL) and *Cowan v Cowan* [2001] EWCA Civ 679, [2002] Fam 97. In *White v White* Lord Nicholls of Birkenhead stated:

> "There is one principle of universal application which can be stated with confidence. In seeking to achieve a fair outcome, there is no place for discrimination between husband and wife and their respective roles."

(See further page 85.)

A Former Wife or Husband who has not Remarried

A "former wife" or "former husband" means a person whose marriage with the deceased was, during the lifetime of the deceased, either:

(a) dissolved or annulled by a decree of divorce or of nullity of marriage granted under the law of any part of the British Islands, or

(b) dissolved or annulled in any country or territory outside the British Islands by a divorce or annulment which is entitled to be recognised as valid by the law of England and Wales (section 25 of the 1975 Act, as amended by the Matrimonial and Family Proceedings Act 1984, and section 25(2) as from 16 September 1985); and

that person has not remarried before the death of the deceased.

Where a decree *nisi* has been granted, but the deceased dies before the decree has been made absolute, the marriage is regarded as subsisting and the claimant is eligible to make a claim as the spouse of the deceased. The court is, however, entitled to have regard to any financial settlement reached between the parties or ordered by the court when considering what, if any, financial provision should be ordered (see further Chapter 9).

Section 44(1) of the Family Law Act 1986 provides that:

> "subject to section 52(4) and (5)(a) of this Act, no divorce or annulment obtained in any part of the British Islands shall be regarded as effective in any part of the United Kingdom unless granted by a court of civil jurisdiction."

Overseas divorce and talaq

The validity of an overseas divorce, annulment or legal separation obtained by means of proceedings must be recognised if the divorce, annulment or legal separation is effective under the law of the country in which it is obtained, and at the relevant date either party to the marriage:

(a) was habitually resident in the country in which the divorce, annulment or legal separation was obtained; or

(b) was domiciled in that country; or

(c) was a national of that country.

(Family Law Act 1986, section 46(1).)

The validity of an overseas divorce, annulment or legal separation obtained otherwise than by means of proceedings must be recognised if the divorce, annulment or legal separation is effective under the law of the country in which it was obtained, and at the relevant date:

(a) each party to the marriage was domiciled in that country; or

(b) either party to the marriage was domiciled in that country and the other party was domiciled in a country under whose law the divorce, annulment or legal separation is recognised as valid; and

(c) neither party to the marriage was habitually resident in the United Kingdom throughout the period of one year immediately preceding that date.

(Family Law Act 1986, section 46(2).)

In *Sulaiman v Juffali* [2002] 1 FLR 479, both parties were Saudi nationals of, and domiciled in, Saudi Arabia. They were married in Saudi Arabia. In 2001 the husband pronounced a bare *talaq* in England and then registered it with a Sharia court in Saudi Arabia, thus dissolving the marriage under Sharia law as applied in Saudi Arabia. The wife issued divorce proceedings in England. The husband contested the proceedings on a number of grounds including the fact the marriage had already been dissolved. It was held, applying the provisions of section 44(1) of the 1986 Act, that, irrespective of the parties' domicile and religion, informal divorces obtained in England and Wales otherwise than by proceedings in a court of civil jurisdiction will not be recognised. A bare *talaq* pronounced in England does not therefore operate to dissolve the marriage because it is not obtained in any proceedings in a court of civil jurisdiction.

In *El Fadl v El Fadl* [2000] 1 FCR 685, [2000] 1 FLR 175, however, it was held that the pronouncement of the *talaq* before witnesses, which was registered by a Lebanese Sharia court that was properly convened and took formal declarations, was a divorce obtained by means of proceedings, although the Sharia court did not have judicial jurisdiction to make it. See also *Wicken v Wicken* [1999] 1 FLR 293, where a letter of divorce was recognised.

For other cases where *talaq* has been considered, see *Quazi v Quazi* [1980] AC 744, [1979] 3 WLR 833, [1979] 3 All ER 897 (HL); *R v Secretary of State for the Home Department, ex parte Ghulam Fatima* [1986] AC 527, [1986] 2 WLR 693, [1986] 2 All ER 32; and *Chaudhary v Chaudhary* [1985] Fam 19, [1984] 3 All ER 1017.

It should be noted that Part II of the Family Law Act 1986 does not apply where Articles 14 to 20 of Council Regulation (EC) No 1347/2000 (of 29 May 2000 on the jurisdiction, recognition and enforcement of judgements in matrimonial matters and in matters of parental responsibility for joint children, Official Journal L 160 of 30.06.2000) apply. These articles require that a judgment given in a Member State relating to divorce, annulment of marriage or legal separation is to be recognised in any other Member State without any special procedure being required; and that recognition may not be refused because the law of the Member State in which recognition is sought would not have allowed the dissolution or annulment of the marriage or a legal separation on the same facts (Article 18).

Article 15(1) of the Regulation provides:

> "A judgment relating to a divorce, legal separation or marriage annulment shall not be recognised:
> (a) if such a recognition is manifestly contrary to the public policy of the Member State in which recognition is sought;
> (b) where it was given in default of appearance, if the respondent was not served with the document which instituted the proceedings or with an equivalent document in sufficient time and in such a way as to enable the respondent to arrange for his or her defence unless it is determined that the respondent has accepted the judgment unequivocally;
> (c) if it is irreconcilable with a judgment given in proceedings between the same parties in the Member State in which recognition is sought;
> (d) if it is irreconcilable with an earlier judgment given in another Member State or in a non-Member State between the same parties, provided that the earlier judgment fulfils the conditions necessary for its recognition in the Member State in which recognition is sought."

Article 16 provides that a court of a Member State may, on the basis of an agreement on the recognition and enforcement of judgments, not recognise a judgment given in another Member State. Under Article 19, "under no circumstances may a judgment be reviewed as to its substance".

Overseas dissolution or annulment

Prior to the enactment of the Matrimonial and Family Proceedings Act 1984, a person whose marriage was dissolved in a foreign country was not eligible to apply for financial provision under the 1975 Act as a former spouse of the deceased. Section 25 of the Matrimonial and Family Proceedings Act 1984 now enables a person whose marriage was dissolved outside England and Wales to apply for an order under section 2 of the 1975 Act.

Application of section 14

In cases where, within twelve months from the date on which a decree of divorce or nullity has been made absolute, or a decree of judicial separation has been granted, a party to the marriage dies and an application for financial relief under sections 23 and 24 of the Matrimonial Proceedings Act 1973 has not been made by the other party to the marriage, or such an application is pending at the time of the death of the deceased, section 14 applies and the claimant may be treated as a spouse of the deceased (see page 28, above).

To qualify as a former spouse, the claimant must not have remarried at the date when proceedings are issued. It matters not whether any such remarriage is void or voidable. Section 25(5) of the 1975 Act provides that:

> "any reference in this Act to remarriage or to a person who has remarried includes a reference to a marriage which is by law void or voidable or to a person who has entered into such a marriage as the case may be, and a marriage shall be treated for the purpose of this Act as remarriage, in

relation to any party thereto, notwithstanding that the previous marriage of that party was void or voidable."

See the Civil Partnership Bill 2004, Schedule 4, for proposed amendments to include similar provisions for same-sex couples.

A Cohabitant of the Deceased

Section 1(1)(ba) and (1A) of the 1975 Act, introduced by the Law Reform (Succession) Act 1995, extended the categories of person who may apply for financial provision to include a cohabitant of the deceased. A cohabitant is, however, eligible to apply as a cohabitant only if the deceased died on or after 1 January 1996, and, during the whole of the period of two years ending immediately before the date when the deceased died, the person was living:

(a) in the same household as the deceased; and

(b) as the husband or wife of the deceased.

This provision was introduced in response to cases such as *Bishop v Plumley* [1991] 1 All ER 236, [1991] 1 WLR 582 (CA), where the claimant had to prove "dependency" in order to succeed. The revised provisions are, however, subject to certain limitations. There are three conditions which must be satisfied to establish eligibility.

First, cohabitation must have continued for the "whole of the two years immediately before the death of the deceased". There are two separate ingredients to this provision:

(a) the whole of the period of two years; and

(b) immediately before the death of the deceased.

The words "whole of the two years" implies that there must have been continuous cohabitation without a break for the full two years and if this cannot be proved the claim will fail. It is submitted, however, that where the evidence establishes that, although the parties may have been physically apart, their separation was not voluntary, the relationship was continuing and the household was being maintained as a single unit for both the deceased and the claimant, the claim should be allowed. To rule otherwise would mean a total disregard of social and economic changes which compel couples to be apart for short periods, for example, where one partner has to work away from home or is posted overseas for a short time, or one partner has to care for a sick relative or has, by agreement, taken a holiday without the other.

Likewise, the second ingredient, "ending immediately before the date when the deceased died", should not, it is suggested, be applied too strictly. If the test relating to claimants under section 1(1)(e) is applied (see page 49), where the language of the statute is "immediately before the death of the deceased", then, if cohabitation has ceased, no matter for how short a period, section 1(1A) may not apply. It is submitted that a common sense approach should be taken and the provision interpreted to allow for circumstances beyond the parties' control which cause cohabitation to cease or to be interrupted immediately before the death of the deceased. The test applied under the Matrimonial Causes Act 1973, to cases of separation for two or five years, where the relationship is not regarded as at an end if separation has been brought about by illness, should be applied.

In *Jelley v Iliffe* [1981] Fam 128, [1981] 2 WLR 801, [1981] 2 All ER 29, Griffiths LJ held that:

> "The words 'immediately before the death of the deceased' in section 1(1)(e) cannot be construed literally as applying to the *de facto* situation at death but refer to the general arrangements for maintenance subsisting at the time of death. So that if for example the deceased had been making regular payments to the support of an old friend, the claim would not be defeated if those payments ceased during a terminal illness because the decease was too ill to make them."

An admission to hospital followed by death in hospital, for example, is a circumstance where the parties would be physically separated immediately before death but neither would have regarded their relationship as at an end. The break in the cohabitation could not be regarded as one of choice and should be disregarded as constituting an act of separation. The issue is not simply whether the deceased and the claimant were physically living together, but whether they remained bound together emotionally and socially and did not consider their relationship at an end (*Gully v Dix*, below).

Although the above two issues were not argued in the case of *Re Watson* [1999] 1 FLR 878, the judgment of Neuberger J supports the view set out above. In *Re Watson*, the claimant and the deceased had had a relationship for over thirty years. From 1995 until April 1996, when the deceased died, the arrangement between them had been that the deceased provided the running living costs for both of them and the claimant looked after the home and contributed towards the service bills. They did not share the same bedroom and did not have a sexual relationship. The deceased was taken into hospital about three weeks before his death. Neuberger J held that:

> "So far as s 1(1A) is concerned, it is not in dispute that 'during the whole of the period of two years ending immediately before the date when [Mr Watson] died Miss Griffiths was living … in the same household as [Mr Watson]. The Treasury Solicitor has not argued that Miss Griffiths' application should fail because this condition was not satisfied during the last three weeks of Mr Watson's life when he was in hospital, and it is right to record that, in my view, that is not an argument which could respectably have been advanced. In the first place as a matter of ordinary language, the fact that someone is in hospital for a period, possibly for a

> long period, at the end of which he dies, does not mean that, before his death, he ceased to be part of the household of which he was part, until he was forced by illness to go to hospital, and to which he would have returned had he not died. Secondly, even if it had involved straining the language of section 1(1A) of the Act to arrive at that result, it would appear to me to be appropriate so to do; it would be contrary to the whole purpose and thrust of the section, if someone, who otherwise fell within it, was wholly deprived of its benefit because the deceased had been forced to spend time in hospital immediately prior to his death. Even if the deceased had returned from hospital for his last few days of life, as not infrequently occurs, a person who otherwise fell within section 1(1A) of the Act might still be deprived of its benefit if the Treasury Solicitor's concession is wrong, because it could then be argued that the deceased and the applicant were not 'living ... in the same household' for 'the whole of the period of two years ending with the death'."

Secondly, the claimant must prove that he or she was living in the same household as the deceased (see *Re Watson,* below). This means living together as one unit, and does not include living in the same property but as two separate independent entities.

The issue is not simply whether the deceased and the claimant were physically living together, but whether they remained bound together emotionally and socially and did not consider their relationship at an end:

> "The relevant word is 'household' not 'house' . . . Thus they will be in the same household if they are tied by their relationship. The tie of that relationship may be made manifest by various elements, not simply their living together under the same roof, but the public and private acknowledgement of the mutual protection and support that binds them together. In former days one would possibly say one should look at the whole *consortium vitae.* For present purposes it is sufficient to ask whether either has demonstrated a settled acceptance or recognition that the relationship is in truth at an end. If the circumstances show an irrevocable breakdown of the relationship, then they no longer live in the same household and the Act is not satisfied. If, however, the interruption is transitory, serving as a pause for reflection about the future of a relationship going through difficult times but still recognised to be subsisting, then they will be living together in the same household and the claim will lie." (Ward LJ in *Gully v Dix,* The Times, 28 January 2004).

In *Gully v Dix*, the claimant, who had lived with the deceased for about twenty-seven years, had left him following an incident when he had threatened her with a knife. She had then remained apart from him for about three months during which time the deceased had telephoned the claimant's daughter on several occasions to ask the claimant to come back. The daughter did not pass on the messages to her mother for fear that she would return to live with the deceased. It was held that on the facts the relationship had not ended. The deceased had genuinely wanted the claimant to return home and the claimant would have returned had she known of the deceased's telephone calls.

Thirdly, the claimant must prove that he or she was living "as the husband or wife of the deceased". This rules out cases where the parties were living in the same household but in a relationship other than that of a husband and wife. It is not necessary to prove that the claimant and the deceased were in a sexual relationship. In *Re Watson* (above, page 34), Neuberger J held that when considering whether two people are living together as husband and wife it would be wrong to conclude that they do so simply because their relationship is one which a husband and wife would have. If the test were as wide as that, then, bearing in mind the enormous variety of relationships that can exist between husband and wife, virtually every relationship between a man and a woman living in the same household would fall within section 1(1A). When considering whether the claimant was living as the wife or husband of the deceased the court should determine the matter by asking whether, in the opinion of a reasonable person with normal perceptions, it could be said that the two people were living together as husband and wife, although the multifarious nature of marital relationships should not be ignored.

In an earlier decision, *Adeoso v Adeoso* [1981] 1 All ER 107, [1980] 1 WLR 1535 (CA), where the court was concerned with the provisions of the Domestic Violence and Matrimonial Proceedings Act 1976, section 1(2), the parties were living together but had not had a sexual relationship with each other for two years. They slept in separate bedrooms. They had not spoken to each other and had communicated with each other only by way of notes. The applicant had stopped cooking and washing for the respondent. The Court of Appeal held that the parties' relationship was comparable to a marriage in the last stages of breakdown, and the fact that the parties had severed their living arrangements did not mean that they were living in different households.

Same-sex cohabitants

Section 1(1A) refers to the claimant living "as the husband and wife of the deceased". "Cohabitant" is not defined in the 1975 Act as amended, but section 62 of the Family Law Act 1996 defines "cohabitants" as "a man and a woman who, although not married to each other, are living together as husband and wife". There is no specific reference to gender in section 1(1A) of the 1975 Act, and therefore the provision is capable of being construed as applying to both heterosexual and homosexual relationships. There are no decided cases on this issue under the 1975 Act. It is submitted that recent decisions under the Rent Act 1977, in matrimonial proceedings, and of the European Court of Human Rights under the European Convention on

Human Rights, suggest that the 1975 Act should apply to same-sex relationships.

In the cases under the Rent Act 1977, the courts have overcome the problem by two separate routes. In *Fitzpatrick v Sterling Housing Association Ltd* [1998] Ch 304, [1997] 4 All ER 991, [1999] 3 WLR 1113, the appellant and the tenant lived together for seventeen years in a loving, faithful, monogamous homosexual relationship. When the tenant suffered a stroke the appellant gave up work and nursed him for eight years. The issue for consideration was whether, as the homosexual partner of the lawful tenant, he was entitled to succeed to a statutory tenancy under the Rent Act 1977, Schedule 1, paragraphs 2(2) and 3(1), as a "person living with the original tenant as his or her wife or husband" or as "a member of the original tenant's family". The Court of Appeal, by a majority, held that the provisions applied only to heterosexual relationships and that only persons who were bound together by ties of kinship could be regarded as "member[s] of the original tenant's family". Ward LJ, in his dissenting judgment, stated that if a gay couple was asked in what manner do they live together, the couple's answer would be not different from that given by a heterosexual couple save only in the one respect – that in their case their sexual relations are homosexual, not heterosexual:

> "no distinction can sensibly be drawn between the two couples in terms of love, nurturing, fidelity, durability, emotional and economic inter-dependence – to name but some and no means all of the hallmarks of a relationship between a husband and his wife.
>
> With regard to the only distinguishing feature, sexual activity, that is a function of the relationship of a husband and his wife, a man and his mistress and it is a function of homosexual lovers. That the activity takes place between members of different sexes or of the same sex is a matter of form not function … I would say that there is no essential difference between a homosexual and a heterosexual couple and accordingly I would find that the appellant had lived with the deceased tenant as his husband or wife …
>
> The common man may be vaguely disapproving of the homosexual relationship which is not for him but having shrugged his shoulders, he would recognise that the relationship was to all intents and purposes a marriage between those partners. They lived a life akin to that of any husband and wife. They were so bound together that they constituted a family."

On appeal, the House of Lords concluded that the appellant could not be treated as the spouse of the deceased tenant because the language of the statutory provisions could be interpreted as referring only to heterosexual relationships, but stressed that this interpretation was confined to the particular provision of the Rent Act 1977.

In *Ghaidan v Mendoza* [2002] EWCA Civ 1533, [2003] 2 WLR 478, [2002] 4 All ER 1162, the Court of Appeal gave a wider interpretation to the words of the statute and held that the words "as his or her wife or husband" should be construed as "as if they were wife or husband".

It could be argued that the decision in *Fitzpatrick* is distinguishable from the provisions of the 1975 Act in that the Rent Act 1977, Schedule 1 paragraph 2 as amended specifically provided that a person living with the original tenant as his or her wife or husband is to be treated as the "spouse" of the original tenant. By contrast, the 1975 Act as amended does not make any reference to a "cohabitant" being treated as a "spouse". Furthermore, there is no reason why the interpretation given to the phrase "as his or her wife or husband" in *Ghaidan v Mendoza* should not be applied to "as the husband or wife of the deceased" in the 1975 Act.

The case of *El-Al Israeli Airlines Ltd v Danilowitz* [1994] Case 712/94 (National Journal of Sexual Orientation Law) Vol 1 p 304, Supreme Court of Ireland, concerned the provision of airline tickets for a married spouse and unmarried cohabitants of different sexes, but not for same-sex partners. Barak VCJ said:

> "the benefit is thus provided to a lasting living-together partnership which displays a strongly tied up social relationship. It is therefore obvious, in my view, that to take this benefit away from homosexual spouses constitutes a discriminatory violation of the equality principle. The differentiating reason standing behind this decision has to do with sexual orientation. But this latter fact was both immaterial and unfair … Does a homosexual cohabitation differ from a heterosexual one, so far as partnership, unity and a social relationship is concerned?"

It could also be argued that the denial of the right to claim under section 1(1A) of the 1975 Act violates the prohibition against discrimination in Article 14 of the European Convention on Human Rights, which provides that:

> "The enjoyment of the rights and freedoms set forth in this Convention shall be secured without discrimination on any ground such as sex, race, colour, language, religion, political or other opinion, national or social origin, association with a national minority, property, birth or other status."

The court is obliged, when construing any statutory provision, to give it an interpretation which is compatible with the Convention rights. It seems that in *Ghaidan v Mendoza* the appellant successfully argued that to give the provision of the Rent Act any other meaning would offend his rights under Article 14. In *Fitzpatrick's* case, although the court considered Articles 8 (the right to respect for family life) and 12 (the right to marry), and in particular the decisions in *Harrogate BC v Simpson* [1986] 2 FLR 91; *X, Y and X v UK* (1997) 24 EHRR 143, [1997] 2 FLR 892, (ECHR), and

Kerkhoven v Netherlands (Application No. 15666/89), 19 May 1992, unreported (ECHR), Article 14 was not argued or considered. As a result of the decisions of the European Court, the government has introduced the Gender Recognition Bill (see page 26) and the Civil Partnership Bill (see page 2). The effect of this legislation, when it comes into force, will have to be considered by practitioners when advising client in same-sex relationships, but in the meantime the above decisions should assist in putting forward an arguable case.

In dealing with cases of transsexuals, both the European Court of Human Rights (in *Goodwin v UK* [2002] IRLR 664, [2002] 2 FLR 487) and the House of Lords (in *Bellinger v Bellinger* – see page 26) have held that the law which restricts the right of a transsexual to enter a valid marriage with another male is inconsistent with Articles 8 and 12 of the European Convention. Article 14 was not considered in these cases, but by analogy, on an analysis of the authorities and the reasons given for the decisions, it is difficult to suggest any basis for arguing that it is fair, just and compatible with the Convention, and particularly Article 14, to deny a homosexual partner, who fulfils all the requirements of the 1975 Act, the same right as a heterosexual partner; or to argue that a same-sex partner should be considered differently from a heterosexual cohabitant and denied the rights extended to heterosexual partners when, as pointed out by Ward LJ in *Fitzpatrick's* case and by Barak VCJ in *El-Al Israeli Airlines Ltd v Danilowitz,* such relationships have all the attributes of a different sex relationship.

Until the law under the 1975 Act is clarified, a claimant in a same-sex relationship may be able to pursue a claim under section 1(1)(e) of the Act (see below).

A Child of the Deceased

A "child" includes:

(a) an illegitimate child;
(b) a child *en ventre sa mere* (i.e., a child who has been conceived but not born at the death of the deceased (section 25(1));
(c) an adult child (*Re Coventry, Coventry v Coventry* [1980] Ch 461, [1979] 2 All ER 815; and *Re Callaghan (Deceased)* [1985] Fam 1, [1984] 3 WLR 1076, [1984] All ER 790);
(d) an adopted child, that is, a child adopted in England and Wales or in any foreign country if the adoption is recognised in England and Wales.

An adopted child

A child of the deceased who is adopted after the death of his biological parent but before making a claim under the 1975 Act is not a child of the deceased within the meaning of section 1(1)(c) of the Act. He is not eligible to make a claim under the Act because, by virtue of section 39(2) of the Adoption Act 1976, on his adoption, he is treated in law as the child of the adopters and as such loses the right to make a claim against the estate of his biological parent. He is, however, eligible to make a claim under the Act as the child of his adoptive parent. By virtue of section 67(1) of the Adoption and Children Act 2002, the status of an adopted child will remain the same when the provisions of the 2002 Act come into force.

Furthermore, section 42(4) of the Adoption Act 1976 does not confer on an adopted child an "interest expectant", as he does not have an enforceable right against the estate of the deceased. The 1975 Act merely confers a right to apply to the court for relief and thus he has a cause of action only (*Re Collins (Deceased)* [1990] 2 All ER 47). The court in *Re Collins* was reinforced in this view by the decision in *Whyte v Ticehurst* [1986] Fam 64, [1986] 2 WLR 700, [1986] 2 All ER 158, where a wife who had applied for financial provision under the 1975 Act died before the hearing of her claim. Her personal representatives applied to carry on with the proceedings on behalf of her estate. In dismissing the application, Booth J stated that the claim under the Act arose from the relationship of the two parties and was a personal one. On the death of the claimant it ceased to exist. In *Re Bramwell (Deceased), Campbell v Tobin* [1988] 2 FLR 263, it was held that the right to apply for financial provision under the Act was a mere hope or contingency and not a cause of action.

The presumption of legitimacy

Where the parents of a child were married to each other at the time of his birth the presumption of legitimacy arises and the husband of the mother is presumed to be the father of the child unless the contrary is proved. The presumption can be relied on to prove parenthood until the presumption is rebutted. A certified copy of the claimant's birth certificate is regarded as sufficient evidence of legitimacy provided it contains the relevant information on parenthood. If an appropriate birth certificate is not available and there is no other evidence to prove the claimant's parenthood, an order for DNA profiling to be carried out could be applied for.

Where a child is born not later than the period of gestation after the marriage has been dissolved, the presumption of legitimacy may arise. In *Re Overbury (Deceased)* [1955] Ch 122, [1954] 3 All ER, a child was born less than nine months from the date when the mother's first marriage was dissolved but during the subsistence of her second marriage. On the basis of the common law presumption of legitimacy the child was presumed to be the child of both the former husband and the mother's current husband. The court ruled, on the evidence, that the child was the legitimate child of the first husband. Today, however, the matter would be established by DNA profiling, not by legal presumption or inference.

Legitimation
Where the parents of an illegitimate child marry then, provided that the father is domiciled in England and Wales at the time of the marriage, the child is legitimated at the date of the marriage (Legitimacy Act 1976, section 2). Where the father is not domiciled in England and Wales at the date of the marriage the child is legitimated if the law of the domicile of the father legitimates the child by marriage (Legitimacy Act 1976, section 3).

A child of a void marriage
Section 1 of the Legitimacy Act 1976 as amended provides that a child of a void marriage, whenever born, shall, subject to subsection 1(2) of and Schedule 1 to the Act, be treated as the legitimate child of his parents if at the time of the insemination resulting in the birth, or where there was no such insemination, the child's conception (or at the time of the celebration of the marriage if later), both or either of the parties reasonably believed that the marriage was valid. For this provision to apply, the father of the child must be domiciled in England and Wales at the time of the birth or, if he died before the birth, he must have been so domiciled immediately before his death (section 1(2)).

The phrase "child of a void marriage" does not extend to an illegitimate child born before the void marriage took place. Such a child is not the child of a void marriage but a child of his parents; the child is not legitimated by the subsequent void marriage of the parents. Section 1(1) applies only to a child born *after* a void marriage has been celebrated (*Re Spence (Deceased)* [1990] Ch 652, [1990] 2 WLR 1430, [1990] 1 All ER 827).

A child born or conceived during the subsistence of the marriage is legitimated notwithstanding the subsequent annulment of the marriage (Matrimonial Causes Act 1973, section 16).

A child born as a result of infertility treatment
Where a child has been conceived as a result of infertility treatment, such as artificial insemination, gamete intra-fallopian transfer (GIFT), or *in vitro* fertilisation (IVF), the legal status of the child, particularly having regard to the provisions of the Human Fertilisation and Embryology Act 1990, needs to be considered. Likewise, the question of who, in law, are the child's legal parents, arises.

Where a child is born as a result of *in vitro* fertilisation or gamete intra-fallopian transfer, or where sperm taken from the husband or partner of the mother is used to inseminate her (AIH), the legal relationship between the child and the parent can be established on the basis of blood ties. The child is the child of the mother and her husband or partner, and if the parents were married, the child would be legitimate.

The Family Law Reform Act 1987, section 27, applied where a child was born to a married woman after 4 April 1988 in England and Wales as a result of artificial insemination of the woman (whose marriage had not at the time been annulled or dissolved), and she was artificially inseminated with the semen of some person other than her husband. In such a case, unless it was proved to the satisfaction of any court by which the matter had to be determined that the husband did not consent to the insemination, the child was treated in law as the child of the parties to the marriage. If the husband had not consented to the insemination of his wife, then he was not regarded as the child's father and the child was fatherless. Section 27 was replaced, as from 1 August 1991, by the provisions of the Human Fertilisation and Embryology Act 1990. Section 28 of that Act, headed "Meaning of 'father'", provides:

(1) This section applies in the case of a child who is being or has been carried by a woman as the result of the placing in her of an embryo or of sperm and eggs or her artificial insemination.

(2) If–

(a) at the time of the placing in her of the embryo or the sperm and eggs or of her insemination, the woman was a party to a marriage, and

(b) the creation of the embryo carried by her was not brought about with the sperm of the other party to the marriage,

then, subject to subsection (5) below, the other party to the marriage shall be treated as the father of the child unless it is shown that he did not consent to the placing in her of the embryo or the sperm and eggs or to her insemination (as the case may be).

(3) If no man is treated, by virtue of subsection (2) above, as the father of the child but–

(a) the embryo or the sperm and eggs were placed in the woman, or she was artificially inseminated, in the course of treatment services provided for her and a man together by a person to whom a licence applies, and

(b) the creation of the embryo carried by her was not brought about with the sperm of that man,

then, subject to subsection (5) below, that man shall be treated as the father of the child.

(4) Where a person is treated as the father of the child by virtue of subsection (2) or (3) above, no other person is to be treated as the father of the child.

(5) Subsections (2) and (3) above do not apply–

(a) in relation to England and Wales and Northern Ireland, to any child who, by virtue of the rules of common law, is treated as the legitimate child of the parties to a marriage, …

(c) to any child to the extent that the child is treated by virtue of adoption as not being the child of any person other than the adopter or adopters.

(6) Where–

(a) the sperm of a man who had given such consent as is required by paragraph 5 of Schedule 3 to this Act was used for a purpose for which such consent was required, or

(b) the sperm of a man, or any embryo the creation of which was brought about with his sperm, was used after his death,

he is not to be treated as the father of the child.

(7) The references in subsection (2) above to the parties to a marriage at the time there referred to–

(a) are to the parties to a marriage subsisting at that time, unless a judicial separation was then in force, but

(b) include the parties to a void marriage if either or both of them reasonably believed at that time that the marriage was valid; and for the purposes of this subsection it shall be presumed, unless the contrary is shown, that one of them reasonably believed at that time that the marriage was valid.

(8) This section applies whether the woman was in the United Kingdom or elsewhere at the time of the placing in her of the embryo or the sperm and eggs or her artificial insemination.

(9) In subsection (7)(a) above, 'judicial separation' includes a legal separation obtained in a country outside the British Islands and recognised in the United Kingdom."

Thus, a child born to a married woman after 1 August 1991 as a result of artificial insemination with the semen of someone other than her husband, is treated as the child of the woman and her husband unless it is shown that the husband did not consent to the artificial insemination (Human Fertilisation and Embryology Act 1990, section 28(2)). Where, however, the parents remain married, the common law presumption of legitimacy arises, because section 28(5) provides that section 28(2) does not apply to any child who, by virtue of the rules of common law, is treated as the legitimate child of the parties to a marriage. If paternity is disputed, the dispute will have to be resolved by the court. If the presumption of legitimacy applies it can be rebutted by evidence which establishes that the person could not be the father, for example, that he was impotent, and if necessary by DNA profiling. In a case in France on 6 November 1997 a court in Paris ordered the exhumation of the body of Yves Montand, the French film actor who had died six years previously, to enable the applicant, who alleged that she was his daughter, to establish paternity.

Where an unmarried woman is artificially inseminated in the course of licensed treatment services provided for her and her partner together, the partner is treated in law as the father of the child (section 28(3)). Where the treatment is provided abroad, and therefore by a non-licence holder, the provisions of section 28(3) do not apply to confer paternity on the man. In such cases the issues which may arise include whether the treatment was provided "together"; whether there was appropriate counselling; and whether the man was warned of the consequences and given a full opportunity to make an informed choice. Similarly, where treatment is provided to a couple together but is administered by a person who is not licensed under the 1990 Act, section 28(3) does apply to confer paternity (*U v W (AG Intervening)* [1998] 1 FCR 526).

On the question whether the treatment services were provided for the couple "together", in *Re B (Parentage)* [1996] 2 FLR 15, the father had given sperm with which the mother was inseminated. At the time of insemination the relationship between the mother and the father had ended. The father accepted that he was the biological father of the twins born to the mother. The issues were whether the parties had been receiving treatment together, and whether the father had consented. On the facts it was found that the father had not given his express consent, but it was held that he was deemed to have given his consent as he and the mother had been receiving treatment together and he had not at any stage before insemination withdrawn his consent.

For paternity to be established where the man has no biological connection with the embryo, the embryo must have been placed in the mother at a time when treatment services were being provided for the couple together. Thus, where the relationship between the couple had ended before the embryo was placed in the mother and the mother had misled the medical authority by falsely representing that the relationship with the man was subsisting, the man was held not to be the legal father of the child by reason of section 28(3) (*Re R (IVF: Paternity of Child)* [2003] 1 FLR 1183).

In *Re Q (Parental Order)* [1996] 1 FLR 369, [1996] 2 FCR 345, an unmarried mother acted as a surrogate mother for a married couple. She gave birth to a child created from the egg of the wife and fertilised by sperm from a donor under a licensed arrangement. Under section 28(6) the donor could not be treated as the father of the child. Section 28(3) did not apply as the husband had not received treatment services together with the woman. It followed that no man could be treated in law as the father of the child.

In *R v Human Fertilisation and Embryology Authority ex parte Blood* [1997] 2 FLR 742, [1997] 2 FCR 501, the claimant wished to be artificially inseminated with sperm taken from her husband at her request by doctors treating him when he was unconscious and receiving treatment in hospital. The sperm was stored in a licensed institution. The husband died. The Human Fertilisation and Embryology Authority refused to release the sperm to the applicant on the ground that no written consent had been obtained from the husband and he had not received counselling as required by the provisions of the 1990 Act. On appeal it was held that the provisions of the

1990 Act had been breached and therefore the sperm should not have been preserved and stored. The court directed that in future those responsible for treating a man and a woman together should take the precaution of having the necessary consent not only to storage, but also to the continuation of treatment if the man should die before the sperm is used. Leave was, however, given for the sperm to be released so that the woman could receive treatment in Belgium. A child born as a result of such treatment is not considered the child of the husband (section 28(2) and (3)).

Where, by mistake of the hospital authorities, the sperm used for IVF treatment was not, as intended, that of the woman's husband but of another man, the husband could not be treated as the father of the child born to the mother as he had not consented to the use of the donor sperm. The presumption of legitimacy was displaced as DNA tests established that the husband was not the father of the child born to the mother (*Leeds Teaching Hospital NHS Trust v A & B* [2003] 1 FLR 1091).

Section 28(6)(b) of the Human Fertilisation and Embryology Act 1990 provides that where:

(a) the sperm of a man who had given the consent required by paragraph 5 of Schedule 3 to the Act was used for a purpose for which such consent was required; or

(b) the sperm of a man, or any embryo, the creation of which was brought about with his sperm, was used after his death,

he is not to be treated as the father of the child.

The effect of this provision is that where a man donates his sperm and consents to its use by a licensed person, the man will not be treated as the child's father. The child will be fatherless.

Section 27 of the 1990 Act provides that a woman who has carried a child as a result of artificial insemination, and no other woman, is treated as the mother of the child. This section is relevant in a case of assisted reproduction if there is any question whether or not a claimant is the child of a deceased female.

The law in this area is evolving and new scenarios will emerge. The cases cited above are provided as an illustration of the difficulties that may arise and the hurdles to be crossed. It is not intended to be a full exposition of the law in this area. It is essential to be vigilant and aware of new developments. In cases of doubt, advice from an expert in this field of law is advised.

A child who is the subject of a parental order

By virtue of section 30 of the Human Fertilisation and Embryology Act 1990, a court is authorised to make a "parental order" providing for a child who is genetically the child of the husband or wife or both, but is carried by a surrogate, to be treated in law as the child of the husband and wife. Before such an order is made the court must be satisfied that:

(a) the couple are married and have attained the age of eighteen years at the date of the making of the order;
(b) they are domiciled in the United Kingdom or in the Channel Islands or the Isle of Man;
(c) the child has had his home with the husband and wife;
(d) the application for an order is made within six months of the birth of the child.

Pursuant to regulations made under the 1990 Act, where a parental order has been made, the Adoption Act 1976, section 39(1)(a), (2), (4) and (6), apply with the appropriate modifications. A child who is the subject of a parental order is treated as the child of the marriage of the couple in whose favour the order is made. The child is not regarded as illegitimate. The provisions of the Adoption Act 1976, section 42 (rules of construction of instruments) also apply to a parental order. Similar provisions will apply when the Adoption and Children Act 2002 comes into force.

Declaration of parentage, legitimacy and legitimation

Any person may apply to the court for a declaration that:
(a) a person named in the application is or was his parent;
(b) he is the legitimate child of his parents;
(c) he has become a legitimated person;
(d) he has not become a legitimated person.

(Family Law Act 1986, as amended by the Family Law Reform Act 1987).

In order to make the application the applicant must establish that he is domiciled in England and Wales on the date of the application, or has been habitually resident in England and Wales throughout the period of one year preceding the application.

The procedure to be followed is set out in the Family Proceedings Rules 1991 (SI 1991 No. 1247, "FPR"). The application is begun by petition issued in the High Court, the county court or the magistrates' court. The petition must contain the information set out in FPR, rule 3.13(1) and, where relevant, FPR, rule 3.16(2). A copy of the birth certificate of the person whose parentage is in issue, and a supporting affidavit verifying the petition, must accompany the petition. At least one month before the petition is filed a copy of the petition and the accompanying documents must be served on the Attorney General (FPR, rule 3.13), who has the right to intervene. The court also has the power at any stage of the proceedings, of its own motion or on the application of any party to the proceedings, to direct that the Attorney General be served with the proceedings.

The respondents to the application are generally the parents if they are alive; or, if deceased, the personal representatives and any other party who may be affected by the declaration, e.g., a beneficiary. FPR, rule 3 and rule 3.16(6) and (8) apply to the joinder of respondents to the application. Service should be as required by FPR, rules 2.9, 9.3 and 10.6 as appropriate.

The respondents to the application must file an answer within twenty-eight days of service of the petition and any reply must be filed within fourteen days thereafter (FPR, rules 2.12 and 2.13). Interlocutory orders and directions may be obtained in accordance with the provisions of FPR, rules 2.13 to 2.42. The hearing is before a judge, and if a declaration is made it is in form M30 if the proceedings are in the High Court or in the county court.

A similar procedure is followed where a declaration of legitimacy or legitimation is sought under section 56 of the Family Law Act 1986. The Family Proceedings Rules 1991 again apply to such an application. Any declaration made is in Form M31.

Any Person Treated as a Child of the Family

Section 1(1)(d) of the 1975 Act provides that an application for an order under section 2 may be made by:

> "any person (not being a child of the deceased) who, in the case of any marriage to which the deceased was at any time a party, was treated by the deceased as a child of the family in relation to that marriage".

See the Civil Partnership Bill 2004, mentioned on page 2, for proposed amendments which would apply to same-sex couples.

"Child of the family" is not defined in the Act. It does not, here, have the meaning given to it in the Matrimonial Causes Act 1973. The Family Law Act 1996 does not provide any new definition of "child of the family".

Unlike under the Matrimonial Causes Act 1973, there is no age limit. An adult child of the deceased has been regarded as a child of the family and entitled to claim under the Act. But for a claim to proceed, the deceased must have been married and the claimant must have been treated by him as a child of the family within that marriage. Whether a claimant falls within this category depends on the facts of the individual case, but the following examples of decided cases may assist.

In *Re Callaghan (Deceased)* [1985] Fam 1, [1984] 3 WLR 1076, [1984] 3 All ER 790, the claimant was a step-son of the deceased. He was six years old when his natural father died. Three years later the deceased came to live in his mother's home as a lodger. Subsequently the deceased and the mother lived together as man and wife. The deceased treated the claimant as his son. In 1960 the claimant married, but continued to maintain a close relationship with his mother and the deceased. In 1972 the claimant's mother and the deceased married. The mother died in 1980. The claimant continued to care for the deceased until his death. In considering the claim, Booth J said:

> "In this case the acknowledgement by the deceased of his own role of grandfather to the plaintiff's children, the confidences as to his property and financial affairs which he placed in the plaintiff, and his dependence on the plaintiff to care for him in his last illness are examples of the deceased's treatment of the plaintiff as a child, albeit an adult child of the

family. All these things are part of the privileges and duties of two persons who, in regard to each other, stand in the relationship of parent and child; it is the existence of that relationship that enables the plaintiff to apply under section 1(1)(d) of the Act. My view is not altered by the fact that, in considering an application by a person coming within section 1(1)(d), the court is required to have regard to the education or training of the applicant and must also consider the extent to which the deceased has assumed responsibility for his maintenance."

In *Re Leach (Deceased), Leach v Leinderman* [1986] Ch 226, [1985] 3 WLR 413, [1985] 2 All ER 754, when the claimant's father remarried the claimant was thirty-two years of age and was living away from home. The claimant never lived with her father and her stepmother in one household. The claimant's father died in 1974, and the step-mother died in 1981. The claimant applied for an order under section 2 of the Act for a half share in the net estate. The claim was allowed because the step-mother had, after her marriage and on the death of her husband, expressly and impliedly assumed the position of a parent towards the claimant. Her treatment of the claimant after the death of the claimant's father was a consideration which the court could take into account as it stemmed from the marriage. In his judgment, Slade J said:

"I do not think it is necessary or appropriate to imply any similar temporal limitation in the construction of section 1(1)(d) of the 1975 Act, which is directing attention solely to the treatment of the child by one party to the marriage. The phrase used is not 'during the subsistence of the marriage', it is the wider phrase 'in relation to the marriage'. It seems to me that the treatment of an applicant by a surviving spouse after the death of the other spouse may be a relevant factor in deciding whether the applicant qualifies under section 1(1)(d), provided that such treatment is referable to or 'stems from' the marriage."

It seems therefore that the treatment by the step-parent of the claimant after the death of the natural parent may be a relevant factor provided that the treatment was "in relation to the marriage".

Where grandparents take on the responsibility of caring for a grandchild, that child may become a child of the family both within the Matrimonial Causes Act 1973, section 52, and within the 1975 Act. In such cases the court considers the matter objectively to determine the relationship between the grandparents and the child, and whether the services were provided by them by way of support in an emergency, or whether they had assumed primary responsibility for the child and cared for the child as their own child (*Re A (A child of the family)* [1998] 1 FLR 347 (CA); see also *Re Debenham (Deceased)*, referred to at page 65).

Where a couple are living together but are not married to each other, a child of one of them cannot be regarded as eligible under section 1(1)(d) because, although there does not have to be a subsisting marriage, the conduct towards the claimant has to be in relation to marriage. It matters not that the conduct relates to events after the death of one of the parties to the marriage.

To summarise therefore:

(a) "child", for the purposes of this section, includes an adult child;
(b) the relevant "treatment" is the behaviour of the deceased towards the claimant;
(c) the treatment must stem from the marriage, and the treatment of the claimant by the surviving spouse after the death of the natural parent is relevant;
(d) the mere display of affection, kindness and hospitality by a surviving step-parent towards a step-child is not sufficient. Proof that the deceased expressly or impliedly assumed the position of a parent towards the claimant, with the attendant responsibilities and privileges of that relationship, may be relevant.

Any Other Person Maintained by the Deceased

Section 1(1)(e) provides for any other person, not included in sections 1(1)(a) to (d), who, immediately before the death of the deceased, was being maintained, either wholly or partly, by the deceased, to apply for an order under section 2 of the 1975 Act for financial provision.

"Being maintained"

Section 1(3) of the 1975 Act provides that a person is to be treated as having been maintained by the deceased, whether wholly or partly, if the deceased, otherwise than for full valuable consideration, was making a substantial contribution in money or money's worth towards the reasonable needs of that person. "Full valuable consideration" does not include marriage or a promise of marriage (section 25(1)).

The 1975 Act does not make any other reference to the meaning of "being maintained", but the provisions which apply to this category of claimant identify what must be established. This includes:

(a) the contribution made by the deceased must have been for the maintenance of the claimant and to provide for his reasonable needs;
(b) the contribution must be substantial;
(c) the payments must have been made immediately before the death of the deceased;
(d) the payments must have been made otherwise than for full valuable consideration;
(e) the nature, extent and purpose of the payments, and the length of time over which they were made, are matters which the court is required to take into account;
(f) that the deceased had "assumed responsibility" for the claimant.

Case law provides some guidance. In *Re Coventry, Coventry v Coventry* [1980] Ch 461, [1979] 3 All ER 815, Goff J referred to cases in which the meaning of maintenance was considered. He said:

> "In particular, in this country there is *Re E, E v E* ([1996] 1 WLR 709, [1966] All ER 44), in which Stamp J said that the purpose was not to keep a person above the breadline but to provide reasonable maintenance in all the circumstances. If I may say so with respect, 'breadline' there would be more accurately described as 'subsistence level'. Then there was *Millward v Shenton* ([1972] 1 WLR 711, [1972] 2 All ER 1025) in this court. I think I need only refer to one of the overseas reports … *Duranceau* ([1952] 3 DLR 714) where, in somewhat poetic language, the court said that the question is 'Is the provision sufficient to enable the dependant to live neither luxuriously or miserably, but decently and comfortably according to his or her station in life?'. What is proper maintenance must in all cases depend upon all the facts and circumstances of the particular case being considered at the time, but I think it is clear on the one hand that one must not put too limited a meaning on it; it does not mean just enough to enable a person to get by, on the other hand, it does not mean anything which may be regarded as reasonably desirable for his general benefit or welfare."

In *Re Beaumont (Deceased), Martin v Midland Bank Trust Co Ltd* [1980] Ch 1144, [1979] 3 WLR 818, [1980] 1 All ER 266, the male claimant and the deceased began living together in 1940 in the deceased's bungalow. In 1964, the deceased retired. In 1966 the claimant retired from full-time work, but continued to work part-time for about ten years. Thereafter he received his state pension. He made regular weekly payments to the deceased for his accommodation and shopping expenses. In all other respects they pooled their resources. The deceased also made it clear to the claimant that the bungalow belonged to her and she paid all the outgoings. She also paid the claimant for any decorating work that the claimant did for her. In dismissing the claim, the court held that on the true construction of the section the court was required to look not at the *de facto* state of maintenance existing at the moment of death, but at the "substantial and enduring" basis or arrangement existing between the parties and the degree of maintenance existing normally and habitually under the arrangement; it must be shown that the deceased had "made a substantial contribution in money or money's worth towards the reasonable needs of the applicant otherwise than for full valuable consideration". Full consideration was not limited to consideration provided under a contract but extended to any contribution. Thus if a couple living together made equal contributions towards the maintenance of each other by bearing one half of the cost, then, although both would be making a contribution towards the reasonable needs of the other they would be doing so for full valuable consideration, and each would be barred from making a claim against the estate of the other.

To satisfy the provision of section 3(4) that the deceased had assumed responsibility for the claimant it is not enough to establish a mere fact of maintaining someone. The assumption of responsibility requires an act on the part of the deceased demonstrating that he had undertaken or assumed some "legal or moral responsibility" for the claimant. In *Re Beaumont,* Sir Robert Megarry VC said:

> "The word 'assumes', too, seems to me to indicate that there must be some act or acts which demonstrate an undertaking or responsibility or the taking of the responsibility on oneself. It may be that in some cases where there is neither a negation of responsibility nor a positive undertaking of it, it will be possible to infer from the circumstances attending the act of maintenance that there has indeed been an assumption of responsibility. But it is for the plaintiff to establish that there has been an assumption of responsibility, and for the defendant to have to rebut any presumption of an assumption of responsibility which is to be drawn from the bare fact of maintenance."

To establish that the deceased had assumed responsibility for the claimant's maintenance, the applicant must show that the deceased had regarded himself as discharging the responsibility to maintain the claimant (*Re B* [1999] Ch 206, [1999] 2 FCR 145). It is the settled basis or general arrangement between the parties as regards maintenance during the lifetime of the deceased which must be considered, not the actual, perhaps fluctuating, variations of it which exist immediately before the death of the deceased. The court has to consider whether the deceased, otherwise than for valuable consideration, was in fact making a substantial contribution in money or money's worth towards the reasonable needs of the applicant on a settled basis or arrangement, which either was still in force immediately before the deceased's death, or would have lasted until death but for the approach of death and the consequent inability of either party to continue to carry out the arrangement.

The court must also balance what the deceased was contributing against what the claimant was contributing. Where the claimant was contributing more than the deceased, or where the contributions were equal, there would generally be no dependency. Where there is any doubt about the balance tipping in favour of the deceased's contribution being the greater, then the claimant is entitled to succeed (*Jelley v Illife* [1981] Fam 128, [1981] 2 WLR 801, [1981] 2 All ER 29).

As a general rule, the fact that the claimant was being maintained by the deceased under an arrangement subsisting at the time of the deceased's death and the deceased was making a substantial contribution in money or money's worth to the reasonable needs of the claimant will raise an inference that the deceased had undertaken to maintain the claimant and had assumed responsibility for the maintenance of the claimant. In such circumstances there would be no need to establish any other overt act to demonstrate the "assumption of responsibility".

All the contributions made, whether in kind or otherwise, are taken into account. In *Jelley v Illife* the claimant was a widower, and had lived with his daughter before he went to live with the deceased. The deceased lived in a house which had been conveyed to her by her children on the understanding that she would leave it to them on her death. The claimant and the deceased shared the accommodation and pooled their resources. The claimant also did the household jobs and the gardening. He lived in the house rent-free. On her death the deceased left all her property to her children and nothing to the claimant. His claim was allowed.

In *Re Wilkinson (Deceased), Neale v Newell* [1978] Fam 22, [1977] WLR 514, [1978] 1 All ER 221, Arnold J, when assessing the value of the contributions made by the claimant, said:

> "It is not very easy, when one is dealing with the question of what is full valuable consideration, to measure in purely financial terms the sort of things which the applicant was doing for the deceased and the sort of thing which the applicant represented to the deceased ... Somehow it seems to me I have to measure those matters in order to see whether, fairly looked at, they were a full valuable requital or return for that which the applicant received from the deceased."

In this case, the sister of the deceased had left her employment at the age of sixty-one to look after the deceased. The deceased had paid for all the food and met the household expenses. The claimant had done the light housework and the cooking. The heavier tasks were carried out by a home help and a sister-in-law. Having carried out a balancing exercise, the court held that the deceased had made a substantial contribution to the claimant's needs, and that the duties that the claimant performed for the deceased could not be regarded as full valuable consideration in return for the contribution made by the deceased.

In *Rees v Newbery and the Institute for Cancer Research* [1988] 1 FLR 1041, for almost ten years before the death of the deceased the claimant had lived in a flat owned by the deceased. He had paid to the deceased rent below the market rent. The deceased had given instructions for a new will which was to provide that the claimant should continue living at the property under the existing arrangements for life. Before the will could be executed, the deceased died. The claim was allowed because the deceased had not only expressly indicated his intention, but the arrangement between the deceased and the claimant before death led to the inference that the claimant had been maintained by the deceased; that he had assumed responsibility for the claimant's maintenance; and that he was making a substantial contribution towards the reasonable needs of the claimant.

In *Re Beaumont (Deceased)* (above, page 50), the court had held that the claimant had to establish some action on the part of the deceased to show that he had undertaken responsibility for the claimant before the claim could succeed, whereas the decision in *Rees v Newbery* suggests that it is open to the court to infer the assumption of responsibility from the surrounding facts, unless the circumstantial evidence suggests that the deceased had made it clear that he did not assume such responsibility or that his actions should not be taken to mean that the support afforded to the claimant would continue. It is not necessary, however, to prove that the deceased had intended to maintain the claimant after his death. Such an intention may be inferred from the conduct of the deceased, particularly where the conduct was such that the claimant had been made wholly or partly dependent on the deceased, as was the case in *Graham v Murphy* [1997] 1 FLR 860. There, the deceased and the claimant had lived together from 1976 until 1993 when the deceased died. The deceased had a substantial income, whereas the claimant was a lorry driver with an average wage of £160 per week. By reason of the deceased's income the couple were able to live a comfortable life including eating out and going for holidays abroad which were paid for by the deceased. In 1990 the deceased became ill. Throughout her illness until her death the claimant cared for and provided support for the deceased. The claim was allowed, although the court referred to it as "quite close to borderline". The provisions of section 2 of the Law Reform (Succession) Act 1995 were then not in force. Had they been, the claimant would have succeeded in any event as a cohabitant of the deceased.

A situation similar to that in *Graham v Murphy* arose in *Bishop v Plumley* (see page 33). In *Re Haig, Powers v Haig* [1979] LS Gaz R 476, the claimant had lived with the deceased as his wife for three years preceding his death. She was given the right to occupy his house rent-free.

In *Bouette v Rose* [2001] 1 FLR 363, [2000] 1 FCR 385, the deceased had suffered severe mental and physical disabilities due to medical negligence at birth, for which she had been awarded damages of £250,000. Her financial affairs were managed by the Court of Protection and her mother, who was the claimant, was appointed receiver. The Court of Protection provided the mother with regular payments in her capacity as receiver for the deceased's maintenance. The deceased died intestate. Her estate passed on intestacy to the mother and father in equal shares. The mother made a claim under the Act. On the father's application, the claim was struck out on appeal from the master's decision; the judge held that the Court of Protection had made payments solely for the deceased's maintenance and that the deceased had not assumed responsibility for her mother's maintenance. On the mother's appeal, the Court of Appeal held that it must have been obvious to the Court of Protection that the payments made to the mother would necessarily be used to meet the mother's financial and material needs, particularly as, on the facts, the mother had made no contribution toward the household expenses. There was nothing absurd in the notion of the Court of Protection acting as the conscience of the patient and making provision for those to whom the patient would have felt a moral obligation if the patient had been of full capacity. On the facts it would have been obvious to the Court of Protection that the payments made to the mother were also providing the financial and material needs of the mother throughout the deceased's life.

In *Malone v Harrison* [1979] 1 WLR 1353, the claimant was the second mistress of the deceased. She had been wholly supported and maintained by the deceased, but he failed to make provision for her. Her claim was allowed.

In *Harrington v Gill* [1983] 4 FLR 265 (CA), the deceased and the claimant had cohabited together for eight years before the deceased's death in the deceased's house. The claimant had retained the tenancy of her council flat. She carried out all the household duties and the deceased had paid all the outgoings. The claimant, who worked, also spent all her earnings on household extras, clothes and other necessaries. She made no contribution towards her board and lodgings. The deceased died intestate and his estate, worth about £65,000, went to his daughter, who was financially comfortable. At the date of the hearing the claimant was seventy-four. Her income consisted of the state pension. She was living in the deceased's house but had surrendered the council tenancy. On appeal it was held that, in considering the needs of the claimant, the court will, among other things, consider the extent to which the deceased had undertaken responsibility for the claimant; the standard of living enjoyed by the claimant during the deceased's lifetime; and the extent to which the deceased contributed to that standard of living. Dunn LJ said:

> "The scheme of the Act, as set out in the sections, is a little complicated, but at the end of the day the court must ask itself the question: What testamentary provision would a reasonable man in the position of this deceased have made for the plaintiff in all the circumstances, including the matters set out in section 3."

In *Re Viner (Deceased), Kreeger v Cooper* [1978] CLY 3091, the claim was by a woman aged seventy-four. She had been widowed for a year before her brother's death, and was left in difficult circumstances. The brother had been persuaded by another sister, to whom he was voluntarily paying £10 per week, partly to maintain the claimant. He agreed to divide the weekly payments of £10 between his two sisters, and grudgingly paid £5 per week to the claimant for six months prior to his death. By his will the deceased left an annuity to his unmarried sister but nothing to the claimant. The residue of his estate was left to a person with whom he had worked. On the facts the claimant succeeded.

Whether the deceased made a substantial contribution to another's reasonable needs depends, therefore, on the circumstances of the parties and their relationship. The deceased's motives or intentions are relevant only when the court is considering the matters set out in section 3(4) and determining whether or not to make any orders for financial provision for the claimant:

> "the benefactor's motives or intentions are irrelevant except insofar as section 3(4) makes them relevant to the court's task of deciding whether or not to make provision for the claimant and if so in what form and what scale." (*per* Walker LJ in *Bouette v Rose,* above, page 53).

"Substantial contribution"

In determining whether the deceased had made a "substantial contribution" to the claimant's needs, the court must approach the problem in the round, apply a common sense approach, and avoid fine balancing computations involving the value of normal exchanges of support in the domestic sense (*Bishop v Plumley,* above). In *Jelley v Illife*, Griffiths LJ said:

> "the court must use common sense and remember that the object of Parliament in creating this extra class of persons who may claim benefit from an estate was to provide relief for persons of whom it could truly be said that they were wholly or partially dependent on the deceased."

Further:

> "Each case will have to be looked at carefully on its own facts to see whether common sense leads to a conclusion that the applicant can fairly be regarded as a dependant."

See also *Bouette v Rose*, above, page 53.

"Immediately before the death of the deceased"

In claims under section 1(1)(e) of the 1975 Act, the relationship between the deceased and the claimant must have been continuing at the date of the death, and the claimant must show that the deceased was maintaining the claimant immediately before the death of the deceased. If the arrangement had ceased before the date of death, the claim will fail no matter how short the period. Thus, where cohabitation between the deceased and the claimant had ended two years before the death of the deceased the claim failed (*Layton v Martin* [1986] 2 FLR 227).

Where the deceased had left his mistress nine days before he died it was held that she was not being maintained by him immediately before his death and the claim failed (*Kourgy v Lusher* [1983] 4 FLR 65).

In *Sen v Headley* [1991] Ch 425, [1991] 2 WLR 1308, [1991] 2 All ER 636, the claimant was obliged to make a claim under the doctrine of *donatio mortis causa* as she was not being maintained by the deceased immediately before his death.

On the other hand, the court does have regard to the circumstances which led to the break. Dependence is not measured in days or weeks, particularly where the separation has been forced or is involuntary, for example where the deceased becomes terminally ill and has to be admitted to hospital. In *Re Beaumont* (above, page 50), Megarry VC said:

> "If one is to reject a mere examination of the *de facto* state of affairs existing at the instant of death, and seek to discover something more substantial and enduring than that, then an assumption by the deceased of responsibility for the maintenance of the applicant seems to me to be the relationship which has to be considered. If immediately before the death of the deceased such an assumption of responsibility by the deceased for the applicant was in existence, and under it the applicant was being maintained, wholly or partly, by the deceased, then the applicant may claim under the Act. In such a case the degree of maintenance would not be whatever degree existed at the instant before death but whatever degree normally and habitually existed under the assumption of responsibility which was then in existence."

In *Re Kirby (Deceased), Hirons v Rolfe* [1982] 3 FLR 249, the court applied the test of "the settled pattern of arrangements between the parties ignoring any transitory interruption owing to changes of circumstances occurring immediately before the death and possibly in anticipation of it". In *Re Watson* (see page 34), although the point was not raised by the Treasury Solicitor, Neuberger J said that if it had, it was not an argument which in his view could respectably have been advanced, and that as a matter of ordinary language, the fact that someone is in hospital for even a long period at the end of which he dies does not mean that "he ceased to be part of the household of which he was a part until he was forced by illness to go to hospital and to which he would have returned had he not died".

It would seem therefore that the court will not apply the words of the section strictly, but consider the facts and the circumstances which led to the separation, and the parties' relationship, and take a broad and practical decision.

Chapter 4

The Basis of the Claim

Ground on which a Claim may be Made

There is only one ground upon which a claim under the 1975 Act may be made, namely that:

> "the disposition of the deceased's estate effected by his will or the law relating to intestacy, or the combination of his will and that law, is not such as to make reasonable financial provision for the applicant."

When determining whether the disposition is such as to make reasonable financial provision for the claimant, the court must have regard to the matters set out in section 3 of the Act; these are discussed in detail in Chapter 5, and the material in this chapter should be read in conjunction with Chapter 5.

"Reasonable Financial Provision"

The statutory definition of "reasonable financial provision" is provided in section 1(2) of the Act. A distinction is drawn between a claimant who is a surviving spouse of the deceased and all other categories of claimant.

Surviving spouse

In respect of a surviving spouse (except where the marriage with the deceased was the subject of a decree of judicial separation and at the date of death the decree was in force and the separation was continuing), reasonable financial means:

> "such financial provision as it would be reasonable in all the circumstances of the case for a husband and wife to receive, whether or not that provision is required for his or her maintenance" (section 1(2)(a)).

The section makes an exception in relation to a surviving spouse who was separated from the deceased under a decree of judicial separation which was in force at the date of death. Such a spouse comes within the provision which applies to all other claimants (see below). If, despite the decree of judicial separation, the parties were living together and therefore the decree of judicial separation was not in force and the separation was not continuing, then the claimant would be entitled to receive financial provision as set out under section 1(2)(a) above.

The Act makes one further exceptional provision in section 14, in respect of a claimant who is a former spouse, but whose ancillary relief application in the matrimonial proceedings has not been considered. The court may, if it thinks just to do so, treat such a claimant as if there had not been a decree of divorce, nullity or judicial separation (i.e., as if that party was still married to the deceased), provided that:

(a) the death of the other party to the marriage occurs within twelve months from the date on which a decree of divorce or nullity of marriage has been made absolute, or a decree of judicial separation granted; and

(b) an application for ancillary relief under the Matrimonial Causes Act 1973 sections 23 and 24 has not been made, or such an application is pending, at the time of the death of the deceased.

See the Civil Partnership Bill 2004, Schedule 4, for the proposed amendments to this provision to extend it to same-sex couples.

Any other claimant

In respect of any other claimant, "reasonable financial provision" means:

> "such financial provision as it would be reasonable in all the circumstances of the case for the claimant to receive for his maintenance." (section 1(2)(b)).

Maintenance and reasonable financial provision compared

In the case of a surviving spouse and a spouse who comes within section 14 of the Act, the statutory definition makes clear that the court's considerations are not restricted to what would be reasonable for the spouse to receive by way of "maintenance". In the words of Oliver LJ in *Re Besterman, Besterman v Grusin* [1984] Ch 458, [1984] 3 WLR 280, [1984] 2 All ER 656:

> "The Inheritance (Family Provision) Act 1938, which firsts introduced the concept of reasonable testamentary provision into English Law, was an Act to provide for the *maintenance* of dependants. The present Act remains such an Act in relation to dependants other than surviving spouses, but this section expressly provides that in the case of a surviving spouse the governing criterion is to be what the court considers to be 'reasonable' provision unqualified by any such consideration. There may, of course, be cases where that reasonable provision in all the circumstances might be restricted to maintenance, but the sub-section makes it clear that the court, in making such reasonable provision, is not to be inhibited by what I may call 'the 1938 concept' that maintenance is the only criterion or, indeed, even that that is the dominant consideration."

In *Re Besterman* the deceased and the claimant were married in 1958 and lived together until the deceased's death in 1976. The deceased had been extremely wealthy, and his wife had enjoyed an extremely high standard of living. Under the deceased's will the widow received personal chattels and a life interest in war stocks, which produced an income of £3,500 per annum.

The principal beneficiary was Oxford University. The widow had no financial resources, other than a state pension. She applied for financial provision to be made for her. An interim order was made, granting her a lump sum of £75,000 to purchase a property, and interim periodical payments of £15,000 per annum. At the substantive hearing a lump sum of £259,000 was awarded to her. The widow appealed on the ground that the provision made for her was considerably less than she might reasonably have expected to receive under the Matrimonial Causes Act 1973, which was a factor the court was required, by section 3(2) of the 1975 Act, to have regard to when calculating reasonable financial provision. On appeal, the lump sum was increased to £378,000. See also page 94.

The following cases further illustrate this special provision in respect of a surviving spouse.

In *Re Bunning (Deceased), Bunning v Salmon* [1984] Ch 480, [1984] 3 WLR 265, [1984] 3 All ER 1, the claimant had married the deceased when she was thirty-five and he was fifty-six years of age. Soon after the marriage, the claimant had given up her job; she had found it impossible to continue working and to run a home and give assistance to the deceased in his business. In 1971 the deceased retired. In 1978 the claimant left him. Between 1968 and 1973 the deceased had given the claimant various capital funds. On his death in 1982 he left various legacies, including legacies to the Royal Society for the Protection of Birds and the Department of Veterinary Medicine at Cambridge University. At the time of his death the widow's assets were estimated at £98,000 and her income consisted of an investment income, the state pension and other pensions. She had an earning capacity. There were no dependants. In considering her claim, the court had regard, as required by section 3(2) of the Act, to the lump sum she would have been awarded on an application under the Matrimonial Causes Act 1973. The court also had regard to her age and the likely length of widowhood and took into account the fact that the assets had been built up largely by the deceased's own efforts before the marriage. In determining what the wife would have received under the 1973 Act the court took into account the husband's likely future needs and on that basis the maximum the widow would have received would have been £36,000. The court would not interfere with the deceased's right to dispose of his assets as he willed save to make reasonable provision for the wife. She was awarded £60,000 which, added to her existing assets, gave her about one half of the total assets of the parties.

In *Re Rowlands (Deceased)* [1984] FLR 813, (1984) 14 Fam Law 280, the claimant widow was ninety years of age. She had lived apart from the deceased for about forty-three years when the deceased died in 1981. She lived with her daughter and son-in-law. The deceased left his entire estate, worth about £100,000, to his two sons. On her application the widow was awarded £3,000. She appealed. The court, in dismissing her appeal, took into account her special position as a surviving spouse and the matters set out in section 3(2) of the Act, but found that she was not able to formulate what her needs were and what she would do if a substantial award was made in her favour. There was no indication how her life would be enhanced if periodical payments or a lump sum were awarded to her.

In *Stead v Stead* [1985] FLR 16, (1985) 15 Fam Law 154, the claimant and the deceased had married when they were fifty-five and sixty-three respectively. The deceased had two children by his first marriage. The parties worked in their farming business and the claimant also worked as a nursery nurse. On their retirement they sold the farm and purchased a new home and thereafter the claimant took in paying guests. The deceased was eighty-eight when he died. By his will he gave his widow a life interest in the home on condition that she discharged all the outgoings, and bequeathed a sum of £60,000 on trust to be invested to give her an income for life. On her claim under the Act she was awarded a lump sum and periodical payments of £1,500 per year.

In *Re Krubert* [1997] Ch 97, [1997] 1 FLR 42 (CA), by his will, the deceased left his widow £10,000 and a life interest in the matrimonial home and in the residuary estate. The trustees were required to hold the residuary estate in trust for the deceased's sister and brother in equal shares. At first instance the widow received what was in effect 85 per cent of the net estate and the brother and sister received legacies of £7,000 each. On appeal, it was held that, in considering an appropriate award for a surviving spouse, the figure resulting from what would have been a section 25 exercise in ancillary relief proceedings under the Matrimonial Causes Act 1973 was merely one of the factors to which the court must have regard, subject to the overriding consideration of what was reasonable in all the circumstances. The Court of Appeal preferred the approach in *Re Besterman*, stating that it was more in accordance with the intention of the Act read as a whole.

Thus, in considering whether to make an order on a claim by a surviving spouse the court will have regard to:

(a) the special provision set out in section 1(2)(a), which is not linked to "maintenance". Maintenance may be a relevant factor but, as stated in *Re Besterman,* it is not the only criterion, nor is it the "dominant consideration";
(b) all the relevant factors referred to in section 3 of the Act;
(c) the standard of living of the parties (*Re Besterman*);
(d) the provision which the claimant might reasonably have expected to receive if, on the day the deceased died, the marriage, instead of being terminated by death, had been terminated by a decree of divorce (section 3(2)(b)); the section 25 of the Matrimonial Causes Act 1973 exercise is, however, only one of the factors to which the court must

have regard, but this is subject to:

(e) the overriding consideration of what would be reasonable in all the circumstances, and

(f) the fact that in a claim under the 1975 Act the court is not concerned with the competing claims of merely two parties to the marriage; other beneficiaries' interests must also be considered.

The judicially separated spouse and the former spouse

A surviving spouse who is judicially separated from the deceased, and a former spouse, are placed in the same category as other claimants. This distinction may well have been made because a judicially separated or divorced spouse would have been entitled to apply for ancillary relief under sections 23 and 24 of the Matrimonial Causes Act 1973, and such an application would have been considered and dealt with under the very wide jurisdiction provided by the 1973 Act. Any claim for financial provision made under the 1975 Act by such a spouse would therefore be additional to the relief already obtained in the matrimonial proceedings (but see section 15 of the Act, which entitles the court to exclude such a claimant from seeking an order under the 1975 Act; see page 129).

Some confirmation for the basis of this distinction can also be found in the special and exceptional provision made by section 14 of the 1975 Act in respect to a claimant whose marriage to the deceased was dissolved or annulled, or who was granted a decree of judicial separation, within twelve months of the date of the deceased's death and the application under the 1973 Act has not yet been made or is still pending.

In view of the court's powers, under the Matrimonial Causes Act 1973, to make capital adjustments between spouses on a divorce, annulment of marriage or judicial separation, there will be few cases in which it is possible for a former spouse to satisfy the condition that the deceased's will or the law of intestacy, or the combination of his will and that law, failed to make reasonable financial provision for the former spouse. The former spouse will have to show exceptional circumstances. These exceptional circumstances were referred to by Ormrod LJ and Purchas LJ in *Re Fullard (Deceased)* [1981] 3 WLR 743, [1981] 2 All ER 796. Purchas LJ said:

> "There must be some exceptional developments or conditions present which would make the analysis of what is reasonable as at the date of the death, which is the time when considerations under the Act must be made, different from the circumstances which existed at the dissolution of the marriage when these matters were carefully canvassed and resolved.
>
> There may well, of course, be developments which would enable an ex spouse to seek relief with some chances of success under this Act. Where there has been a long period of time since the dissolution of the marriage in circumstances in which a continuing obligation to support the ex spouse has been established by an order of the court, by consent, or

> otherwise, under which periodical payments have been, and continue to be made up to the date of death there may be circumstances such as envisaged by counsel for the applicant, where the death itself unlocks a substantial capital sum of which the testator should have been aware and from which had he made a will, at the time immediately before his death, he ought, within the criteria of the 1975 Act have made provision. There may be other incidents of further accretion of wealth but I doubt that the mere fact of accretion of wealth after the dissolution of the marriage would justify an application. An application would only be justified if all the circumstances of the case and all the considerations set out in the Act, made it reasonable that the testator should have made some provision as at the time of his death for the applicant."

The test in such cases is whether the former wife is reasonably provided for, and it is only if she is not so provided for that the court will interfere. See also *Whiting v Whiting* [1988] 2 FLR 189.

The following are some of the cases in which the former spouse's claim was considered. They illustrate the distinctly different principles which apply to such claims.

In *Re Talbot* [1962] 1 WLR 1113, [1962] 3 All ER 174, the claimant was fifty-two. Her marriage to the deceased had been annulled and on her application for ancillary relief an order by consent was made in her favour for her maintenance at the rate of £432 per annum. A year later she gave birth to a child of whom the deceased was not the father. The deceased nevertheless continued to maintain the claimant. The deceased remarried and had three children by his second wife, all of whom were minors at the date of his death. His estate, worth £19,397, was left to his second wife. When dismissing the claimant's claim Baker J said:

> "Before I sit in the testator's chair to amend his last will, I must be satisfied that he has not been reasonable in his solution to the dilemma which faced him. Would any testator have done other than did the deceased in the circumstances which existed immediately before his death? I think not. Such a man would regard interference with his disposition as an unwarranted statutory and judicial defeat of his intentions. It may be said that all testators who fail to make provision for a former wife are unreasonable if a substantial maintenance order is suddenly to be cut off at death. But that problem should be decided by the ordinary canons of human behaviour and decency, balancing generosity against parsimony and the duty to a family against the claim of an ex-wife."

In *Re Eyre* [1968] 1 WLR 530, [1968] 1 All ER 968, when allowing the claimant's claim, Lane J had regard in particular to:

(a) the fact that there was an order for secured maintenance in her favour;

(b) whether the first wife should be accorded financial equality with the widow. He came to the view that there was no such general rule, even when there was nothing to choose between them so far as conduct was concerned, as there were many other factors to be considered; and

(c) the fact that an accretion of wealth to the estate had occurred since the first marriage ended.

In *Lusternik v Lusternik* [1972] Fam 125, [1972] 2 WLR 203, [1972] 1 All ER 592, the claim succeeded because the deceased had not made a full, frank and honest disclosure of his means.

In *Re Crawford (Deceased)* [1983] 4 FLR 273, the deceased and his former wife were divorced in 1968. A consent order was made, under which the deceased was required to pay the claimant, by way of maintenance, one third of his gross salary less the mortgage and the insurance on the former matrimonial home, where the claimant lived. In addition, the deceased was obliged to pay the outgoings on the property. In 1975 the former matrimonial home was sold and another property purchased for the claimant. The deceased thereafter failed to make the payments under the order. The deceased remarried and had two children, who were both dependants at the date of his death. On his retirement, the deceased received a lump sum of £69,767, which was paid into a joint account with his second wife. He also received an index-linked pension. In 1979, on the deceased's suggestion, the claimant made an application for a lump sum order on a "clean break" basis. Before the application was heard the deceased died. The claimant did not receive anything from his estate. The trustees of the pension fund, however, paid to the widow £72,402.12, which did not form part of the net estate. She also received an indexed linked pension, as did her two children; again, these did not form part of the net estate. Her pension was £10,369, and the children's was £8,644.92. She also received £46.27 state pension per week and £10.50 child allowance per week. In addition, the widow had an interest in one half of the former wife's house and a life interest in the other half under the will. She also had capital of £69,767.21 and the lump sum from the pension fund. The claimant had capital of £1,500 and state benefits of £34.28 per week.

It was conceded that the deceased had failed to make reasonable financial provision for the claimant and that a lump sum should be awarded. The issue related to the amount which should be awarded, and in deciding the amount the questions were:

(a) whether the court should take into account the financial benefits accruing to the beneficiaries of the estate of the deceased or to the claimant by reason of the death of the deceased but which did not form part of his estate;

(b) whether there were any special principles to be applied by the court in determining whether or not to exercise its discretion under section 9 of the 1975 Act to treat the severable share in joint property as part of the net estate (see page 114);

(c) if the court decided to exercise its discretion under section 9, whether the former wife's house should be treated differently from the net estate merely by virtue of its being joint property; and

(d) if the needs of the former wife remained the same, whether it was reasonable for her to receive the same provision out of the estate as was agreed or ordered by the court during the deceased's lifetime.

The court held that:

(a) section 3(1)(c) of the 1975 Act directed the court to take into account the financial resources and financial needs which any beneficiary of the estate of the deceased had, so that the lump sum of £72,402 paid to the second wife, the pension of £10,369 per annum that she received and the capital of £69,767 which she had in the building society were financial resources which the court was entitled to take into consideration in deciding the claim;

(b) there were no special principles which ought to guide the court in considering its discretion under section 9, as that section sets out everything which is necessary for the purpose of guiding the court;

(c) if the court exercised its discretion and ordered the deceased's share in the joint property to be treated as part of the net estate, it should not be treated differently;

(d) it should not be assumed that provision for a former wife under the Act was the same as a periodical payments order under the Matrimonial Causes Act 1973, as different considerations applied under the two enactments. In assessing the amount to be awarded to the former wife, the court had to look at all the matters set out in section 3(1)(a) to (g) and section 3(2)(a) and (b);

(e) on the facts of the case, the former wife needed an annuity of £4,000 per annum, which would cost £35,000 and, in the circumstances, an order under section 9 of the Act was justified.

See also *Re Farrow (Deceased)* [1988] 1 FLR 205, (1987) 17 Fam Law 14.

Where, however, a former wife's claims for income and capital have been finally settled, she is unlikely to succeed in obtaining an order under section 2. In *Brill v Proud* [1984] Fam Law 59 (CA), the parties had obtained, upon a decree, a consent order in full and final settlement of their claims for financial relief. The former wife had, under the terms of the settlement, received the former matrimonial home in return for a small lump sum. Her income was higher than her husband's. On his death she made a claim which failed.

The Meaning of "Maintenance"

There is no definition of "maintenance" in the 1975 Act, but case law provides guidance on the approach of the courts on what can be regarded as reasonable maintenance.

"Maintenance" includes payments which directly or indirectly enable the claimant in the future to discharge the cost of living. It does not include a capital sum to enable the claimant to discharge his tax liability (*Re Dennis (Deceased), Dennis v Lloyds Bank* [1981] 2 All ER 140).

The fact that the claimant is in necessitous circumstances is not enough (*Re Coventry (Deceased), Coventry v Coventry* [1980] Ch 461; [1979] 3 All ER 815 (CA). In *Re Coventry* the claimant was the only child of the deceased. He returned home when he was twenty-six. Shortly afterwards, the mother left home and she lived separately from the deceased. The son looked after the home, did all the tasks and contributed towards the general outgoings. When he married his wife took over the task, but the marriage broke down. A year later the deceased died intestate. His entire estate passed to his widow. The son, who was on a low income and had no savings, made a claim. His claim failed.

"Maintenance" does not mean whatever may be desirable for the claimant's general benefit or welfare (*Re Coventry*).

"Maintenance" means what is sufficient to enable the claimant to live decently and comfortably according to the station in life to which she has been called. It does not merely mean enough to bring the claimant to subsistence level, but it does not mean sufficient to give the claimant a life of luxury (Ewbank J in *Re Debenham (Deceased)* [1986] 1 FLR 404, (1985) 16 Fam Law 101, adopting the decision in *Re Duranceau* [1952] 3 DLR 714). In *Re Debenham* the claimant was an unwanted child of the deceased, who had always been aloof, distant and cruel to the claimant. The claimant was brought up by her grandparents in South Africa. When she was twenty-one she came to England to see her mother but she was totally rejected by her. Subsequently, the mother had led her to believe that she would be "all right" if anything happened to the mother. The deceased left the claimant a legacy of £200, and most of the residue of her estate was left to six charities. The claimant was fifty-eight, and epileptic and a sick woman. She and her husband lived on a pension of £500 per annum and state benefits. In allowing her application the court had regard to the matters set out in section 3; the fact that there were no other claimants; and the fact that the deceased had no obligations or responsibilities to the charities. The court considered that the deceased owed the claimant a moral obligation and responsibility and awarded her a lump sum of £3,000 and periodical payments of £4,500 per annum. The case was distinguished from that of *Re Coventry* (above). See also *Re Scott-Kilvert (Deceased), Robinson v Bird* [2003] 2 All ER (D) 190, on luxury items not coming within the meaning of "maintenance".

"Maintenance" means no more or less than the claimant's and his family's way of life and well-being, his health and financial security. In *Graham v Murphy* [1997] 1 FLR 860, on the facts, it was decided that maintenance did not mean that the claimant should be provided with a lavish lifestyle or such as would relieve him from working, or such as would provide him with a high standard of life for the rest of his life.

Some moral obligation of maintenance over and above blood ties must be established. In *Re Goodchild, Goodchild v Goodchild* [1997] 1 WLR 1216, [1997] 3 All ER 63, [1997] 2 FLR 644, the deceased and his wife had executed simultaneous wills in favour of the survivor of them and then in favour of their adult son. After his wife's death the deceased remarried and made a new will leaving his entire estate to his second wife. On the son's claim, it was held that the wills were not mutually binding but that when the first wife made her will it had been on the clear understanding that her husband would give effect to their mutual intention. That gave rise to a moral obligation to provide for the son. The deceased was in breach of that obligation which left the son in financial difficulties; in those circumstances the court must ensure that adequate financial provision was made for the son to provide for his reasonable needs for maintenance and support.

It is not enough to establish relationship and necessity. A child must also establish special circumstances, which must be relevant to the issues before the court. Moral obligation is the most obvious special circumstance although not the only one (*Re Abrams* [1996] 2 FLR 379). In *Re Pearce (Deceased)* [1998] 2 FLR 705 (CA), the deceased's son had worked hard on the deceased's farm without pay and was told repeatedly by the deceased that he would leave the farm to him. The deceased and his wife divorced and the deceased started cohabiting with the defendant. The deceased made a will leaving all his property to her. She subsequently moved out but the deceased did not alter his will. The son was on a low income. He had five children and lived in a property which required considerable improvement. The court found that the deceased owed a moral obligation to his son and had not made reasonable financial provision for him.

In *Re Hancock (Deceased)* [1998] 2 FLR 346, the deceased did not make any provision for one of his daughters because sufficient funds were not available, but stipulated that, in the event of his wife's predeceasing him, his money was to be divided between his beneficiaries, which included his daughter. The deceased's assets included a plot of land, which was valued at £100,000, and which he left to his other children. The land was sold at a price higher than had been expected and the children received a windfall. The daughter's claim succeeded on the basis that the deceased's will clearly indicated that he would have made provision for her if he had believed he had sufficient assets available. A periodical payments order of £3,000 per annum was awarded.

For other examples where an award was made, see *Rees v Newbery and the Institute for Cancer Research* [1988] 1 FLR 1041, and *Re Watson* [1999] 1 FLR 878.

Failure by the deceased to provide for the claimant during the claimant's minority does not entitle the claimant to apply for financial provision from the deceased's estate when he becomes an adult (*Re Jennings (Deceased)* [1994] Ch 286, [1994] 3 All ER 27 (CA)).

In *Re Christie (Deceased), Christie v Keeble* [1979] Ch 168, [1979] 2 WLR 105, [1979] 1 All ER 546, an order was made to redress the balance between the two children of the deceased. The court interpreted section 1(2)(b) thus:

> "In my judgement, the financial provision that is thus contemplated is not necessarily financial provision that would be 'required' for the applicant's maintenance. The contrast between paragraphs (a) and (b) of section 1(2), in my judgment, makes it clear. Nor in my judgment does the use of the word 'maintenance' carry with it any implication that the applicant, in order to qualify, must be in any way in a state of destitution or financial difficulty. Nor in my judgment, is it useful to refer to the test as being an objective test, whatever that word may mean, in the context of this Act which directs the court to consider the particular and personal matters set out in section 3.
>
> In my judgment the word 'maintenance' refers to no more and no less than the applicant's way of life and well-being, his health, financial security and allied matters such as the well-being, health and financial security of his immediate family for whom he is responsible."

Other cases where the court has made an award include cases where the claimant is mentally disabled and on state benefits. State benefits have been disregarded in considering whether reasonable financial provision had been made for the claimant by the deceased. In *Re Collins* [1990] Fam 56, [1990] 2 All ER, the deceased died intestate. The claimant was her daughter who was mentally subnormal, unemployed and on state benefit. She was awarded £5,000 and her entitlement to state benefit was disregarded.

The fact that the claimant is on state benefit should not preclude the person from seeking or being granted an award unless, as occurred in *Re E, E v E* [1966] 1 WLR 709, [1966] 2 All ER 44, the estate is so small that it would not benefit anyone to make any awards. Since those under disability, particularly those with mental disability, are often treated in the community, an award can provide them with some basic needs and comfort which would otherwise not be available. See *Hanbury v Hanbury* (page 97), where an award of £39,000 was settled on a discretionary trust. Where a person is on benefit, and particularly where the recipient of such benefit is under some disability, it is essential to ascertain the maximum capital which a person is entitled to have and still remain eligible for benefit.

In deciding the reasonableness of the provision made by the testator the court will apply the objective test.

Chapter 5

Matters to which the Court is to Have Regard

Introduction

As explained in the previous chapters, there are certain preliminary issues on which the court has to be satisfied before it can go on to consider and determine a claim under the Inheritance (Provision for Family and Dependants) Act 1975, namely whether the claim has been issued within the time limit prescribed by the Act or following leave to bring such a claim out of time; and whether the claimant is eligible to bring the claim.

If the court is satisfied on the preliminary issues, section 3 of the 1975 Act comes into play. It requires the court to have regard to all the matters set out in the section in determining whether the disposition of the deceased's estate effected by his will or the law of intestacy, or the combination of his will and that law, is such as to make reasonable financial provision for the claimant; and, if the court considers that reasonable financial provision has not been made, in determining whether and in what manner it exercises its powers under section 2.

When determining a claim for an order under section 2 of the Act, the court must therefore proceed in three stages:

(a) the court must decide whether the disposition of the deceased's estate effected by his will or the law of intestacy, or both, makes reasonable financial provision for the claimant;
(b) if such reasonable financial provision has not been made, the court must decide whether or not to exercise its powers under the Act; and
(c) if it does decide to exercise its powers, it must decide in what manner it should do so.

The requirements of section 3 are mandatory. In determining the issues, the court must take into account all the matters set out in section 3(2) and have regard to those facts as known *at the date of the hearing* (section 3(5)). See *Re Coventry, Coventry v Coventry* [1980] Ch 461, [1979] 3 All ER 815 and *Re Rowlands (Deceased)* [1984] FLR 813, (1984) 14 Fam Law 280. The court therefore requires up-to-date information about the parties' circumstances and the values of all assets, including those of the parties. When dealing with the claim, the court should not:

> "interfere with a testatrix's or testator's disposition merely because the judge may think that he would have been inclined, if he were in the

position of the testator or testatrix, to make some provision for a particular person. I think that the court has to find that it was unreasonable on the part of the testatrix or the testator to make no provision for the person in question, or that it was unreasonable not to make a larger provision."
(*Re Styler, Styler v Griffiths* [1942] Ch 387, [1942] 2 All ER 201, *per* Morton J; see also *Re Talbot* [1962] 1 WLR 1113, [1962] 3 All ER 174).

The Criteria under Section 3

The matters which the court is required to take into account in deciding whether reasonable financial provision has been made, and if not, whether and in what manner to exercise its powers, vary according to the status of the claimant. There are general matters which apply to all claimants. There are additional factors to which the court must have regard in relation to a claim by:

(a) a surviving spouse;
(b) a former spouse;
(c) a cohabitant of the deceased;
(d) a child of the deceased or a child of the family; and
(e) any other person who was being maintained by the deceased.

A surviving spouse

In the case of a claim by a surviving spouse of the deceased the court must have regard to the following matters:

(a) the financial resources and financial needs which the claimant has or is likely to have in the foreseeable future;
(b) the financial resources and financial needs which any other claimant for an order under section 2 of the 1975 Act has or is likely to have in the foreseeable future (see *Re Debenham* [1986] 1 FLR 404, (1985) 16 Fam Law 101, above, page 65);
(c) the financial resources and financial needs which any beneficiary of the estate of the deceased has or is likely to have in the foreseeable future (see *Re Besterman*, page 58, and *Re Debenham* (above));
(d) any obligations and responsibilities which the deceased has towards any claimant for an order under section 2 or towards any beneficiary of the estate of the deceased (see *Rajabally v Rajabally* [1987] 2 FLR 390, page 96);
(e) the size and nature of the estate of the deceased (for the definition of "net estate" see Chapter 7, and see *Re Besterman* (above);
(f) any physical or mental disability of any claimant for an order under section 2 or any beneficiary of the deceased;
(g) any other matter, including the conduct of the claimant or any other person, which in the circumstances of the case the court may consider relevant;
(h) the age of the claimant and the duration of the marriage;

(i) the contribution made by the claimant to the welfare of the family of the deceased, including any contribution made by looking after the home or caring for the family;
(j) the provision which the claimant might reasonably have expected to receive if, on the day on which the deceased died, the marriage, instead of being terminated by death, had been terminated by a decree of divorce. See also *Re Besterman* (above) and *Re Bunning*, page 59.
(section 3(1) and (2)).

See the Civil Partnership Bill 2004, Schedule 4, for the proposed amendments to include similar provisions for same-sex couples.

A former spouse of the deceased who has not remarried and cohabitants
Where the claimant is a former spouse of the deceased who has not remarried, the court must have regard to:

(a) the financial resources and financial needs which the claimant has or is likely to have in the foreseeable future;
(b) the financial resources and financial needs which any other claimant for an order under section 2 of the 1975 Act has or is likely to have in the foreseeable future (see *Re Debenham*, above);
(c) the financial resources and financial needs which any beneficiary of the estate of the deceased has or is likely to have in the foreseeable future (see *Re Besterman* and *Re Debenham,* above);
(d) any obligation and responsibilities which the deceased has towards any claimant for an order under section 2 or towards any beneficiary of the estate of the deceased (see *Rajabally v Rajabally,* page 96);
(e) the size and nature of the estate of the deceased (for the definition of "net estate" see Chapter 7, and see *Re Besterman,* above);
(f) any physical or mental disability of any claimant for an order under section 2 or any beneficiary of the deceased;
(g) any other matter, including the conduct of the claimant or any other person, which in the circumstances of the case the court may consider relevant;
(h) the age of the claimant and the duration of the marriage, or, in the case of a cohabitant, the length of the period during which the claimant lived as the husband or wife of the deceased and in the same household;
(i) the contribution made by the claimant to the welfare of the family of the deceased, including any contribution made by looking after the home or caring for the family.
(section 3(1) and (2)).

See the Civil Partnership Bill 2004, Schedule 4, for the proposed amendments in relation to same-sex couples whose relationships have been dissolved or annulled.

A child of the deceased

In the case of a claim by a child of the deceased the criteria under section 3 are as follows:

(a) the financial resources and financial needs which the claimant has or is likely to have in the foreseeable future;
(b) the financial resources and financial needs which any other claimant for an order under section 2 of the Act has or is likely to have in the foreseeable future (see *Re Debenham,* above, page 65);
(c) the financial resources and financial needs which any beneficiary of the estate of the deceased has or is likely to have in the foreseeable future (see *Re Besterman*, page 58 and *Re Debenham*, page 65);
(d) any obligations and responsibilities which the deceased has towards any claimant for an order under section 2 or towards any beneficiary of the estate of the deceased (see *Rajabally v Rajabally*, below, page 96);
(e) the size and nature of the estate of the deceased (for the definition of "net estate" see Chapter 7, and see *Re Besterman,* above, page 58);
(f) any physical or mental disability of any claimant for an order under section 2 or any beneficiary of the deceased;
(g) any other matter, including the conduct of the claimant or any other person, which in the circumstances of the case the court may consider relevant;
(h) the manner in which the claimant was being, or in which he might have expected to be, educated or trained.

(section 3(1) and (3)).

A person treated as a child of the family

Where the claim is made by a person (not being a child of the deceased) who was treated by the deceased as a child of the family, the court must take into account:

(a) the financial resources and financial needs which the claimant has or is likely to have in the foreseeable future;
(b) the financial resources and financial needs which any other claimant for an order under section 2 of the Act has or is likely to have in the foreseeable future (see *Re Debenham*, above, page 65);
(c) the financial resources and financial needs which any beneficiary of the estate of the deceased has or is likely to have in the foreseeable future (see *Re Besterman,* page 58 and *Re Debenham*, page 65);
(d) any obligations and responsibilities which the deceased has towards any claimant for an order under section 2 or towards any beneficiary of the estate of the deceased (see *Rajabally v Rajabally,* below, page 96);
(e) the size and nature of the estate of the deceased (for the definition of "net estate" see Chapter 7, and see *Re Besterman,* above, page 58);

(f) any physical or mental disability of any claimant for an order under section 2 or any beneficiary of the deceased;
(g) any other matter, including the conduct of the claimant or any other person, which in the circumstances of the case the court may consider relevant;
(h) the manner in which the claimant was being, or in which he might have expected to be, educated or trained;
(i) whether the deceased had assumed any responsibility for the claimant's maintenance and if so, the extent to which and the basis upon which the deceased assumed that responsibility, and the length of time for which the deceased discharged that responsibility;
(j) whether, in assuming and discharging that responsibility, the deceased did so knowing that the claimant was not his own child; and
(k) the liability of any other person to maintain the claimant.
(section 3(1) and (3)).

Any other person who was being maintained by the deceased
In the case of a claim by any other person who, immediately before the death of the deceased, was being maintained, either wholly or partly, by the deceased, the court must have regard to:
(a) the financial resources and financial needs which the claimant has or is likely to have in the foreseeable future;
(b) the financial resources and financial needs which any other claimant for an order under section 2 of the Act has or is likely to have in the foreseeable future (see *Re Debenham*, above, page 65);
(c) the financial resources and financial needs which any beneficiary of the estate of the deceased has or is likely to have in the foreseeable future (see *Re Besterman,* page 58 and *Re Debenham,* page 65);
(d) any obligations and responsibilities which the deceased has towards any claimant for an order under section 2 or towards any beneficiary of the estate of the deceased (see *Rajabally v Rajabally*, below, page 96);
(e) the size and nature of the estate of the deceased (for the definition of "net estate" see Chapter 7, and see *Re Besterman,* above, page 58);
(f) any physical or mental disability of any claimant for an order under section 2 or any beneficiary of the deceased;
(g) any other matter, including the conduct of the claimant or any other person, which in the circumstances of the case the court may consider relevant;
(h) the extent to which, and the basis upon which, the deceased assumed responsibility for the maintenance of the claimant, and the length of time for which the deceased discharged that responsibility.
(section 3(1) and (4)).

Financial Resources and Needs

The financial resources and needs of the claimant(s) and the beneficiaries must be considered (section 3(1)(a) to (c)). Section 3(6) of the Act provides that in considering the "financial resources" of any person the court must take into consideration the person's "earning capacity"; and in considering the financial "needs" of any person, account must be taken of that person's "obligations and responsibilities".

Financial resources

Information about the parties' present and foreseeable resources should be disclosed to the court. This includes information not only about current earnings, but about future prospects. Earnings from investments, such as dividends from shareholdings, interest on savings and income from other sources, must be provided. In respect of a person receiving state benefits, it is necessary to consider the different types of benefit and the amounts of each type to which the person is entitled. Any pension rights, whether a state pension or under an occupational or private pension, are relevant. Information about, and valuations of, capital and other assets, including real property, savings, shareholdings and any other item of value, are required. Any entitlement under an insurance policy should be disclosed, including the surrender value and its value on maturity.

Form E, which is used in applications for ancillary relief, provides a good guide to the information required and can be referred to in section 2 claims cases, as a way of ensuring all the relevant evidence is collected. Form E is available on the website of the Court Service: (www.courtservice.gov.uk).

Financial needs

The needs of a claimant or beneficiary depend on his or her standard of life and the extent to which the deceased provided for that standard. In a claim by a surviving spouse or cohabitant, the lifestyle enjoyed by the claimant and the deceased, to which the deceased contributed, is highly relevant. Whether those needs can be met, however, depends on the size of the estate and the competing claims of other claimants and beneficiaries. It is not the function of the court to re-write the deceased's will, but to carry out a balancing exercise between the competing interests, while giving effect to the deceased's intention.

The 1975 Act requires the court to consider both present and foreseeable future needs. It is under this head that information relating to the parties' future prospects, in terms of both income and capital, is relevant. In addition, the needs of those for whom the claimant or beneficiary is and will continue to be responsible, for example, children, an adult disabled child and other members of the family, are relevant. Any other liability which the claimant or a beneficiary has is also a relevant factor. Where a claimant or beneficiary or his dependant is suffering ill-health, medical evidence should be provided about the person's present condition and the prognosis; in appropriate cases it may be useful to adopt the approach taken in personal injury cases (see *Hanbury v Hanbury*, page 97).

"Financial needs" means reasonable requirements, and in assessing this factor the court may take into account the standard of living enjoyed by the claimant during the lifetime of the deceased, and the extent to which the deceased contributed to that standard (see *Harrington v Gill,* page 54; *Stead v Stead,* page 60; *Malone v Harrison,* page 54; *Re Besterman*, page 58; and *Re Bunning*, page 59).

When considering whether the deceased has made reasonable financial provision for the claimant, the court is concerned with whether the provisions made or not made were reasonable in the circumstances as they existed, and not as the deceased may have thought they existed. See *Millward v Shenton* [1972] 1 WLR 711, [1972] 2 All ER 1025, where the claimant was suffering from *dystrophia syotonica* and was an invalid living on benefits, while his mother made no provisions for any of her six children as she believed they were self-supporting.

The Deceased's Obligations and Responsibilities

The obligations and responsibilities which the deceased had towards the claimant or beneficiary, to be taken into account when considering a claim, must have existed immediately before the death of the deceased. A claim by an adult child of the deceased, without any evidence to show special circumstances, will generally fail, and failure by the deceased to provide for his child during the child's minority does not entitle the child, when he is an adult, to found a claim.

In *Re Jennings (Deceased)* [1994] Ch 286, [1994] 3 All ER 27 (see also page 67), the claimant's father had not made any financial contribution for the claimant's maintenance during his minority and had had no contact with him. The father died without leaving any other children or other dependants. He left his estate to remote relatives and three charities. The claimant lived comfortably. At first instance the judge had held that he was entitled to take into account the deceased's total failure to fulfil his financial and moral obligations towards the claimant during his minority and awarded the claimant £40,000 to enable him to reduce his mortgage. On appeal it was held that Parliament had not intended that the 1975 Act should revive defunct obligations and responsibilities as a basis for a claim under the Act. As a general rule, the obligations and responsibilities of the deceased referred to in section 3(1)(d) are those which the deceased had immediately before his death, and if the claim did not come within paragraph (d) it could not be brought under the general provision of section 3(1)(g). Blood relationship between a parent and child did not impose a continuing moral obligation which could found a claim under the Act. Furthermore, on the facts, the claimant had failed to satisfy the test in section 1(1)(b) that the provision was necessary for his maintenance to enable him to discharge the cost of his daily living at the standard appropriate to him. See also *Williams v Johns* [1988] 2 FLR 475.

The morality of a claim, or the deceased's moral obligation, though not always enough to substantiate a claim, may be relevant when weighing up all the other factors under section 3 and carrying out the balancing exercise. In the case of an adult child it is not necessary to show exceptional circumstances. While a claim by an adult child who is able to support himself, without any other relevant circumstances, is unlikely to succeed, it does not follow that a claim by an adult child will always fail. The test is whether, after applying the section 3 criteria to the particular facts of the case, which include the deceased's obligations towards the claimant, it is established that the deceased did not make such provision as would be reasonable in all the circumstances of the particular case for the claimant to receive for his or her maintenance. The Act does not in any way restrict the interpretation to be given to the word "obligations".

Re Coventry, Coventry v Coventry [1980] Ch 461, [1979] 3 All ER 815 is often cited as authority that an adult child of the deceased is not entitled to make a claim unless it can be shown that there are exceptional circumstances; reliance for this proposition is placed on the judgment of Oliver J where he said:

> "applications for maintenance by able-bodied and comparatively young men in employment and able to maintain themselves must be relatively rare and need to be approached, I would have thought, with a degree of circumspection."

But the learned judge also said:

> "It cannot be enough to say, 'Here is a son of the deceased; he is in necessitous circumstances; there is property of the deceased which could be made available to assist him, but which is not available if the deceased's dispositions stand: therefore those dispositions do not make reasonable provision for the applicant'. There must it seems to me, be established some sort of moral claim by the applicant to be maintained by the deceased, or at the expense of his estate, beyond the mere fact of a blood relationship, some reason why it can be said that, in the circumstances, it is unreasonable that no or no greater provision was in fact made."

In *Re Debenham (Deceased)* [1986] 1 FLR, (1985) 16 Fam Law 101, the deceased had never recognised her obligations towards the claimant, her daughter, whom she had rejected since her birth, and consistently repulsed efforts by the daughter to form a relationship with her, although she had indicated to the claimant that she would be well provided for in her will. The deceased left the claimant £200, even though she was aware that her daughter was an epileptic and unable to work; her life expectancy was lower than average and she and her husband lived on a small income. The deceased left the rest of her estate to six animal charities to whom she had no obligations. It was held that although the deceased did not owe any legal obligation to the claimant who was an adult, she owed her moral obligation and responsibility.

Case law supports the view that the deceased's moral obligation to the claimant justifying an award may be established where promises were made; or where the deceased took advantage of the services of the claimant; or by evidence of the deceased's conduct towards the claimant, as occurred in *Re Debenham*; or where the deceased had said that he owed the claimant such an obligation. In *Re Abrams (Deceased)* [1996] 2 FLR 379, a claim was made by an adult son of the deceased. The son had worked for the deceased in the family business for many years at a low wage in expectation that one day it would be his. He had been forced by the mother's ill-treatment of him to leave the business. The court found that moral obligation was the most obvious circumstance to be taken into account and that, on the facts of the case, the deceased's moral obligation or special circumstances and failure to make provision had been overwhelmingly established to justify an award.

In *Re Pearce* [1998] 2 FLR 705, the claimant, the deceased's son, had worked hard on the deceased's farm without pay and was told by the deceased that he would leave the farm to his son on his death. The deceased, on his divorce, formed a relationship with the defendant. He made a will leaving all his property to the defendant. She then left him and did not live with him again. The deceased did not change his will. The claimant was on a low income and lived with his wife and five children in a home which was in need of substantial improvements. It was held that the deceased had a moral obligation to his son to make financial provision for him.

In *Espinosa v Bourke* [1999] 1 FLR 747, an award was made even though the claimant had left her father when he was aged eighty-seven, to be cared for by his grandson and the cleaner. The court made the award on the basis that, in considering the section 3 criteria, it had to consider that the claimant had initially left her employment to care for her father for eight years; had not been in formal employment for a considerable period; and was in financial need. The deceased had also promised his wife that he would leave the wife's portfolio of shares to his daughter and he therefore had an obligation arising from that promise to make provision for his daughter.

See also *Re Callaghan (Deceased)* [1985] Fam 1, [1984] 3 WLR 1076, [1984] 3 All ER 790, where the deceased, who had been cared for by his adult step-son, was held to have owed the step-son considerable obligations.

In *Re Rowlands (Deceased)* [1984] FLR 813, (1984) 14 Fam Law 280, a daughter of the deceased had cared for her mother, who was bed-ridden, in very difficult circumstances. The court held that, although the deceased owed an obligation towards his wife, the daughter's claim failed.

In *Re Hancock* [1998] 2 FLR 346, the deceased, when not making any provision for the claimant, who was one of his daughters, had expressed that he would have done so if there had been sufficient money available, and had made provision that if his wife predeceased him, his money was to be divided between his children, including the claimant. The estate received a windfall as a result of the sale of a plot of land. It was held that, in determining the claim, the windfall should be taken into account, along with the expressed obligation of the deceased.

It may be possible to establish a claim grounded in moral obligation on the basis of estoppel, where the deceased's actions led and encouraged a person to act in the belief thereby arising, as occurred in *Re Goodchild, Goodchild v Goodchild* (page 66).

Moral obligation is also owed by the deceased where the claimant is mentally disabled or suffers from disability, or where the claimant cared for a disabled child. See *Hanbury v Hanbury* (page 97), where the claimant, an adult child of the deceased, was physically and mentally disabled and the deceased had deliberately taken steps to avoid a claim by his daughter. See also *Re Wood (Deceased), Wood v Wood* [1982] LS Gaz R, 774 and *Bouette v Rose* (page 53).

In the case of a claim by a former spouse, the deceased does not owe any obligation or responsibility where there has been a "clean break" settlement by agreement or court order; indeed the court may specifically have directed, pursuant to section 15 of the 1975 Act, that neither party is entitled, on the death of the other, to apply for financial provision under section 2 of the Act. Where, however, a continuing obligation has been imposed by an order made on marriage breakdown, or it becomes evident that the deceased had not given a full and frank disclosure of his assets, it could be argued that the deceased owed the former spouse obligations and responsibilities (see further Chapter 9).

The Size and Nature of the Net Estate

For the meaning of "net estate" see Chapter 7, and *Re Besterman, Besterman v Gruisin,* page 58.

Where the estate is large, there may not be much difficulty in meeting the competing claims of the claimants and the beneficiaries, particularly where the deceased did not owe any obligations or responsibilities to beneficiaries, as where the beneficiary is a charity (*Re Besterman* and *Re Debenham* (page 75), or a remote relative. Where, however, the estate is modest, the insufficiency of the funds available to meet the competing claims, particularly having regard to the cost of litigation, must be considered. See *Re Gregory, Gregory v Goodenough* [1970] 1 WLR 1455, [1970] 1 All ER 497, where the estate was worth about £2,500; and *Re Harker-Thomas* [1969] P 28, [1968] 3 WLR 1267, [1968] 3 All ER 17, where it was worth about £6,082. Difficulties may also arise where it is not possible to realise the "book" value of assets, or where an asset is tied as in the case of the matrimonial home which provides a home for, say, a child.

Any Physical or Mental Disability of any Claimant or Beneficiary

The cases of *Re Debenham* (page 75); *Hanbury v Hanbury* (page 97), *Re Wood, Wood v Wood* (above) and *Millward v Shenton* (page 74), are good examples of cases in which an award was justified. Inheritance claims, like personal injury claims, should be meticulously prepared, so that the court is provided with all appropriate medical evidence and evidence about the costs of care.

Any Other Relevant Matter Including Conduct

Section 3(1)(g) of the 1975 Act provides that the court must take into account any other matter, including the conduct of the claimant and any other person which, in the circumstances of the case, the court may consider relevant. "Other relevant matters" may include the deceased's reasons for disposing of his estate as he did, the deceased's wishes in respect of his assets, and mutual wills.

The deceased's reasons

Section 1(7) of the Inheritance (Family Provision) Act 1938, as amended, had required the court to consider the testator's reasons "so far as ascertainable" for making the dispositions contained in his will (if any), for refraining from disposing of his estate, or for not making any provision for a dependant. The court could admit documentary evidence, other evidence of facts, and oral statements by the deceased for the purpose of ascertaining or inferring the deceased's reasons for making or not making financial provision for the claimant. The court was not obliged, however, to comply with the deceased's wishes. This is demonstrated by the following cases, in which the court considered evidence of the deceased's reasons but rejected them when determining a claim for financial provision from the deceased's estate. The cases may also be a useful guide on the nature of the evidence which may be relied on in claims under the 1975 Act where the deceased's reasons are regarded as relevant to the issues before the court.

In *Re Vrint, Vrint v Swain* [1940] Ch 920, [1940] 3 All ER 470, the court permitted a document, which had been formulated by the deceased's solicitors and approved by the deceased in connection with his former wife's application for maintenance in the magistrates' court, to be adduced in evidence for the purposes of inferring the deceased's reasons for not making any provision for her.

In *Re Pugh, Pugh v Pugh* [1943] Ch 387, [1943] 2 All ER 361, the deceased by his will left his farm, worth £5,000, to his grandson and the residue, valued at about £1,800, to his widow. In support of her claim the widow sought to rely on the evidence that, about four months before his death, the deceased had told his solicitors that he intended to alter his will. Thereafter, he had told the claimant that he intended to leave everything to her. That intention was repeated by him on many occasions, including as he was passing into unconsciousness, just before his death. It was held that the statements amounted to statements of intention and could not be described as the deceased's reasons for not making any further provision.

In *Re Smallwood, Smallwood v Martins Bank* [1951] Ch 369, [1951] 1 All ER 372, on the widow's application for financial provision under the 1938 Act, a statement by the son of the deceased about what the deceased had said to him about the claimant was admitted, on the basis that section 1(7) of the 1938 Act extended to evidence of facts from which the court could infer the deceased's reasons for making or not making any provision.

In *Re Clarke, Clarke v Roberts* [1968] 1 WLR 415, [1968] 1 All ER 451, the deceased had agreed with his wife, the claimant, that they would live with his mother as a temporary measure. The mother's conduct, however, forced the claimant to leave the home, but she told the deceased that they ought to have their own home. The deceased did not respond. He died leaving a legacy of £1,000 to the claimant and the residue to his mother. His reasons for not making any further provision for the applicant were that she had agreed that the matrimonial home should be his mother's home, and that she had left and set up home on her own. The court considered those reasons, but found that it was the deceased who had broken the terms of the agreement and that the deceased's moral obligation to the claimant as his wife had not ceased.

In *Re Preston, Preston v Hoggarth* [1969] 1 WLR 317, [1969] 2 All ER 96, the deceased gave, as his reasons for not making any provision for his wife, the fact that she was responsible for their separation by returning to Australia with her daughter. Notwithstanding the reasons given, the claimant was awarded a lump sum. See also *Re Gregory, Gregory v Goodenough* (page 78) and *Millward v Shenton* (page 74).

The 1975 Act, by contrast with the 1938 Act, does not provide that the deceased's reasons for making or not making any provision is a factor to be considered by the court when determining a claim under section 2. Section 3(1)(g), however, requires the court to have regard to "any matter which in the circumstances of the case the court may consider relevant". This is wide enough to include the deceased's reasons for making or not making any financial provision in his will for a claimant, but such considerations must be taken in the context of all the circumstances of the case. If the court considers it relevant, it will weigh that evidence against all the other factors which the court is enjoined to take into account.

Goff LJ referred to the deceased's reason as a relevant factor in *Re Coventry* (above, page 50), in the following terms:

> "Indeed I think any view expressed by a deceased person that he wishes a particular person to benefit will generally be of little significance because the question is not subjective but objective. An express reason for rejecting the applicant is a different matter and may be relevant to the problem."

In *Re Leach (Deceased), Leach v Linderman* [1986] Ch 226, [1985] 3 WLR 413, [1985] 2 All ER 754, the claimant obtained an award against her deceased's step-mother's estate despite the fact that she had never lived in her step-mother's household and was never maintained either wholly or partly by her. One of the factors in her favour was that there was considerable evidence that the deceased intended to make a will in the step-daughter's favour.

In *Re Hancock* (page 66) the deceased had recorded that, had there been sufficient funds available, he would have made provision for the claimant., and a clause in the will expressed his wish that his widow should make provision by her will for the claimant. A plot of land forming part of the deceased's estate was sold for development for a substantial sum of money, by the beneficiaries under his will. The Court of Appeal accepted the approach adopted in *Re Coventry* by Goff LJ and said:

> "That principle of course governs the approach of the court to the assessment required to be made by the court of the reasonableness of the provision or lack of provision. A good reason to exclude a member of the family has to be a relevant consideration. However, in my view, the recognition by the testator of the status of members of his family and his goodwill towards them and in this case towards the plaintiff are factors which it is proper to take into account under s 3(1)(g) and it is for the court to give such weight to those factors as may in the individual case be appropriate."

It seems therefore that, in appropriate cases, a statement of the deceased's wishes or reasons for making or not making financial provision may be a relevant factor which the court will consider in weighing up all the matters set out in section 3 and carrying out a balancing exercise.

The claimant's wish to pass assets to beneficiaries of choice

In *Re Adams v Lewi*s [2001] WLTR 493, the court made an award which took into account the surviving spouse's wish to have sufficient assets to pass on to beneficiaries of her choice. The court made that allowance by applying the section 1(2)(a) test, under which there is no requirement that the award be restricted to the reasonable maintenance of the surviving spouse; and on the basis of section 3(2) which requires the court to have regard to the provision which the surviving spouse might have expected to receive if, on the day on which the deceased died, the marriage, instead of being terminated by death, had been terminated by a decree of divorce. The court also considered *White v White* [2001] AC 596, [2000] 2 FLR 981 (HL), stating that where the estate of the deceased is substantial and there is a surplus of assets, the application of the principles in *White v White* may be appropriate and may not do injustice to those who may have competing claims, but where the estate is modest or small, it would create injustice to do so. Consideration has to be given to the fact that, notwithstanding section 3(2), where the marriage has terminated by divorce, there are only two parties to the proceedings whose interests the court has to consider, subject to the claims of the minor children if any; and the parties, or one of them, may have the earning capacity to increase the asset from which the payments may be made.

In claims under the 1975 Act the assets from which an award may be made are limited to the net estate, and the interests of other beneficiaries have to be considered. Of the criteria set out in section 3, no one factor has greater significance or priority than any other. The court's duty is to strike a balance between the competing claims of the surviving spouse; any other claimants, who may be minor children of the deceased; a cohabitant of the deceased; disabled children, both adult and minor; and other beneficiaries. It is not the court's function to rewrite the deceased's will or to make what it considers to be an equitable distribution of the estate.

Mutual wills

It may be that the deceased entered into an agreement to make a mutually binding will and as a result could not dispose of his estate, or part of it, other than on the basis of that agreement. This is known as the doctrine of "mutual wills". The doctrine applies only where the agreement to enter into mutual wills is reinforced by undertakings that the wills shall not be revoked. If the first testator dies having made a will in compliance with the agreement, the agreement becomes binding on the second testator, and gives rise to an equitable obligation to give effect to the mutually agreed disposition(s). A "floating trust" is created, and the personal representatives of the second testator are obliged to administer it.

Where the legal formalities relating to mutual wills have not been complied with, but the parties believed that they had created mutually binding wills, a constructive trust is implied to prevent the second testator from dealing with the deceased's assets in a way which is incompatible with the agreement *(Healey v Brown* [2002] 19 EG 147, [2002] WTLR 849). The case of *Re Goodchild* (above, page 66) illustrates the practical difficulties which arise in relation to such wills. See further Chapter 21.

Conduct

"Conduct" under the 1975 Act does not have the same meaning as under the

Matrimonial Causes Act 1973. Cases where the conduct of the deceased and the claimant have been considered are referred to above under "obligations and responsibilities". Other examples of relevant conduct include cases:

(a) where the parties had been divorced for many years and the claimant had concealed her financial position, which had resulted in her continuing to receive maintenance from the deceased at a level higher than that to which she was entitled (*Re Harker-Thomas,* page 78);

(b) where the claimant's conduct in leaving the deceased, rejecting his numerous requests for a reconciliation, her continued separation for a long period and her loss of interest in the deceased were taken into account (*Re Gregory, Gregory v Goodenough,* (page 78);

(c) where a long period of separation diminished the value of the order made: *Re Rowlands* (page 59);

(d) where the deceased had concealed or been secretive about his financial position. In *Re W (Deceased)* (1975) 119 SJ 439, *The Times*, 22 April 1975, the deceased had deserted the claimant. After the parties divorced the deceased had been secretive about his financial position, as a result of which the claimant did not apply for maintenance. On his death the deceased left his residual estate, valued at £28,000, to two female friends in equal shares. Rees J took account of the deceased's secretive conduct; the fact that he had accumulated capital at the expense of the claimant; the claimant's precarious financial position; and the effect on the claimant of the breakdown of the marriage.

Proprietary estoppel

The conduct of the deceased in encouraging the claimant to believe that he or she would acquire an interest in his estate and thereby, upon that belief, to act to his or her detriment, can give rise to estoppel upon which a claim may be based. To establish constructive trust in a case of proprietary estoppel, whereby a court of equity would prevent a person from relying on his legal rights when it would be unconscionable for him to do so, the claimant must prove:

(a) that the claimant had a belief at all material times that he or she would receive the property which is the subject of the action;

(b) that that belief was encouraged by the deceased; and

(c) that, in reliance on that belief and assurance, the claimant acted to his or her detriment.

Although the case of *Re Basham (Deceased)* [1986] 1 WLR 1498, [1987] 1 All ER 405, [1987] 2 FLR 264, was not a claim under the 1975 Act, it concerned the question of family provision, the conduct of the deceased and the assurances he gave during his lifetime. The circumstances and the result of the case, however, may be of relevance in claims under the 1975 Act. The claimant was the step-daughter of the deceased. She had lived with the deceased from the age of fifteen when her mother married the deceased, and, together with the claimant's husband, they had formed a very closely knit family. The claimant, her husband and their children had assisted the deceased in his business and had worked for the deceased for no reward. The deceased had given the claimant assurances that he would leave her all his estate and that she and her family should have no worries about money. Her understanding was that she would inherit his property. When the claimant's husband wished to move to Lincolnshire to a better job, he was persuaded not to do so by the deceased. He was also persuaded by the deceased not to apply for planning permission on a plot of land he owned with a view to selling it. The claimant also cooked and cleaned for the deceased for the rest of his life and spent a considerable amount of time and money on him. Allowing the claimant's claim, Edward Nugee QC, sitting as a Deputy High Court Judge, said:

> "Where a person (A) has acted to his detriment on the faith of a belief, which was known to and encouraged by another person (B), that he either has or is going to be given a right in or over B's property, B cannot insist on his strict legal rights if to do so would be inconsistent with A's belief. The principle is commonly known as proprietary estoppel, and since the effect of it is that B is prevented from asserting his strict legal rights it has something in common with estoppel. But in my judgment, at all events, where the belief is that A is going to be given a right in the future, it is properly to be regarded as giving rise to a species of constructive trust, which is the concept employed by a court of equity to prevent a person from relying on this legal rights where it would be unconscionable for him to do so. The rights to which proprietary estoppel gives rise and the machinery by which effect is given to them, are similar in many respects to those involved in cases of secret trusts, mutual wills and other comparable cases in which property is vested in B on the faith of an understanding that it will be dealt with in a particular manner."

See also *Re Goodchild, Goodchild v Goodchild* (page 66), where the doctrine of estoppel was relied on to establish "moral obligation", and Chapter 21.

Factors Relevant to a Surviving Spouse

Age

The age of a surviving spouse is relevant in assessing his or her earning capacity. Also relevant is whether or not, and, if so, the extent to which, the surviving spouse is caring for a minor child. If the surviving spouse was not gainfully employed during the marriage, age is relevant in considering whether that person could train or retrain so as to earn an income to meet some or all of his or her own needs. In such a case provision may be made for a modest sum to enable the spouse to adjust to the new situation and to take up or resume gainful employment. Cases decided under the

Matrimonial Causes Act 1973 should be considered, and see *Khan v Khan* [1981] 2 FLR 131, where an order was made while the wife trained and obtained employment; and *Attar v Attar (No 2)* [1985] FLR 653, where a wife was given a lump sum representing two years' maintenance. Where the spouse is middle-aged or elderly, it will be relevant whether or not the spouse has lost the potential to earn income; see *Robertson v Robertson* [1983] 4 FLR 387, where a wife had not lost the potential to work.

The duration of the marriage
The duration of marriage is also significant. Where the marriage has lasted a long time, with the parties living together and bringing up a family, a substantial award may be justified. Where the parties to the marriage are not young, although the marriage may have been short, the effect on the spouse is relevant in assessing an award which is just in all the circumstances of the case. The surviving spouse may have given up employment or lost pension rights and other benefits in order to care for the deceased.

Where the surviving spouse is young and the marriage was short, whether or not there are children, the shortness of the marriage is taken into account. Premarital cohabitation and any contribution made during that period should also be taken into account. Conversely, any period during which the spouses were separated should be deducted in calculating the length of the marriage.

Where the marriage was long but the parties lived separate and apart, although not divorced, the period of separation is a relevant factor; see *Re Rowlands* (page 59) where the separation was for forty-three years. In *GW v RW* [2003] EWHC 611, [2003] 2 FLR 108, a period of pre-marriage cohabitation and a period of estrangement during the marriage were both taken into account in calculating the length of the marriage; it was stated that a twelve-year period of marriage with two children could not be regarded as a long marriage, but a twenty-year marriage would fall into that category.

The claimant's contribution to the welfare of the family
The contribution made by a spouse by looking after the home and caring for the family is given as much weight as that of the spouse who goes out to work. Greater value ought not to be placed on the contribution of the breadwinner than that of the homemaker as a reason for an unequal division of assets between the spouses. Sterile suggestions that the breadwinner's contributions were greater than the homemaker's should be avoided The nature of the contributions was different and incommensurable and each should be recognised as of no less value than the other: *Lambert* v *Lambert* [2002] EWHC Civ 1685, [2002] 1 FCR 673, [2003] 1 FLR 139. A spouse's contribution to the husband's business which assisted in making the business prosperous must be given due weight (*Conran v Conran* [1997] 2 FLR 615, [1998] 1 FCR 144).

What the claimant might reasonably have expected

Section 3(2) of the 1975 Act provides that, in a claim by a surviving spouse of the deceased, the court should, unless at the date of death a decree of judicial separation was in force and the separation was continuing, have regard to the provision which the claimant might reasonably have expected to receive if, on the day on which the deceased died, the marriage, instead of being terminated by death, had been terminated by divorce. This implies an exercise under section 25 of the Matrimonial Causes Act 1973, although this provision is not the only, or the paramount, factor to be considered by the court. It is one of eight other factors among all the other circumstances of the individual case. The House of Lords' decision in *White v White* (page 81) and the principles set out in that case now form the basis of the court's approach to applications for financial relief under the 1973 Act, although it should be noted that *White v White* was a "big money case" and the principles set out there should not be applied inflexibly, but tailored to the individual circumstances of each case and to the value of the assets available for distribution. This is particularly significant in cases under the 1975 Act. The general principles which emerge from the decision in *White v White,* bearing in mind that in that case the assets substantially exceeded the needs, and the court's observations were made in that context, are:

(a) the objective of the court is to achieve a fair outcome;

(b) in seeking to achieve a fair outcome, there is no place for discrimination between husband and wife and their respective roles. Whatever the division of labour between the spouses, fairness requires that this should not prejudice or advantage either party;

(c) the non-financial contributions made to the welfare of the family and the loss of opportunity to acquire and develop money-earning qualifications and skills should be recognised;

(d) where the wife has made a non-financial contribution to the family she is entitled to a fair settlement which is not confined to her reasonable needs;

(e) the "*Duxbury* calculations" (*Duxbury v Duxbury* [1972] Fam 62, [1990] 2 All ER 77, [1987] 1 FLR 7) are not always a reliable guide and do not take account of the parental wish to pass money to the next generation;

(f) property acquired before marriage, inherited property or property acquired from sources external to the marriage should be treated differently from assets acquired by the joint efforts of the spouses, referred to as "matrimonial property";

(g) a presumption of equal division would not be an impermissible judicial gloss on the statute;

(h) equality of division should be the yardstick and, as a general rule, should be departed from only if there are good reasons for doing so.

Good reasons for departing from equality should be articulated.
Since the decision in *White v White*, further guidance on the interpretation of these principles have been given in a number of cases. In *Dharamshi v Dharamshi* [2001] 1 FLR 736, the wife received between 35 per cent and 41 per cent of the assets. In *H v H* [2001] EWCA Civ 653, [2001] 3 FLR 628 she received 42 per cent. In *D v D (Lump Sum: Adjournment of Application)* [2001] 1 FLR 633, the principles in *White* were applied. In *N v N (Financial provision: sale of company)* [2001] FLR 69, the court ordered the sale of the husband's business, which was an income-producing asset. In *Foster v Foster* [2003] EWCA Civ 565, the Court of Appeal upheld the district judge's attempts to give back to the parties what they had brought into the marriage at the value at the date of the marriage, and divide equally the proceeds generated during the marriage from property dealings. In *GW v RW* (above, page 84), a period of cohabitation before the marriage was treated as equivalent to marriage; it was accepted that some departure from equality was justified as the husband had brought to the marriage a developed career and high earnings capacity, which was unmatched by anything the wife had contributed, and the husband's assets had grown during the separation. The wife was awarded 40 per cent of the assets.

The equality principle has been applied in a number of other cases, but in each of these cases the assets were substantial. It is submitted that these cases may impact on cases under the 1975 Act where the estate is large and there is a surplus available. Where the estate includes assets acquired before the marriage, or acquired by inheritance or sources outside the marriage, applying *White v White,* such assets ought to be treated differently from "matrimonial assets". Where the estate is sufficiently large it may be appropriate to apply this principle, but where the funds are insufficient to meet the claims, it may not be.

Factors which Apply to a Former Spouse or Cohabitant
In the case of a claim by a former spouse or co-habitant, the matters to which the court must have regard are, save for the deemed marriage issue, the same as for a surviving spouse; see above**.** Where a "clean break" settlement was made, it will be rare for a claim under the 1975 Act to be made, or, if made, to succeed, unless there is a continuing liability, or a secured provision order has been made, or there are exceptional circumstances: *Barrass v Harding* [2001] 1 FLR 138, (2000) WTLR 1071. See also *Parnall v Hurst and Others* [2003] WTLR 997, where a former wife whose marriage to the deceased was dissolved after twenty-nine years and the deceased was ordered to make periodical payments of £500 per year, issued a claim under the 1975 Act. An application to strike out was refused as the claim was not regarded as "doomed" to fail.

In summary, case law suggests that the following matters are relevant to a claim under the 1975 Act by a former spouse or cohabitant:

(a) a clean break settlement where there is no continuing obligation;
(b) whether there was a relationship between the deceased and the former wife since the divorce which could suggest a moral obligation to provide for her;
(c) special or exceptional circumstances;
(d) the time that has elapsed since the parties separated and since the divorce and the final settlement;
(e) whether there is any evidence to suggest that a full and frank disclosure was not made, or that the deceased has been secretive about his financial affairs which led the former wife to receive less than she might have received.

The following have been found *not* to amount to special circumstances or reasons to allow a claim:

(a) that the former wife received less under different legislation than she might have received when the deceased died;
(b) that the deceased's estate is substantial;
(c) that the former wife is in straitened circumstances or suffering ill-health.

Chapter 6

The Powers of the Court

Introduction

Once the court is satisfied that the claimant is eligible to make a claim under the Inheritance (Provision for Family and Dependants) Act 1975 and that the disposition of the deceased's estate effected by his will or the law of intestacy, or the combination of his will and that law, is not such as to make reasonable financial provision for the claimant, the court may make any one or more of the following orders in favour of the claimant:

(a) an order for the making to the claimant, out of the net estate of the deceased, of periodical payments, for such term as may be specified in the order;

(b) an order for the payment to the claimant, out of that estate, of a lump sum of such amount as may be specified;

(c) an order for the transfer to the claimant of such property comprised in that estate as may be specified;

(d) an order for the settlement, for the benefit of the claimant, of such property comprised in that estate as may be specified;

(e) an order for the acquisition, out of property comprised in that estate, of such property as may be specified and for the transfer of the property so acquired to the claimant, or for the settlement thereof for his benefit;

(f) an order varying any ante-nuptial or post-nuptial settlement (including such a settlement made by will) made on the parties to a marriage to which the deceased was one of the parties, the variation being for the benefit of the surviving party to that marriage, or any child of that marriage, or any person who was treated by the deceased as a child of the family in relation to that marriage.

(section 2(1)).

In certain circumstances, the court may make an interim order for periodical payments and a lump sum payment out of the net estate (section 5; see page 99).

Each of the above orders may be made out of the net estate as defined in section 25(1), including property which forms part of the net estate by virtue of orders made under sections 8 to 12 (see Chapter 7).

For examples of the orders which may be made, see pages 236 to 240.

Periodical Payments Order

An order for periodical payments specifies the term for which the order is to run (section 2(1)). When making such an order, the court may:

(a) specify in the order the amount to be paid;
(b) express the amount to be paid to be such sum as is equivalent to the whole, or a specified portion, of the income of the net estate;
(c) direct that a specified part of the net estate be appropriated or set aside for meeting periodical payments, and express the amount of such periodical payments to be equivalent to the whole of the income of such part of the net estate.

(section 2(2)).

No larger part of the net estate than is sufficient, at the date of the order, to produce the income required may be set aside or appropriated (section 2(3)). The power of appropriation is in addition to any power conferred by the deceased's will or given by the court to the personal representatives under its jurisdiction to make consequential orders and give directions. Alternatively, the court may provide for the amount of the periodical payments, or any of them, to be determined in any other way as the court thinks fit (section 2(2)).

Commencement date

There are three possible dates from which an order for periodical payments can commence:

(a) the date of the deceased's death, when the right to make the claim accrued;
(b) the date when proceedings were commenced, when the right to make the claim was exercised;
(c) the date the order is made, when the court finally determines the merit of the claim.

There is no rule that an order for periodical payments must be backdated to commence from the date of the deceased's death. The matter is one for the discretion of the court. In the absence of exceptional circumstances, the court will be reluctant to backdate the order to a date earlier than the date the proceedings were commenced. Even when backdating is considered appropriate, the court would be mindful not to backdate the order to such an extent that it results in a substantial lump sum having to be paid.

Sometimes the court may consider it appropriate to make a small capital sum to obviate the need to backdate an order for periodical payments *(Re Debenham (Deceased)*, page 65; *Re Farrow (Deceased)*, page 91). Where the claimant has no financial resources and is in receipt of state benefits, it is a matter for the court's discretion whether or not to backdate the order. Each case turns on its own facts, but orders have been made notwithstanding the fact that the claimant was in receipt of state benefits and may have had to pay back the benefits received. The case of *Lusternik v Lusternik* [1972]

Fam 125, [1972] 2 WLR 203, [1971] 1 All ER 592 is an example where an order was backdated although the claimant had been in receipt of state benefits. In that case the deceased and the claimant were divorced and an order for periodical payments of £6.00 per week was made following the divorce. The claimant continued to maintain both a social and a business relationship with the deceased. The deceased made a will in 1960 leaving his share in a company to the claimant for life. Six weeks before his death in December 1964 he revoked his will by codicil and left her a legacy of £500 and the residue to his executrix. The net estate was valued at £10,000. When the claimant made her application she was unable to work and in ill-health. When her appeal was heard she was in receipt of retirement pension and supplementary benefit of £9.60 per week. The trial judge made an order in her favour of £6.00 per week backdated to February 1970. On appeal the order was increased to £8.00 per week. On the issue of backdating, Cairns LJ said:

> "As to back dating, I do not accept the contention of counsel for the applicant that there is any rule that *prima facie* the payments should be backdated to the death. This was certainly not laid down as a rule in the case he cited, *Askew v Askew*. There Marshall J held that it was a matter of discretion in each case; and indeed I think that is the necessary wording of the Act. Where an applicant has not brought proceedings until several years after probate was granted, I should not, in the absence of very special circumstances consider it right to backdate the order to a date earlier than that of the originating summons. And again where, as here, the proceedings have extended over some four years from the date of the originating summons to that of the order, I should not consider it right to backdate the order to the date of the summons unless it is shown that there had been some deliberate obstruction by the respondent in the course of the proceedings. One should I think guard against backdating the order for periodical payments to such an extent as in effect to add to it a lump sum order substantial in relation to the size of the estate. In this case, if there had been no provision at all for the applicant in the will, I should have been disposed to backdate the order for two years or perhaps two and a half years. But taking account of her legacy of £500, I think that the registrar and the judge were right here in choosing the shorter period. By my reckoning, the arrears calculated (now) at £8.00 per week and making an allowance for the interim payments which were ordered and which I understand were made between February and May 1971, will be about £480, payable within a week or two, and I do not think it would be fair to the respondent to increase that sum."

In *Askew v Askew* [1961] 1 WLR 725, [1961] 2 All ER 60, the court was directly concerned with the question of whether the fact that the former wife had been receiving state benefits afforded a ground for postponing the commencement date of the payments ordered. Marshall J said:

> "It falls to the court to consider whether in the section itself there is any indication or guide to the proper date from which the payments should be made out of the estate. The right which the former wife has established is described in s. 3(1) as a right of 'reasonable provision for her maintenance after his death' and I have no doubt whatever that a court in its discretion would if the circumstances of any particular case warrants it, make an order that there is a right arising immediately after death in all circumstances. In my judgment this section gives the court a discretion, and it would be incumbent on the court to consider all the factors in the case before deciding on any date from which the first payment under the section should be made."

In *Re Goodwin (Deceased), Goodwin v Goodwin* [1969] 1 Ch 283, [1968] 3 WLR 558, [1968] 3 All ER 12, however, the court, in exercising its discretion, considered the matter on the basis that if the will had made reasonable provision, that provision would have taken effect from the testator's death. Accordingly, the court ordered that payments should commence from the death of the testator. The court treated any state benefits which were received by the claimant as a matter which was extraneous to the issue before the court. See also *Stead v Stead* [1985] FLR 16, (1985) 15 Fam Law 154, where payments were backdated to the day after the testator's death; and *Re Farrow (Deceased)* [1988] 1 FLR 205, (1987) 17 Fam Law 14, where, in backdating the payments, the court took into account all the relevant factors.

The decision in *Re Goodwin* was not cited in *Lusternik v Lusternik* and appears to suggest that, generally speaking, the discretion should be exercised in favour of backdating the order to the date of death. Since, however, the Act is silent on the date from which an order for periodical payments should commence, and the court's power is any event discretionary, it is submitted that, in exercising its discretion, the court should have regard to all the circumstances of the case, including any delay in issuing proceedings; any delay resulting from deliberate obstruction by the respondent to the claim; any payments made to the claimant under an interim order; and any benefits received by the claimant under the will. The provision which the will should have made is and should be one of the considerations, and not the premise from which the court ought to start.

When an immediate order is not required, but it is anticipated that provision will be required in the future, the court may adjourn the application (*Re Franks, Franks v Franks* [1948] Ch 62, [1947] 2 All ER 638).

Setting aside and appropriation of property

Section 2(3) of the 1975 Act gives the court the power to direct that such part of the net estate as may be specified be set aside or appropriated for the making, out of the income from such property, of the payments ordered by the court. But the section also restricts the court's power to anticipate the future needs of the claimant, in that it prohibits setting aside or appropriating any part of the net estate larger than would be sufficient at the date of the order to produce, from the income thereof, the amount ordered by the court. The future needs of the claimant must, therefore, be dealt with by an application for variation of the periodical payments order (see page 102), but when varying the order, the court has no power to bring in new property to meet any increase.

Supplementary orders and conditions
By virtue of section 2(4) of the 1975 Act, the court may make such consequential and supplementary provisions to an order as it thinks necessary or expedient for the purposes of giving effect to the order, or for securing that the order operates fairly as between the beneficiaries of the estate of the deceased.

The court may attach conditions to an order for periodical payments, as it did in *Re Lidington, Lidington v Thomas (No 2)* [1940] Ch 927, where, on making provision for periodical payments for the widow of the deceased, the court required her to undertake to maintain the children during their minority. In *Re Pointer, Pointer v Shonfiel v Edward* [1941] Ch 60, the court awarded the daughter of the deceased the income of one fifth of the residuary estate or the sum of thirty shillings per week, whichever was the smaller, during her life, subject to section 1(2)(b) of the Inheritance (Family Provision) Act 1938, namely in the particular circumstances of her disability ceasing, but subject to the condition that her daughter should inform the trustees if she received at any time a sum in excess of 200 shillings from any source.

Secured order
The Act does not specifically make any provision for a secured periodical payments order. But in view of the wide powers conferred on the court under section 2(4) for the purpose of giving effect to its order, it is suggested that, as in matrimonial financial relief applications, a secured periodical payments order could be made if the court considers it is justified. Further, in appropriate cases, the court may consider making provision for an annuity to be set up.

Duration of the order
An order for periodical payments and interim periodical payments in favour of a former spouse or judicially separated spouse where the separation is continuing at the date of death, ceases to have effect on the remarriage of the claimant, save in respect of any arrears outstanding (section 19(2)). The Act does not make such restrictive provision in the case of a surviving spouse, but, following the Matrimonial Causes Act 1973, it would be usual for the

order to terminate upon the remarriage of the spouse.

It is now the practice, on making an order for periodical payments in matrimonial proceedings, to provide for the termination of the order on the cohabitation of the recipient of the payment with another. It is suggested that an order for periodical payments made under the 1975 Act in favour of a widow(er) should likewise provide for a cut-off date. The Matrimonial Causes Act 1973, section 29, restricts the duration of a financial provision order in favour of a child until his eighteenth birthday, save in the circumstances referred to in the section. It is submitted that, when making an order under the 1975 Act, the court should follow the same principle. This would ensure that distribution of the estate to any other beneficiary can take place. It is always open to the claimant to apply for a variation of the order if circumstances justify it.

Lump Sum Order

An order for a specified lump sum to be paid out of the net estate may be made on a claim under the 1975 Act. It can also be made on an application under section 6 of the 1975 Act for the variation or discharge of an order for periodical payments (see page 102). A lump sum ordered under section 6, however, may be made only out of any "relevant property", to the original claimant or to any such person who has applied or would, but for section 4 of the Act, be entitled to apply for an order under section 2 of the Act (see page 8).

In claims under the 1975 Act it is more common for the court to award a lump sum payment rather than periodical payments. This is because a lump sum provides finality for both the claimant and the other beneficiaries, and allows the personal representatives to administer the estate without the additional costs of operating trusts, which would have to be created to provide income to meet a periodical payments order.

Instalment order

Pursuant to section 7(1) of the 1975 Act, where a lump sum is ordered under section 2(1)(b) or section 6(2)(b), the court has power to order that the lump sum be paid by instalments of such amount as may be specified in the order.

Variation of order

The court also has power to vary a lump sum order, whether made under section 2 or 6 of the Act, but the power is limited in that the order may be varied only on the application of:

(a) the person to whom the lump sum is payable;
(b) the personal representatives of the deceased; or
(c) the trustees of the property out of which the lump sum is payable.

Further, the order may be varied only by altering:

(a) the number of instalments payable;

(b) the amount of any instalment; and
(c) the date on which any instalment becomes payable.

Assessing the amount to be awarded
The factors taken into account in arriving at the amount to be awarded under a lump sum order depend on the circumstances of each case, and in particular the matters set out in section 3 (see Chapter 5).

Where a capital sum is provided to produce an income, an important factor to be taken into account in assessing the amount to be awarded is the fact that the claimant is forgoing the right to apply for variation; an adjustment in favour of the claimant should therefore be made to compensate for the loss of that right. This is particularly likely to be the case where the estate is large. Other factors for which the court should make allowance are inflation and future contingencies. In the words of Oliver LJ in *Re Besterman (deceased), Besterman v Grusin* [1984] Ch 458, [1984] 3 WLR 280, [1984] 2 All ER 656:

> "… houses decay, circumstances change, the cost of living increases and the value of money falls, or certainly the history of the last ten years leads us to believe. Furthermore, although, happily, the plaintiff appears in good health, there is an inevitable health hazard with advancing age, and having regard to the fact that this lady is the widow of a more than ordinarily wealthy man, reasonable provision would in my judgment require that she should have access to a sufficient sum of money to ensure beyond any reasonable doubt that she is relieved of any anxiety for the future. It is a criticism of the annuity purchase approach to the problem that the income which it is intended to provide is provided only if an annuity is actually purchased which is not, in general, a course which a prudent adviser would advise in an age of inflation and that postulates that there can be no resort to capital in the event of emergency … The relevant consideration is the extent of the lump sum and that ought (at any rate where as here the estate is ample for the purpose and scarcity of funds is not an inhibiting factor) to take account of the fact that the plaintiff is (whether or not of her volition) giving up the right to return to the court for a variation of the provision in the event of unforeseen contingencies. I think that the absence, which is inherent in a lump sum order, of an opportunity to return to the court does mean that, in assessing the lump sum, the court must take rather greater account than might otherwise be the case of contingencies and inflation. I accept the submission of junior counsel for the plaintiff that reasonable provision, in the case of a very large estate such as this and wholly blameless widow who is incapable of supporting herself, should be such as to relieve her of anxiety for the future. I say 'in the case of a very large estate' not because there is any difference in principle but simply because the existence of a large estate makes that which is desirable also practically possible. It has been pointed

out more than once that the calculation in cases of this sort is, of necessity, not one where any precision is possible, but for my part I take the view that reasonable provision in this case would dictate that in addition to the secure roof over her head, the widow should have available to her a capital sum of sufficient size not simply to enable her to purchase an adequate annuity according to her present needs but to provide her with the income which she needs and a cushion in the form of available capital which will enable her to meet all reasonable foreseeable contingencies. What that sum is, is a matter for judgment but I think that in it we are entitled to take into account that, though the plaintiff is quite content with her present residence it is in fact somewhat more modest than she might be thought to be entitled to expect to be provided for her by a husband in the financial position of the deceased."

The fact that a lump sum may enable the claimant to provide for someone else should not govern the amount ordered to be paid. In *Preston v Preston* [1982] Fam 17, [1981] 3 WLR 619, [1982] 1 All ER 41 (a case under the Matrimonial Causes Act 1973), Brandon J said that the lump sum awarded to the wife should not include an amount for the future maintenance of her son.

In assessing the amount of the lump sum to be awarded the court has sometimes capitalised periodical payments which it has awarded. In *Malone v Harrison* [1979] 1 WLR 1353, the court used a multiplier and multiplicand as applicable in personal injuries actions. In *Re Besterman* (above) the court used the amount of capital which would be needed to generate the income required to satisfy the claimant's needs. See also *Re Bunning (Deceased), Bunning v Salmon*, page 59. If the circumstances justify it, it may be appropriate to apply the *Duxbury* calculations (*Duxbury v Duxbury*, see page 85) or the *Ogden Tables (Actuarial Tables with Explanatory Notes for Use in Personal Injury and Fatal Accident Cases,* Michael Ogden, Stationery Office Books, 1994) to achieve the right result.

It should be borne in mind that no hard and fast rule has been applied and there is no case which sets out any guidelines. The court's decision turns on the particular facts of the case before it and the application of the principles set out in section 3.

Transfer of Property Order

Section 2(1)(c) of the 1975 Act empowers the court to order the transfer to the claimant of such property comprised in the net estate as may be specified in the order. This power is similar to that contained in the Matrimonial Causes Act 1973, section 24. As in matrimonial proceedings, there is no power to order a transfer of property on an application for periodical payments, but on a variation of a periodical payments order the court may order a transfer of property under section 6(2)(c) (see further page 103).

Where an order for transfer of property in favour of a claimant is justified, but would mean that the needs of the other beneficiaries would not be met because the other assets are insufficient, the court may order the transfer subject to a legacy in favour of a beneficiary. In *Rajabally v Rajabally* [1987] 2 FLR 390, the testator, who was survived by his widow, their two sons and a son of his first marriage, left his estate, consisting of the former matrimonial home, to his widow and the three children in equal shares. The widow lived in the house with two of her sons. The eldest son suffered from mental illness, lived in council accommodation and his only source of income was state benefits. The widow made a claim under the 1975 Act. During the proceedings the eldest son was prepared to take provision under the will by being bought out at a valuation. The two younger children were prepared to give assurances that they would not insist on their rights under the will. The court took the view that the widow should be provided with real security in the house, but that account had to be taken of the limited means and uncertain future of the eldest son. The balance was struck by transferring the house to the widow absolutely, but subject to a legacy in favour of the eldest son to be raised by a mortgage on the property. See also *Re Christie (Deceased), Christie v Keeble* [1979] Ch 168, [1979] 2 WLR 105, [1979] 1 All ER 546.

Settlement of Property Order

The power to order property comprised in the net estate to be settled for the benefit of the claimant is derived from section 2(1)(c) of the 1975 Act. There is no power to vary or discharge such an order once made. If it is envisaged that the purpose of the settlement may alter in the future, powers of appointment and variation, and the power to invest and purchase property, can be provided. The deed of trust should be tailored to meet the particular circumstances of the case and the deed should be drafted with care to cover contingencies and changes of circumstances which may occur in the future.

The nature of the settlement which the court orders depends on the circumstances of the case. Where the settlement is in favour of a child, it will provide for the needs of the child during his minority. In the case of a widow it could be limited until such time as she remarriages or cohabits.

The power to settle property is particularly useful where the deceased did not make provision for a mentally disabled child, particularly an adult child, in the belief that the child would be adequately provided for by the state. In view of the policy of providing care in the community for those who are disabled, a financial provision order in the form of a settlement would provide for a better quality of life within the community than would otherwise be possible. In such cases the court should consider making a settlement of property order; and, if necessary, an order for the acquisition of property and its settlement upon a discretionary trust so as to permit the whole or any part of the income from the trust fund to be applied for the maintenance, care and benefit of the claimant as the trustees in their discretion deem fit.

In *Hanbury v Hanbury* [1999] 2 FLR 255, the deceased's daughter was physically and mentally disabled with a mental age of about twelve. She was living with and cared for by her mother, supported by social services. At the time of his death the deceased was making maintenance payments under a court order to the daughter, but he had, from choice, not had any contact with her since she was four years old. Having sought legal advice on how to defeat his daughter's claim, the deceased had transferred his property into, and acquired investments in, the joint names of himself and his second wife and had arranged for investment trust holdings to be bought in the second wife's sole name. Applying the powers it had under sections 9 and 10, the court treated the severable share of the jointly owned property as part of the net estate of the deceased and took the net estate to include a one-half share of the investment holding and of the joint accounts. The court took into account the fact that the daughter's needs would eventually be met by placement in a residential home. It ordered the costs of such placement to be met by settling £39,000 in a discretionary trust, with the daughter as principal beneficiary, so that her state benefits by way of income support would not be prejudiced.

Re Abrams (Deceased) [1996] 2 FLR 379 is another case where the court used the power to settle property to make appropriate provision for a claimant out of the net estate. In *Re Abrams,* at the date of the hearing, the claimant's business had failed and he had entered into an individual voluntary arrangement under Part VIII of the Insolvency Act 1986. It was a term of the individual voluntary arrangement that any capital sum received by the claimant's estate should be paid to the creditors. The claimant's home had been repossessed and he was unemployed. To ensure that the provision ordered by the court was received by the claimant, the court ordered a settlement to be effected under section 2(1)(d) of the Act whereby 50 per cent of the estate would be settled on the claimant for life on protective trusts, the life interest importing the statutory trusts under section 33 of the Trustee Act 1925, so that the income would be paid to the claimant for life; but if he became bankrupt or sought to alienate his interest, the life interest would be determined and replaced by a discretionary trust for the claimant and his immediate family.

Acquisition of Property Order

Section 2(1)(e) of the 1975 Act gives the court power to make an order for the acquisition of property comprised in the net estate, and for the acquired property to be transferred to the claimant; or for the settlement of such property for the benefit of the claimant. Once made the order may not be varied (section 6(9)). This power can be useful where the claimant is handicapped (see above) or a minor and needs a home. Where this power is used, the order may also provide for the settlement of the acquired property on trust.

Variation of Nuptial Settlements

Section 2(1)(f) of the 1975 Act provides that the court may vary any ante-nuptial or post-nuptial settlement (including such a settlement made by will) made on the parties to a marriage to which the deceased was one of the parties, the variation being for the benefit of the surviving spouse to that marriage, or any child of that marriage, or any person who was treated by the deceased as a child of the family in relation to that marriage.

As under the Matrimonial Causes Act 1973, this power can be exercised only in favour of the limited classes of person referred to in the subsection, namely:

(a) a party to that marriage;
(b) a child of that marriage; and
(c) a child who was treated by the deceased as a child of the family in relation to that marriage.

The 1975 Act does not define ante-nuptial or post-nuptial settlements, but it seems that the settlement need not be a classic marriage settlement, nor is it necessary for the settlement to be expressed to be a marriage settlement, because the court will look at the substance not the form. In *Hargreaves v Hargreaves* [1926] P 42, [1926] All ER 195, such a settlement was defined as one which was made "in contemplation of, or because of, marriage and with reference to the interests of married people and their children". It must be a settlement in relation to a marriage of the deceased (section 2(1)(f)), although marriage need not be the principal motive for making the settlement. The settlement must, however, be made in contemplation of the particular marriage, not marriage generally.

Under the analogous provision in matrimonial proceedings it has been held that every acquisition by a husband and wife of a matrimonial home in their joint names constitutes a post-nuptial settlement (*Brown v Brown* [1959] P 86, [1959] 2 All ER 266; *Thompson v Thompson* [1986] Fam 38 and *Dinch v Dinch* [1987] 1 WLR 252, [1987] 1 All ER 818 (HL)). In *E v E (Financial Provision)* [1990] 2 FLR 233, during the course of the marriage, a property for which the husband's father had provided the funds was settled on discretionary trusts of which the husband and the wife were beneficiaries; it was held that the settlement constituted a post-nuptial settlement.

To determine whether a nuptial settlement has been made, account should be taken of all the relevant facts to identify the substance of the transaction: *Parrington v Parrington* [1951] 2 All ER 916. The motive for entering into the settlement is irrelevant: *Prescott (formerly Fellowes) v*

Fellowes [1958] P 260, [1958] 3 WLR 288, [1958] 3 All ER 55. Any variation must be for the benefit of the claimant.

In *Dixit v Dixit* CAT June 23 [1988] (CA), the testator made no provision in his will for his widow or for the children of his second marriage. There was, however, an investment property, which was held in trust, the effect of which was to give the widow a life interest in one half and, contingent on their attaining the age of eighteen years, the other half to the two children of the testator's second marriage. Waite J gave the widow a full life interest in the property and provided for the children by granting them an interest in another property which passed under the will of the deceased. The Court of Appeal held that the order made by the judge could not stand as he had failed to consider the tax implications, but did not decide whether Waite J had power under section 2(1(f) to "switch" the trusts. This appears to be the only case under the 1975 Act on the point. It seems, however, that the power of variation will be exercised to benefit the surviving spouse provided the settlement related to that marriage. Where the marriage was dissolved but the decree absolute was made within twelve months of the death of the deceased, then, since the court has the power under section 14 to treat the former spouse in the same category as a surviving spouse, an appropriate settlement may be varied for that spouse's benefit.

It has been suggested that the decision in *Brooks v Brooks* [1996] 1 AC 375, [1995] 3 All ER 257, [1995] 2 FLR 13, which was a case decided under the Matrimonial Causes Act 1973, would apply to a claim made under the 1975 Act, to enable the court to treat a pension scheme as a post-nuptial settlement. But in matrimonial proceedings, the court cannot now make a variation of settlement in relation to a pension (known as a *Brooks* order) (Matrimonial Causes Act 1973, section 24(1)(c) and (d) as amended by the Welfare Reform and Pensions Act 1999, Schedule 3 paragraph 3). There are no decided cases on the subject under the 1975 Act.

Interim Orders

On an application under section 2 of the 1975 Act the court has power to order interim payments to be made, out of the net estate, of such sum or sums, and if more than one, at such intervals, as the court thinks reasonable.

Conditions precedent

Before the court can make an interim order it must be satisfied that:

(a) the claimant is in immediate need of financial assistance but it is not yet possible to determine what order (if any) should be made under section 2; and

(b) property forming part of the net estate of the deceased is or can be made available to meet the needs of the claimant.

Since the power to make the order is discretionary, the claimant must also prove that it would be just in all the circumstances of the case for the court to exercise its discretion. For a case where both a periodical payments order and a lump sum order were made on an interim application, see *Re Besterman (Deceased),* page 94.

In *Re Ralphs, Ralphs v District Bank* [1968] 1 WLR 1522, [1968] 3 All ER 285, the deceased's second wife had left him after a marriage which had lasted about nine years. By his will the deceased left her the income from a sum of £8,000. To his daughter he left an income of £13,000 and capital of £3,000 and the residue he left to his son. The daughter was destitute. The second wife applied for financial provision. An interim order was made in her favour, the court holding that in the great majority of cases where some benefit is given to the claimant by the will there can be no good reason for withholding it pending the hearing of the summons.

Matters to be considered

Section 5(3) of the 1975 Act provides that in determining what order, if any, should be made under the section, the court shall, so far as the urgency of the case admits, have regard to the same matters as those to which the court is required to have regard under section 3 of the Act. In exercising its discretion the court has regard to the fact that the purpose of any order it makes is to hold the situation as reasonably and fairly as possible until the determination of the final application.

Orders that can be made

The court's power to make interim orders is limited to ordering such sum or sums as the court thinks reasonable. This would include an order for periodical payments and a lump sum order, but not a property transfer order. The court may, however, make an order for a lump sum payment to enable the claimant to purchase a home, as occurred in *Re Besterman* (above). The court may impose conditions and restrictions, and determine the duration of any interim orders it may make. It may order that any sum paid to the claimant shall be treated, to such an extent and in such manner as may be provided, as having been paid on account of any payment provided for by that order (section 5(4)). When making an interim order therefore, the court may seek an undertaking that if, say, the claimant's financial circumstances change, the claimant should notify the personal representatives so that an application for variation of an interim order can be applied for.

The court has power to vary an interim order under the provisions of section 5(1).

By virtue of section 5(2), when making an interim order, the court may provide for:

(a) payments of such amount as may be specified in the order;
(b) payments equal to the whole of the income of the net estate or of such portion thereof as may be specified;

(c) payments equal to the whole of the income of such part of the net estate as the court may direct to be set aside or apportioned for the making out of the income thereof of interim payments, or may provide for the payments or any of them to be determined in any other way as the court thinks fit.

Personal representatives and interim orders
Section 20(2) of the Act provides that where the personal representative of a deceased person pays any sum directed by an order under section 5 of the 1975 Act to be paid out of the net estate, he shall not be under any liability by reason of the estate's not being sufficient to make the payment, unless at the time of making the payment he had reasonable cause to believe that the estate was not sufficient. In *Re Ralphs, Ralphs v District Bank* (above), Cross J laid down the following guidelines for personal representatives faced with an application for an interim order:

> "They should form their own view, with the assistance, of course, of their legal advisers, as to the payments which can properly be made, and if they are not prepared to make such payments on their own responsibility they should ask the parties who might conceivably be affected – whether applicant of residuary legatee – for their consent. If such consent is not forthcoming the executors can apply to the court for leave to make the payment in question and the court, if it thinks that any withholding of consent was unreasonable, could throw the costs of the application on the party to blame."

Consequential and Supplemental Orders
When making any of the orders referred to under section 2(1), the court also has power, under section 2(4), to make such consequential and supplemental provisions as it thinks necessary or expedient for the purposes of:

(a) giving effect to the order;
(b) securing that the order operates fairly as between one beneficiary of the deceased and another.

There are no limitations on the very wide scope which the court has under this provision. Without in any way restricting the court's power under this subsection, section 2(4) particularises four specific orders which the court can make under this provision, namely:

(a) order any person who holds any property which forms part of the net estate of the deceased to make such payment, or transfer such property, as may be specified in the order;
(b) vary the disposition of the deceased's estate effected by the will or the law of intestacy, or by both the will and the law relating to intestacy, in such manner as the court thinks fair and reasonable having regard to the provisions of the order and all the circumstances of the case;
(c) confer on the trustees of any property which is the subject of an order

under section 2 such powers as appear to the court to be necessary or expedient;

(d) confer on the trustees of any property which is the subject of an order under section 2 such powers as appear to the court to be necessary and expedient.

The powers given under this provision can be used to impose conditions on a substantive order made under section 2 to define, restrict or regulate the order made. For instance, where a periodical payments order is made the court may direct the claimant to inform the personal representatives of any change in the financial circumstances of the claimant; or it may grant the claimant the right to occupy a property subject to making payment for use and occupation. The specific power under section 2(1)(d) enables the court to extend the authority given to trustees under the will to meet the particular requirements of the case.

The court's power under section 2(4) to make consequential directions for the purpose of giving effect to the order, or to secure that the order operates fairly between the beneficiaries, enables the court to apportion the incidence of any orders between different classes of beneficiary or between the same class. Usually, the awards are made out of the residuary estate, but where this is not possible the court apportions the burden between pecuniary legatees and residuary legatees. See *Bunning, Bunning v Salmon* [1984] Ch 480, [1984] 3 WLR 265, [1984] 3 All ER 1; and *Malone v Harrison* [1979] 1 WLR 1353.

The court is not bound by any express declaration of the deceased as to how an award should be borne; although awards are usually made out of the residuary estate this is not always the case. In *Re Preston, Preston v Hoggarth* [1969] 1 WLR 317, [1969] 2 All ER 961, the testator provided in his will that in the event of his widow making a claim, it was his wish that the award should be discharged out of the provision made for his grandchildren. The court held that it had power not only to apportion the burden of the award as regards respective classes of beneficiary, but also to throw the burden unequally between beneficiaries in the same class.

In exercising its discretion, the court should have regard to the claims of beneficiaries who would be claimants under the Act and those who do not qualify. It should also have regard to the intention of the deceased, whether expressed or presumed: *Re Simson, Simson v National Provincial Bank* [1950] Ch 38, [1949] 2 All ER 826. Finally, the court should have regard to the matters which influence the court in deciding whether or not the deceased has made reasonable financial provision for the claimant.

Variation, Discharge, Suspension and Revival of Orders

Where the court has made an order for periodical payments under section 2(1)(a) (the "original order"), it has power to vary or discharge that order; to suspend any provision of it temporarily; and to revive the operation of any provision so suspended (section 6(1)). An application to vary an order may be made only in respect of a periodical payment orders. An order varied once may be varied again: *Frickler v Frickler* [1982] 3 FLR 288.

Who may apply
An application under section 6 of the 1975 Act for variation, discharge, suspension or revival of an order for periodical payments may be made by any one of the following persons:

(a) a person who has applied for an order under section 2, or who would have been entitled to apply for an order under section 2 were it not for the time limit for applications imposed by section 4 of the Act;
(b) the personal representatives of the deceased;
(c) the trustees of any relevant property;
(d) any beneficiary of the estate of the deceased.
(section 6(5)).

Orders which can be made
On an application for variation of the original order the court may:

(a) provide for the making, out of any relevant property, of such periodical payments and for such term as may be specified in the order, to any person who has applied, or would but for section 4 of the Act be entitled to apply, for an order under section 2 of the Act (whether or not, in the case of any claim, an order was made in favour of the claimant);
(b) provide for the payment, out of any relevant property, of a lump sum of such amount as may be specified, to the original recipient or to any such person as is mentioned in (a) above;
(c) provide for the transfer of the relevant property, or such part thereof as may be specified, to the original recipient or to any such person as is referred to in (b) above; (section 6(2));
(d) make orders under section 6(3) (see below);
(e) give consequential directions as it thinks necessary and expedient having regard to the provisions of the order (section 6(8)).

There is no power, on an application for variation under section 6 of the 1975 Act, to make any of the following orders:

(a) a settlement of property under section 2(1)(d);
(b) a variation of an ante-nuptial or post-nuptial settlement (section 2(1)(e));
(c) dealing with the deceased's severable share of property on a joint tenancy under section 9;
(d) dealing with dispositions intended to defeat applications for financial provision under section 10;
(e) under section 11 in respect of contracts to leave property by will.

Where an order for periodical payments is to cease:

(a) on the occurrence of an event (other than the remarriage of a former spouse) specified in the order, or

(b) on the expiration of a period specified in the order,

and no application for variation has been made before the occurrence of the specified event or the expiration of the specified period, as the case may be, then if, before the end of the period of six months from the date of the occurrence of that event or of the expiration of that period, an application is made for variation, discharge, suspension or revival, the court may make any order which it would have had power to make if the application had been made before that date. The order in such an instance may be made in favour of:

(a) the original recipient;

(b) any other person who has applied for an order under section 2; or

(c) any person who would have been entitled to apply for an order under section 2 of the Act were it not for the time limits for application imposed by section 4 of the Act.

It appears from section 6(3) and (5) that a person who was debarred from making an application under section 2 by reason of the limitation period imposed by section 4, or a person whose original application was unsuccessful, may nevertheless apply for the variation of an order made in favour of another.

In an application falling within section 6(3), the court has power to make any order which it would have had power to make if the application had been made in time. An order varying the original order may be made only within the limits of the "relevant property" available. It follows that an increase in periodical payments or other variation can occur only in limited circumstances, such as:

(a) if there is an increase in income available from the relevant property;

(b) if another recipient dies, thus releasing the payments in respect of him; or

(c) there is a reduction in payments to another recipient.

Meaning of "relevant property"

Section 6(6) of the 1975 Act defines "relevant property" as follows:

(a) property the income of which is at the date of the order applicable, wholly or in part, for the making of periodical payments to any person who has applied for an order under the 1975 Act, or

(b) in the case of an application under section 6(3) in respect of payments which have ceased to be payable on the occurrence of an event or the expiration of a period, property the income of which was so applicable immediately before the occurrence of that event or expiration, as the case may be.

Matters to be considered
In exercising the power to vary, the court must have regard to all the circumstances of the case, including any change in those circumstances and any change in the matters to which the court was required to have regard under section 3 of the Act when making the original order (section 6(7)).

Lewis v Lewis [1977] 1 WLR 409, [1997] 3 All ER 992 concerned the construction of section 31 of the Matrimonial Causes Act 1973, which gives the court power to vary or discharge a periodical payments order in divorce proceedings. It was held that, in considering an application for variation, the court is not confined to looking at any change in the means of the parties since the original order was made, but is required to look at the actual means of the parties as they stand at the time when the case is before the court, and to approach the matter as it were fixing the payment *de novo*.

An order can be varied to take account of inflation: *Frickler v Frickler* [1982] 3 FLR 288.

Time limits
Save for the limitation in section 6(3) (see page 104), an application for the variation, discharge, suspension or revival of the original order may be made at any time. Section 6(3) relates to periodical payments which are to cease on the occurrence of an event or the expiration of a specified period. An application relating to such an order must be made within six months of the event's occurring or the expiration of the specified period. There is no power to extend this period. In all other cases, however, the court is entitled to consider any delay which has occurred in making the application.

Commencement of the order
An order made by virtue of section 6(3) may be directed to take effect from:
(a) the date of the occurrence of the specified event;
(b) the expiration of the specified period; or
(c) such later date as may be specified by the court.

Orders under the Matrimonial Causes Act 1973
Section 31(6) of the Matrimonial Causes Act 1973 provides that, in respect of a secured periodical payments under the 1973 Act, or an order under section 24A(1) of that Act which requires the proceeds of sale of property to be used for securing those payments, an application may be made for variation or discharge of the order; or the suspension of the order temporarily; or to revive the operation of any provision so suspended. The application may be made by the person entitled to payments under the periodical payments order or by the personal representatives of the deceased person.

Section 16 of the 1975 Act incorporates a similar provision, enabling an application by the person entitled to secured periodical payments, or the personal representatives of the deceased, to apply to vary or discharge that periodical payments order or to revive the operation of any provision thereof which has been suspended under section 31 of the 1973 Act. The powers exercisable by the court under this section in relation to an order are also exercisable in relation to any instrument executed in pursuance of the order (section 16(3)).

In *Re Eyre* [1968] 1 WLR 530, [1968] 1 All ER 968, although the court was not directly concerned with the provisions of section 16, it took into account the fact that there was an order in favour of the applicant, who was the former spouse of the deceased, for secured periodical payments. On the facts it was concluded that:

> "an order for secured maintenance should not properly be treated as a pre-determination of what a survivor is to receive after the death of a former spouse, although it is necessarily an important factor to be considered in every application under section 26."

(Note that this was a pre-1975 Act decision.)

Unless the court extends the time limit, an application under section 16 must be made within six months from the date on which representation with regard to the estate was taken out.

In exercising its powers under section 16, the court must have regard to all the circumstances of the case, including any order which the court proposes to make under section 2 or 5 of the 1975 Act and any change (whether resulting from the death of the deceased or otherwise) in any of the matters to which the court is required to have regard when making a secured periodical payments order (section 16(2)).

Where a person against whom a secured periodical payments order was made has died, and an application is made under section 31(6) of the Matrimonial Causes Act 1973 for the variation or discharge of that order, or for the revival of the operation of any provision thereof which had been suspended, the court has the power to direct that the application under section 31(6) be deemed to have been accompanied by an application for an order under section 2 of the 1975 Act (section 18(1)(a)).

The Children Act 1989, Schedule 1, paragraph 7, makes comparable provisions whereby secured periodical payments orders in favour of children which continue after the death of the payer may be varied after the death of the payer, on the application of the surviving parent or guardian of the child or any person in whose favour a residence order in respect of the child is in force. The personal representatives of the deceased also have a right to apply.

In exercising its powers the court must have regard to all the circumstances of the case, including the changed circumstances resulting from the death of the payer (Children Act 1989, Schedule 1, paragraph 7(5)).

Maintenance agreements

Where a claim for an order under section 2 of the Act is made to the court by any person who was, at the time of the death of the deceased, entitled to payments from the deceased under a maintenance agreement which continued after the death of the deceased, the court has power to vary or revoke the agreement if an application is made under section 17 by either the payee or the personal representatives (section 17(1)).

Section 17(4) defines "maintenance agreement" as follows:

> "In this section 'maintenance agreement' in relation to a deceased person means any agreement made, whether in writing or not whether before or after the commencement of this Act, by the deceased with any person with whom he entered into marriage, being an agreement which contained provisions governing the rights and liabilities towards one another when living separately of the parties to that marriage (whether or not the marriage has been dissolved or annulled) in respect of the making or securing of payments or the disposition or use of any property, including any rights and liabilities with respect to the maintenance or education of any child, whether or not a child of the deceased or a person who was treated by the deceased as a child of the family in relation to that marriage."

To fall within the definition, the agreement must be one made between parties to a marriage.

The Children Act 1989, Schedule 1, paragraph 10, contains provisions whereby a maintenance agreement in favour of a child, which provides for the continuation of payments after the death of one of the parties, may be varied or revoked by the High Court or the county court on the application of the surviving party or the personal representatives of the deceased. The application must not, however, except with the leave of the court, be made after the end of the period of six months beginning with the day on which representation in regard to the estate of the deceased is first taken out (Children Act 1989, Schedule 1, paragraph 11(3)). A grant limited to settled land or to trust property is left out of account when calculating when representation was first taken out, unless a grant limited to the remainder of the estate has previously been made or is made at the same time (Children Act 1989, Schedule 1, paragraph 11(2)).

As in the case of an application under section 16, where a party to a maintenance agreement within the Matrimonial Causes Act 1973, section 34, has died, the agreement being one which provided for the continuation of payments after the death of one of the parties, and an application is made under the Matrimonial Causes Act 1973, section 36(1), for alteration of the agreement under section 35, the court has the power to direct that the application under section 36(1) be deemed to have been accompanied by an application for an order under section 2 of the 1975 Act.

Where the court gives a direction under section 18(1)(a) or (b) that the application under the Matrimonial Causes Act 1973 is deemed to be accompanied by an application for an order under section 2 of the 1975 Act, it has power, in the proceedings on the application under section 31(6) or 36(1), to make any order which the court would have had power to make under the 1975 Act if the application under section 31(6) or 36(1) had been made jointly with an application for an order under section 2 of the 1975 Act. The court also has power to give such consequential directions as may be necessary for enabling the court to exercise any of the powers available to the court under the Act in the case of an application under section 2. (Section 18(2) of the 1975 Act.)

The court does not have the power to direct that an application under the Matrimonial Causes Act 1973, section 31(6) and 36(1), is deemed to have been accompanied by an application for an order under section 2 if an order has been made under section 15(1) of the 1975 Act (see Chapter 9).

In exercising its powers the court must have regard to all the circumstances of the case, including any order the court proposes to make under section 2 or section 5, and any change (whether resulting from the death of the deceased or otherwise) in any of the circumstances in the light of which the agreement was made (section 17(2)).

Injunctive Relief

In *Andrew v Andrew* [1990] 2 FLR 376, it was held that the court does not have power to restrain tortious conduct in relation to an application under the 1975 Act. The substantive issues raised in the proceedings were not for assault, trespass or any other cause of action based on tort or an invasion of a legal right; therefore the applicant was not, under section 38 of the County Courts Act 1984, entitled to any injunctive relief. Section 38 has since been amended by the Courts and Legal Services Act 1990 to confer wide injunctive powers on the county court. It now provides that, subject to certain exceptions, the county court may make any order which could be made by the High Court if the proceedings were in the High Court. Any such order may be made either unconditionally or on such terms and conditions as the court thinks just.

Furthermore, in *Burris v Azadani* [1995] 1 WLR 1372, [1995] 4 All ER 802, it was held that both the High Court and the county court have jurisdiction to grant injunctions in wide terms to restrain conduct that was not in itself tortious or otherwise unlawful if such an order was reasonably regarded as necessary for the protection of a claimant's legitimate interests.

Since the 1975 Act provides for a transfer of property order, the court would have jurisdiction to make any orders to prevent any dealing with property and to make any orders which would ensure that property is preserved until the claim before the court is finally disposed of. Before making such an order, the court will need to be satisfied that the claimant has an arguable case for an order under section 2, and that it would be just in all the circumstances of the case to exercise the court's discretion.

Chapter 7

The Net Estate

Introduction

Section 2 of the Inheritance (Provision for Family and Dependants) Act 1975 gives the court power to make orders for financial provision out of the *net estate* of the deceased. The definition of "net estate" under the 1975 Act replicates the definition in section 5(1) of the Inheritance (Family Provision) Act 1938 Act, but is wider in scope in three respects:

(a) any property may be treated as part of the net estate if the court considers it just so to order;
(b) "net estate" includes property held on a joint tenancy which can be treated as forming part of the net estate by the court, overriding the law of survivorship (section 9); and
(c) the court may order that "net estate" also includes any property which forms part of a transaction intended to defeat an application for financial provision.
(Sections 10 and 11).

Section 25(1) of the 1975 Act nevertheless restricts the meaning of "net estate". This chapter deals with the definition of "net estate" in section 25(1), and the provisions which permit the court to treat certain property as part of the net estate if necessary to make an award for financial provision under the Act.

Definition

Section 25(1) defines the "net estate" from which any order for financial provision may be made as follows:

(a) all property which the deceased had power to dispose of by his will (otherwise than by virtue of a special power of appointment), less his funeral, testamentary and administration expenses, debts and liabilities, including any inheritance tax payable out of his estate on his death;
(b) any property in respect of which the deceased held a general power of appointment (not being a power exercisable by will) which has not been exercised;
(c) any sum of money or other property which is treated for the purposes of the Act as part of the net estate of the deceased by virtue of section

8(1) or (2) of the Act (see below);

(d) any property which is treated for the purposes of the Act as part of the net estate of the deceased by virtue of an order made under section 9 of the Act (see page 114);

(e) any sum of money or other property which is, by reason of a disposition or contract made by the deceased, ordered under section 10 or 11 of the Act to be provided for the purposes of the making of financial provision under the Act (see Chapter 8).

"Property" is defined as including any *chose in action*.

Property which the Deceased had Power to Dispose of by Will

This category corresponds to that set out in section 5(1) of the 1938 Act. Creditors take priority over beneficiaries and dependants. Property subject to a special power of appointment is excluded.

Section 25(2) of the Act provides that, for these purposes, a person who is not of full age and capacity is treated as having power to dispose by will of all property of which he would have had power to dispose by will if he had been of full age and capacity.

Section 25(3) provides that any reference in the Act to provision out of the net estate of a deceased person includes a reference to provision extending to the whole of that estate.

Property under a General Power of Appointment

Where the deceased had a general power of appointment which he could have exercised by will, and either he did not exercise the power, or did so by will, in either case, the property subject to the power forms part of the net estate of the deceased.

Nominated Property

Section 8(1) provides that where a deceased person has, in accordance with the provision of any enactment, nominated any person to receive any sum of money or other property on his death, and that nomination is in force at the time of his death, that sum of money, after deducting any inheritance tax payable thereon, or that property to the extent of the value thereof at the date of death of the deceased after deducting any inheritance tax payable, is treated as part of the net estate of the deceased.

Section 8(1) also provides that nothing in the section renders any person liable for having paid that sum or transferred that property to the person named in the nomination in accordance with the directions given in the nomination. This provision exempts from liability the person transferring property on a nomination, but such transfer should not be made until six months after the grant was first taken out.

Two conditions apply to any nomination made by the deceased before it can be treated as forming part of the net estate. These are that the nomination must be in force at the time of the deceased's death; and must be in accordance with the provision of any enactment.

Insurance policies and pension schemes
A nominated policy under an insurance scheme which is effected pursuant to a contract does not form part of the net estate. Under such a policy, a member of the scheme may nominate a beneficiary, within a designated class of permitted beneficiaries, to whom the benefit is payable on the member's death. The nominations under these schemes are not effected pursuant to any statute, and the benefits payable therefrom fall outside the definition of net estate. If the benefits under such a scheme automatically fall into the estate of the deceased they form part of the net estate. If the pension benefits automatically pass to the deceased's widow or widower they are not included in the net estate.

Private occupational pension schemes are not operated pursuant to any enactment and so fall outside section 8. It is debatable whether public sector schemes fall within the ambit of section 8. Any capital or income, however, which is paid to a beneficiary in consequence of a pension scheme will be considered by the court when it takes into account the financial resources and financial needs of a beneficiary of the estate.

This point was raised in *Re Cairnes (Deceased), Howard v Cairnes* [1983] FLR 225, (1982) 12 Fam Law 177. The preliminary issue was whether, on the true construction of section 25(1), a death benefit fell within the meaning of net estate. The claimant was the deceased's mistress. The defendant and the deceased were married in 1954. They were divorced in 1976. After the divorce, the deceased lived, on and off, with his former wife and with the claimant, until his death. On the divorce the deceased had agreed with his wife that he would give her £80 per month and that he would share the household expenses of the matrimonial home while he lived there. In addition he gave her £18 per week and paid the hire instalments on the television and the washing machine. The deceased's employment was pensionable. Under the terms of the pension scheme a member could nominate a beneficiary, within a designated class, to whom benefits would accrue on the member's death. The designated classes were:

(a) a member's wife; and
(b) any person who, in the opinion of the insurance company, was, immediately prior to the member's death, in receipt of any regular weekly or monthly voluntary payment from the member for the ordinary necessities of life.

The deceased had nominated his wife as beneficiary. The nomination of the beneficiary or its cancellation required the trustees' consent, as did any variation of the nominated beneficiary.

On the deceased's death the claimant, the deceased's mistress, applied for an order under the 1975 Act. She contended that the proper time for determining whether a beneficiary fell within the designated class was at the time of death, and therefore the nomination of the former wife as beneficiary was no longer effective and the fund fell into the residuary estate. Further, in any event, under the terms of section 25(1), the words "net estate" were to be construed as widely as possible. The court rejected these submissions on the grounds that:

(a) even if the entitlement to the death benefit vested only at the testator's death, the former wife was still within the designated class of beneficiary because she was receiving regular payments from the deceased and was dependent upon him, within (b) above;

(b) the death benefit did not come within paragraph (a) of the definition of "net estate" in section 25(1) because the power of the testator to dispose of the death fund was circumscribed. He did not have the power to dispose of the fund which was in the control of the trustees;

(c) the death benefit could not be construed as part of the net estate within paragraph (c) of the definition because section 8(1) required the nomination to be "in accordance with the provision of any statute".

Accordingly, on the preliminary issue, it was held that the death benefit was not part of the net estate.

Donatio Mortis Causa

Donatio mortis causa is a gift made by a person in contemplation of death but which does not take effect until the death of the donor.

Section 8(2) of the Act provides that where any sum of money or other property is received by any person as *donatio mortis causa* made by the deceased person, that sum of money, after deducting any inheritance tax payable, or that other property, to the extent of the value thereof at the date of the death of the deceased after deducting any inheritance tax payable, is treated for the purposes of the Act as part of the net estate of the deceased.

For a gift to be regarded as *donatio mortis causa*, four conditions need to be satisfied:

(a) the gift must be made in contemplation of the death of the donor;

(b) the gift must be made on condition that it becomes absolute and irrevocable only on the death of the donor;

(c) the subject matter of the gift, or something that represents the gift, must have been delivered to the donee or someone on his behalf, with the intention of parting with it;

(d) the property must be capable of passing by *donatio mortis causa*. Any property which can be transferred by delivery or some suitable document can be given.

See further Chapter 21.

Donatio mortis causa of land is now possible: *Sen v Headley* [1991] Ch

425, [1991] 2 WLR 1308, [1991] 2 All ER 636.

If the gift is made unconditionally, it does not form part of the net estate unless it can be proved that it was made with the intention of defeating a claim for financial provision under the 1975 Act (see Chapter 8).

Section 8(2) exempts from liability any person who has paid a sum of money or transferred property in order to give effect to the *donatio mortis causa*.

On whether a *donatio mortis causa* of movable property outside the jurisdiction forms part of the net estate, see Dicey and Morris, *Conflict of Laws*.

Property held on Joint Tenancy

Where a deceased person was, immediately before death, entitled to a joint tenancy of any property, the court, for the purposes of facilitating the making of financial provision for the claimant, may, under section 9, order that the deceased's severable share of the property or the value thereof immediately before his death, should, to such an extent as appears to the court to be just in all the circumstances of the case, be treated for the purposes of the Act as part of the net estate of the deceased (section 9(1)). This provision extends to a *chose in action* (section 9(4)) and therefore includes assets held in a joint account or by way of joint insurance policy, and other joint investments. It should be noted, however, that:

(a) where it is intended to make an application under section 9 to treat the deceased's severable share of a joint tenancy as part of the net estate, the application must be made within the period of six months from the date on which representation with respect to the deceased's estate was first taken out. There is no power to extend the time limit (section 9(1)). This is another reason why it is advisable to apply for a standing search (see page 11) immediately upon the death of the deceased;

(b) unlike the provisions of section 3 of the Act which are mandatory, the power to order severance under section 9 is discretionary, and the discretion will be exercised only to such extent as appears to the court to be just in all the circumstances. Section 9 does not set out any other specific matters which the court is to take into account in exercising its discretion. See *Kourgky v Lusher* [1983] 4 FLR 65, (1982) 12 Fam Law 86 and *Re Crawford (Deceased)* [1983] 4 FLR 273;

(c) in determining the extent to which any severable share is to be treated as part of the net estate of the deceased, the amount of inheritance tax payable in respect of that severable share must be taken into account (section 9(2));

(d) where the court severs the deceased's share, it does not render any person liable for anything done by him before the order was made (section 9(3)). This provision protects any person or organisation, a bank or insurance company for example, from liability to account for any money paid out before the order is made. Section 9 does not, however, restrict the court's power to make an order that the severable share of the joint tenancy should form part of the net estate to any particular stage of the proceedings. It would therefore be advisable to seek such an order before the final hearing, to ensure that the property is preserved in the hands of the survivor and is available if necessary towards any orders the court may make. The alternative is to obtain an undertaking that the property will not be dissipated, disposed of or otherwise dealt with until the determination of the claim. A further alternative is to apply for an injunction forbidding the person or organisation from dealing in any way with the property until the determination of the substantive claim;

(e) a joint tenancy may be severed by notice in writing or by any act done which has the effect of severing the joint tenancy.

Severance

Section 9 of the Act applies only to property which is subject to a joint tenancy at the date of the deceased's death. If the joint tenancy was severed before death then the provisions of section 9 do not apply. The question whether or not the joint tenancy has in fact been severed may arise. In *Hawkesley v May* [1956] 1 QB 304, [1955] 3 WLR 569, [1955] 3 All ER 353, a settled fund was held on a trust which provided that, on attaining the age of twenty-one, the applicant and his sister would became absolutely entitled to the fund as joint tenants. The question was whether the joint tenancy had been severed, and her share transferred to her, when the sister wrote a letter requesting that the dividends be paid into her bank account. Holding that the tenancy had been severed Havers J stated:

> "there are a number of ways by which a joint tenancy may be severed. In *Williams v Hensman* [1861] Sir W Page Wood VC in the course of his judgement said 'a joint tenancy may be severed in three ways: in the first place, an act of any one of the persons interested operating upon his own share may create severance as to that share. The right of each tenant is a right by survivorship only in the event of no severance having taken place of the share which is claimed under the *jus accrescendi*: each one is at liberty to dispose of his own interest in such manner as to sever it from the joint fund – losing, of course, at the same time, his own right by survivorship. Secondly, a joint tenancy may be severed by mutual agreement. And in the third place, there may be severance by any course of dealing sufficient to intimate that the interests of all were mutually treated as constituting a tenancy in common. When a severance depends on an inference of this kind without any express act of severance it will not suffice to rely on an intention, with respect to the particular share, declared only behind the backs of the other persons interested. The first

> method indicated, namely an act of any one of the person interested operating upon his own share, obviously includes a declaration of intention to sever by one party."

In *Re Draper's Conveyance, Nihan v Porter* [1969] 1 Ch 486, [1968] 2 WLR 166, [1967] 3 All ER 853, property was conveyed to a husband and wife as joint tenants in October 1951. The parties divorced and the decree absolute was made in March 1966. On 11 February 1966 the wife issued proceedings under section 17 of the Married Women's Property Act 1882 for an order for sale of the property and the division of the net proceeds. It was held that the joint tenancy was severed by the issue of the proceedings, coupled with the affidavit in support of it which clearly evinced an intention on the part of the wife to sever the tenancy.

In *Harris v Goddard* [1983] 1 WLR 203, [1983] 3 All ER 242, the issue was whether a prayer in a petition for divorce for a property adjustment order operated as a notice in writing to sever the joint tenancy. Before the application was heard the husband died in a road traffic accident. The executors and the children of the deceased's first marriage sought a declaration that the tenancy had been severed and that they were entitled to one half of the net proceeds of sale. In holding that the prayer in the petition did not take effect as a severance notice Lawton LJ said:

> "When notice in writing of a desire to sever is served pursuant to s 36(2) [of the Law of Property Act 1925], it takes effect forthwith. It follows that a desire to sever must evince an intention to bring about the wanted result immediately. A notice in writing which expresses a desire to bring about the wanted result at some time in the future is not, in my judgement, a notice in writing within s 36(2). Further, the notice must be one which shows an intent to bring about the consequences set out in section 36(2), namely that the net proceeds of the statutory trust for sale shall be held upon trust which would have been requisite for giving effect to the beneficial interests if there had been an actual severance. I am unable to accept the submission of counsel for the plaintiffs that a notice in writing which shows no more than a desire to bring the existing interest to an end is a good notice. It must be a desire to sever which is intended to have the statutory consequences. Paragraph 3 of the prayer of the petition does no more than invite the court to consider at some future time whether to exercise its jurisdiction under section 24 of the 1973 Act, and if it does, to do so in one or more of three different ways. Orders under section 24(1)(a) and (b) could bring co-ownership to an end by ways other than by severance."

Dillon LJ stated:

> "Joint ownership is a form of co-ownership or concurrent ownership of property. Its special feature is the right of survivorship, whereby the right to the whole of the property accrues automatically to the surviving joint

tenant or joint tenants on the death of any one joint tenant. Severance is, as I understand it, the process of separating off the share of a joint tenant, so that the concurrent ownership will continue but the right of survivorship will no longer apply. The parties will hold separate shares as tenants in common. The joint tenancy may come to an end through other acts which destroy the whole ownership e.g. if one joint tenant acquires the entire beneficial interest of the other joint tenant(s) so as to become solely and absolutely entitled beneficially to the property, or by all the joint tenants joining in resettling the property on other trusts not involving concurrent ownership; but such acts do not involve severance and would not be called severance of the joint tenancy. In *Draper's Conveyance* the relief claimed by the originating summons which had been issued and by the affidavit in support included, as Lawton LJ has pointed out, a claim that the property might be sold and the proceeds be divided equally in accordance with the rights of the parties. This plainly involved severance of the beneficial joint tenancy as I understand the term 'severance'.

In the present case however, paragraph 3 of the prayer in the petition merely seeks relief in the most general and unparticularised terms under s. 24 of the Matrimonial Causes Act 1973. Apart from the fact that any relief for Mrs Harris under s. 24 lay in the future and was contingent on the court exercising its discretion under the section in her favour, she had not yet specified what she desired by the time Mr. Harris died, and the general prayer in her petition could have been satisfied by relief which did not involve severance, e.g. an order extinguishing Mr Harris's interest in the property and directing that the property be vested in Mrs Harris as sole absolute beneficial owner, or an order directing a resettlement of the property on Mr and Mrs Harris successively and not as concurrent owners. Therefore the petition in this case cannot be notice of a desire to sever the joint tenancy."

Valuing the deceased's severable share

By section 9 of the Act, the value of the property out of which the court can make an order for financial provision under section 2 is limited to the value of the deceased's severable share immediately before the death of the deceased but after deduction of any inheritance tax which is payable thereon. The crucial date therefore for assessing the value of the severable share is "immediately before the death" of the deceased.

In *Powell v Osbourne* [1993] 1 FLR 1001, [1993] 1 FCR 797, the Court of Appeal was concerned with the interpretation of "immediately before death". The deceased and his wife were divorced but the decree *nisi* had not been made absolute as there were pending ancillary relief proceedings. The deceased lived with his mistress. About two months before the deceased's death he and his mistress purchased a property as beneficial joint tenants. The property was subject to a substantial mortgage. There was also a joint collateral endowment policy. The house was the only property out of which any provision for the widow could be made. It was argued that, immediately before the death of the deceased, the policy had no surrender value. It acquired a value on death and therefore should be disregarded in valuing the deceased's assets. The Court of Appeal rejected this argument on the basis that it is at the moment immediately before death that a joint tenancy can be severed, and that if death were certain the value of the policy immediately before the death of the deceased would be equal to the proceeds of the policy when it matures.

It follows from this decision that the value of the property for the purposes of making an order under section 2 will be assessed after setting off the value of the policy at death against the mortgage debt on the property so as to give the deceased's share in the property a significant value.

Exercise of the court's discretion

The power granted to the court under section 9 is discretionary, but the Act does not set out any specific criteria to which the court should have regard when exercising its discretion, save that it may exercise its discretion:

(a) only for the purposes of facilitating the making of financial provision for the claimant; and

(b) only to such extent as appears to be just in all the circumstances.

The language of the section is so broadly phrased that it gives the court a very wide discretion in respect of the matters it may take into account when making its decision, the objective of which is to ensure that justice is done.

In *Kourgky v Lusher* [1983] 4 FLR 65, (1982) 12 Fam Law 86, Wood J stated that the words "facilitating and making financial provision for the applicant" should not be understood to narrow the broad discretionary power given by section 9. In considering the application the court will necessarily take into account the financial needs and resources of the parties. With the increase in divorce and cohabitation, it seems inevitable that the courts will be concerned with cases where the property which is the subject matter of the application provides a home for the deceased's families, or with assets which provide, as far as possible, financial security for such families and step-families. Since the court's duty when exercising its discretion is to impart justice having regard to all the circumstances of the case, it seems unlikely that the courts will take from Peter to give to Paul where the assets are inadequate.

In *Re Crawford (Deceased)* [1983] 4 FLR 273, the court applied the provisions of section 3 and took into account financial benefits to the beneficiaries under the will of the deceased. In *Kourgky v Lusher* (above), Wood J approached the exercise of discretion by considering the matters set out under section 25 of the Matrimonial Causes Act 1973. Although those matters resemble those under section 3 of the 1975 Act, they are not identical in all respects. It is submitted that it is questionable whether it is appropriate to introduce the provisions of the 1973 Act, which concerns matters following the breakdown of a marriage, to claims for financial provision under the 1975 Act, where the circumstances are necessarily different, and the statutory bases for determining the applications are set out in different enactments.

In *Jessop v Jessop* [1992] FLR 591, the property was owned jointly by the deceased and his mistress. The value of the property had risen considerably between the death of the deceased and the date of the final hearing. Although the value to be taken into account is the value immediately before the death, in determining the claim, Nourse J took into account the income, expenditure and capital resources of the parties when making an order for the payment of £10,000 to the deceased's widow. It would appear that, where the court is asked to take into account the deceased's severable share in any property, it does not follow that the whole of the property will be treated as part of the net assets of the deceased. Whether the court will treat the severable share as part of the net estate, and if so, to what extent, depends on the particular circumstances and what appears, in those circumstances, to be just. In some cases part of the value may be sufficient to meet the justice of the case. In others, as in *Hanbury v Hanbury* [1999] 2 FLR 255, the whole of the share may be treated as part of the net estate.

Where the deceased had an interest in property abroad, much will turn on the laws of succession of the country in question, and whether the deceased made a valid will according to the law of the that country or died intestate.

Chapter 8

Dispositions Intended to Defeat Financial Provision

Introduction

Provision is made in the Inheritance (Provision for Family and Dependants) Act 1975 to prevent a person from defeating its measures by making a disposition of his assets during his lifetime or contracting to do so after his death. The powers of the court in respect of such evasion or avoidance, and the duties of personal representatives and the protection afforded to them, are set out in sections 10 to 13 of the 1975 Act. These provisions may be invoked only if the court is satisfied that the exercise of its powers under section 10 would facilitate the making of financial provision for the claimant.

Inter Vivos Dispositions

Where a claim for financial provision is made under section 2 of the 1975 Act, the claimant in those proceedings may apply to the court for an order under section 10(2) of the 1975 Act that the donee of an *inter vivos* disposition (whether or not at the date of the order he holds any interest in the property disposed of to him or for his benefit by the deceased) provide, to the claimant, for the purposes the making that financial provision, such sum of money or property as may be specified in the order.

Conditions precedent for an order

Before the court may make an order under section 10(2) of the 1975 Act, it must be satisfied that:

(a) less than six years before the date of his death, the deceased, with the intention of defeating an application for financial provision under the Act, made a disposition; and

(b) full valuable consideration for that disposition was not given by the donee to whom, or for the benefit of whom, the disposition was made, or by any other person; and

(c) the exercise of the power conferred by section 10 would facilitate the making of financial provision for the claimant under the Act.

Meaning of "disposition"

The section is wide in its terms; section 10(7) of the 1975 Act defines "disposition" to include:

> "any payment of money (including the payment of a premium under a policy of assurance) and any conveyance, assurance, appointment or gift of property of any description, whether made by an instrument or otherwise."

On the other hand, the Act specifically excludes:

(a) any provision in a will, any such nomination as is mentioned in section 8(1) of the Act (see page 111) or any *donatio mortis causa* (see page 113); or

(b) any appointment of property made, otherwise than by will, in the exercise of a special power of appointment.

The transactions under (a) are excluded because they form part of the "net estate" pursuant to other provisions in the Act. Property which is the subject of a special power of appointment and is disposed of *inter vivos* is excluded by reason of the fact that it was never part of the deceased's "net estate".

In *Clifford v Tanner*, unreported, CAT, 10 June 1986, the deceased had a right under a covenant to occupy a house belonging to his daughter. He released the right to his daughter without full valuable consideration. It was held that the release of the right to occupy came within the definition of disposition, as a "gift of property of any description".

Section 10(8) also excludes any disposition made in respect of any property before the commencement of the 1975 Act on 1 April 1976.

"Full valuable consideration"

Section 25(1) provides that "valuable consideration does not include marriage or a promise of marriage". The consideration need not, however, have been provided by the donee. It could have been provided by "any other person" (section 10(2)(b)).

Intention of defeating a claim

For a disposition to come within the provisions of section 10 the claimant must satisfy the court that, in making the disposition, the deceased had the intention of defeating a claim for financial provision under the 1975 Act (section 10(2)). Section 12(1) of the 1975 Act provides that this condition should be fulfilled if the court is of the opinion that, on a balance of probabilities, the intention of the deceased (though not necessarily his sole intention) in making the disposition was to prevent an order for financial provision being made under the Act, or to reduce the amount of the provision which might otherwise be granted.

The intention to defeat a claim need not be the sole intention, but there must be some evidence of an intention to defeat such a claim. In *Re Kennedy (Deceased), Kennedy v Official Solicitor* [1980] CLY 2820, the deceased transferred his house to his mistress in consideration of natural love and affection. The deceased's wife issued proceedings for divorce in which she indicated her intention to apply for ancillary relief, but before the decree *nisi* was pronounced, he died. A few months later the mistress died too. It was held that it was not essential to show that the 1975 Act or its provisions were present in the mind of the deceased when he entered into the transaction which was called into question, but there had to be evidence that he intended to defeat a claim made after his death against the estate.

In *Dawkins v Judd* [1986] 2 FLR 360, the deceased had transferred the matrimonial home to his daughter by his first marriage for £100, and left a will leaving his entire estate to the daughter. Bush J had no difficulty, when applying the test set out in section 12, in reaching the conclusion that the sale of the house to the daughter was entered into with the intention, though not necessarily the sole intention, of defeating a claim for financial provision. See also *Hanbury v Hanbury* [1999] 2 FLR 255 for another example where intention was found proved.

The evidence of such an intention need not be in writing. It may be by way of oral statements made by the deceased or derived from the circumstances of the disposition. The value of the property in issue at the time of the disposition; the value of any consideration given for the property; and the relationship between the deceased and the donee are all matters which are relevant and which must be taken into account. The standard of proof required to show intention is the civil standard of proof, that is, on the balance of probabilities.

The court's powers to make orders

If the conditions referred to above are satisfied, and subject to the provisions of sections 12 and 13 of the 1975 Act, the court's order will be directed to the donee to provide the asset, be it money or property, to meet the financial provision the court makes in favour of the claimant. The court may order the donee of an *inter vivos* disposition to provide such money or other property as may be specified for the purposes of making financial provision for the claimant, whether or not, at the date of the order, the donee retains any interest in the property disposed of to him or for his benefit by the deceased (section 10(2)).

If the donee of the *inter vivos* disposition is dead, the court can proceed to make the appropriate orders in like manner against the personal representatives of the donee (section 12(4)).

It will be seen that the provisions of section 10 affect the donee, not the property given to the donee. If the donee is dead the action can be made or continued against his estate. The court does not, however, have power to make any orders under section 10 in respect of any property which has been distributed by the personal representatives. Furthermore, a personal representative is not liable for having distributed any such property before he has notice of the making of a claim under the 1975 Act in which an application is made under section 10, on the grounds that he ought to have taken into account the possibility that such an application would be made (section 12(4)).

Section 10(3) provides that where an order is made under section 10(2), as respects any disposition which consisted of the payment of money to or for the benefit of the donee, the amount of any sum of money or the value of any property ordered to be provided must not exceed the amount of the payment made by the deceased, after deducting any inheritance tax borne by the donee in respect of that payment.

Where the disposition consisted of the transfer of property (other than a sum of money) to or for the benefit of the donee, the amount of any sum of money under section 10(2) must not exceed the value, at the date of the death of the deceased, of the property disposed of by him to or for the benefit of the donee (or if that property has been disposed of by the person to whom it was transferred by the deceased, the value at the date of disposal thereof), after deducting any inheritance tax borne by the donee in respect of the transfer of that property by the deceased (section 10(4)).

Thus, if the donee purchases property or shares with the money paid to him, neither the increase in the value of the property or shares, nor the income from the investment, would need to be accounted for (section 10(3)). The value will be the value at the date of disposal or at the death of the deceased, after the deduction of inheritance tax. The value of the property is the capital value, and does not include income from the property which may have accrued since the disposition was made to the donee. The donee will have to provide only such sum of money or property as will meet the financial provision order made by the court in favour of the claimant.

Donee's right to apply

By virtue of section 10(5) of the 1975 Act, if an application is made for an order under section 10(2) of the Act, the donee of the property in question can apply for the court to substitute, for the disposition which is the subject of the application, another disposition made to him by the deceased. Certain preconditions must be fulfilled. Section 10(5) provides that where an application (the "original application") is made for an order in relation to such a disposition, then if on application under section 10(5) the court is satisfied of certain matters, the court may exercise, in relation to the person to whom or for whose benefit that other disposition was made, the powers which the court would have had under section 10(2) if the original application had been made in respect of that other disposition. The matters of which the court must be satisfied are that:

(a) less than six years before the date of the death of the deceased, the deceased, with the intention of defeating an application for financial provision under the Act, made a disposition other than the disposition which is the subject of the original application; and
(b) full valuable consideration for that other disposition was not given by the person to whom, or for the benefit of whom, that other disposition

was made or by any other person,

Where the claim includes an application for an order under section 10 it is desirable to give notice of the proceedings to the donee, so that the donee has the opportunity to apply to be joined as a party to the proceedings and to be heard before decisions are made which affect him and his rights and interests. The *bona fides* of the donee can be dealt with as a preliminary point in appropriate cases. This course would also be beneficial to the claimant because it would enable the claimant to seek disclosure from the donee and, if necessary, preserve the property until the determination of the claim, by obtaining an undertaking or an order prohibiting the disposal, transfer or other dealing with the property.

Matters to be considered by the court

In determining whether to exercise its powers under section 10(2) of the 1975 Act, and in what manner to exercise its powers, the court must have regard to the following matters:

(a) the circumstances in which the disposition was made;
(b) the valuable consideration which was given;
(c) the relationship, if any, of the donee to the deceased;
(d) the conduct of the donee;
(e) the financial resources of the donee; and
(f) all the other circumstances of the case.
(section 10(6)).

Contracts to Leave Property by Will

The 1975 Act, section 11, gives the court jurisdiction to order any sum of money or other property bequeathed in a will by virtue of a contract to make a will, to be made available for the purposes of facilitating the making of a financial provision order, provided that the conditions in section 11 are satisfied.

Conditions precedent for an order

Before the court can make any of the orders under section 11(2) in respect of a contract to leave property by will to another, it must be satisfied that:

(a) the deceased made a contract by which he agreed to leave by his will a sum of money or other property to any person, or by which he agreed that a sum of money or other property would be paid or transferred to any person, out of his estate; and
(b) the deceased made this contract with the intention of defeating an application for financial provision under the 1975 Act; and
(c) when the contract was made, full valuable consideration for that contract was not given or promised by the person with whom or for whose benefit the contract was made ("the donee") or by any other person; and

(d) the exercise of the powers conferred by section 11 would facilitate the making of financial provision for the claimant under the Act.

Contract

The Act is silent on the meaning of "contract" and therefore the assumption is that the word must be given its ordinary legal meaning. It could, though, be argued that the Act did not intend the term "contract" to have the ordinary legal interpretation because the provisions of section 12(2) envisage a situation where "no valuable consideration" is given. Thus, where the deceased made a promise or representation to leave property by will, and as a result the promisee or representee acted to his detriment, there may not be an enforceable contract, but if the evidence suggests that the doctrine of proprietary estoppel arises, there may be an enforceable claim against the estate. The same may be so if a constructive trust is implied by the agreement.

Section 11 extends to a contract by which the deceased agreed that his personal representatives would pay a sum of money or transfer other property out of his estate.

The 1975 Act did not come into force until 1 April 1976 and therefore does not apply to contracts made before that date. Unlike the provisions of section 10, where only dispositions made less than six years before the date of death may be subject to an order, there are no time limits in respect of contracts to leave property by will. Time may, however, be relevant to the issue of the deceased's intention in making the contract.

Any arrangement which applies in the case of intestacy falls outside section 11, because the section refers to a contract by which the deceased agreed to leave a sum of money or other property "by will".

Intention to defeat a claim

The claimant must satisfy the court that, in making the contract, the deceased had the intention of defeating a claim by the claimant for financial provision out of the estate under the 1975 Act. Section 12(2) also provides that, with respect to any contract made by the deceased where no valuable consideration is given or promised by any person, then it is to be presumed, unless the contrary is shown, that the deceased made the contract with the intention of defeating a claim for financial relief under the Act. Section 25(1) provides that "valuable consideration" does not include marriage or a promise of marriage. The statutory presumption is rebuttable by the donee on production of evidence to show that the deceased did not have the intention to defeat any claim for financial provision by the claimant, but that his motives were sincere and genuine.

The intention to defeat a claim implies a fraudulent dealing and the question then arises whether the standard of proof required to prove such intention should be that applicable where fraud is alleged; but section 12(1) states that the standard to be applied is that of the "balance of probabilities". In some respects the donee is at a disadvantage because in most cases the motives of the deceased cannot be tested by direct evidence from the deceased, by contrast with the position in applications under section 37 of the Matrimonial Causes Act 1973.

As in cases under section 10, the test that the court would need to apply is whether the intention of the deceased (though not necessarily his sole intention) in making the contract was to prevent an order for financial provision being made under the Act, or to reduce the amount of the provision which might otherwise be granted (section 12(1)). It would seem that the court, in applying the test, would be concerned with the deceased's intention subjectively; and that, in determining whether the required intention existed, the deceased would be taken to intend the natural consequences of his acts. All facts, statements and declarations made at, before or after the act was done are relevant in determining the state of mind of the deceased.

Full valuable consideration

For the meaning of "full valuable consideration" see section 25(1), page 121. The consideration need not have been provided by the donee as long as it was provided at the time the contract was made. It could have been provided by any other person on the donee's behalf (section 11(2)(c)).

Orders which may be made under section 11

If the conditions outlined above are satisfied the court may make any one or more of the following orders to facilitate the making of financial provision under section 2 for the claimant:

(a) if any money has been paid, or any other property has been transferred to or for the benefit of the donee in accordance with the contract, an order directing the donee to provide, for the purposes of the making of that financial provision, such sum of money or other property as may be specified in the order;

(b) if the money or all the money has not been paid, or the property or all of the property has not been transferred, in accordance with the contract, an order directing the personal representatives not to make any further payment or transfer any property or further property, as the case may be, or directing the personal representatives to make such payment or transfer such property only as may be specified in the order.

(section 11(2)).

The court may also give such consequential directions as it thinks fit (including directions requiring the making of any payments or the transfer of any property) for giving effect to the order or for securing a fair adjustment of the rights of the persons affected thereby (section 12(3)).

Where money has been paid

Where the personal representatives of the deceased have made payment of money or transferred property to the donee in accordance with the contract, the court can order the donee to provide such sums of money or transfer such property as will facilitate the making of a financial provision order. The order does not attach to the specific sum of money or property as had been transferred.

Where money has not been paid

If the terms of the contract have not been fulfilled (whether wholly or partially) by the personal representatives, the court may forbid them from making payment and from transferring such of the money or the property as may be specified in the order. If the donee of the contract by will has died, the court can proceed to make the appropriate orders against the personal representatives of the donee (section 12(4)). The court cannot, however, make any of the orders set out in section 11 in respect of any property which has been distributed by the personal representatives. Nor are the personal representatives liable for having distributed any such property before they had notice of the making of the claim which included an application for an order under section 11, on the ground that they ought to have taken into account the possibility that such an application would be made (section 12(4)).

Position of a donee who is a trustee

The court's power to make any orders under section 10 and 11 against a trustee is limited to such sum as is, at the date of the order, in the hands of the trustee, or the value at that date of any property which represents that money. In the case of any property transferred, it is limited to so much of that property as is, at the date of the order, in the hands of the trustee and the value at that date of any property (section 13(1)).

As in the case of the personal representatives of the donee, the trustee is exempt from liability for having distributed any money or other property on the ground that he ought to have taken into account the possibility that such an application would be made (section 13(2)).

Restrictions on the court's powers

The court may exercise its powers in relation to any contract made by the deceased only to the extent that the court considers that the amount of any sum of money paid or to be paid, or the value of any property transferred or to be transferred in accordance with the contract, exceeds the value of any valuable consideration given or to be given for the contract. The property transferred or to be transferred under the contract is to be valued at the date of the hearing.

Matters to be considered by the court

The court has a discretion whether or not to make an order under section 11. In determining whether or not to exercise its powers and, if so, in what manner to exercise them, the court must have regard to the following matters:

(a) the circumstances in which the contract was made;
(b) the relationship, if any, of the donee to the deceased;
(c) the conduct of the donee;
(d) the financial resources of the donee; and
(e) all the circumstances of the case.
(section 11(4)).

Rights of persons to enforce the contract

Section 11(5) of the Act provides that where the court makes an order under section 11(2) in relation to any contract, the contractual rights of the donee to enforce that contract or to recover damages, or to obtain other relief for the breach, is subject to any adjustment made by the court under section 12(3). The contractual relief is available to the extent only as is consistent with the court's order.

Chapter 9

Matrimonial Proceedings and Disentitlement Orders

Section 15 of the Inheritance (Provision for Family and Dependants) Act 1975, as amended by the Matrimonial and Family Proceedings Act 1984, provides that where a court in England and Wales grants a decree of judicial separation, or of divorce or nullity of marriage, it may, either then, or at any time thereafter, if it considers it just to do so, exclude the right of the parties to apply for an order under section 2 of the 1975 Act.

The order may be made before or after the decree is made absolute. If it is made before the decree has been made absolute, it does not take effect until the decree has been made absolute (section 15(2)).

Thus, where, on an application for ancillary relief in matrimonial proceedings, a "clean break" provision is made, consideration should be given to whether an order, disentitling the parties from making any claim for an order under section 2 of the 1975 Act against the estate of the other, would also be appropriate.

Section 25 of the Matrimonial and Family Proceedings Act 1984 extends the power to make an order under section 15 to marriages which have been dissolved or annulled overseas; where the parties have been legally separated; and where a court in England and Wales has made an order for ancillary relief under section 17 of the Matrimonial and Family Proceedings Act 1984. On the making of an order under section 17 of the 1984 Act in respect of a marriage which has been dissolved or annulled overseas, or where there has been a decree of judicial separation, the court, if it considers it just to do so, may, on the application of either or both parties to the marriage, order that the other party to the marriage shall not, on the death of the other, be entitled to apply for an order under section 2 of the 1975 Act.

Where an order under section 15 or 15A has been made, on the death of the other party to the marriage, the court should not entertain any application under section 2 of the Act against the estate of the deceased.

There are two conflicting decisions of the Court of Appeal on how the court should approach an application for an order under section 15 of the 1975 Act. In *Re Fullard (Deceased)* [1982] Fam 42, [1981] 3 WLR 743, [1981] 2 All ER 796, when considering the implications of section 15 in an application under the 1975 Act Ormrod LJ stated:

> "I regard section 15 as a form of insuring against applications under the 1975 Act which some people may very reasonably wish to do, having made financial provision of a capital nature for the former spouse. People obviously have other commitments – second wives (or husbands) and children and so on. I do not regard section 15 as materially affecting the question the court has to answer as the condition precedent to these applications."

In *Whiting v Whiting* [1988] 2 FLR 189, however, following the divorce of the parties, a consent order was made for financial provision for the wife and children. Subsequently the husband applied, under section 31(7) of the Matrimonial Causes Act 1973, for a variation of the order for periodical payments for the wife and for an order under section 15(1) of the 1975 Act. His application was dismissed. On appeal it was held that, before the court can consider it just to make an order, it must be presented with some indication of what the estate is likely to consist of and some details of the person(s) whom the applicant considers to have a prior claim on the estate. Balcombe LJ said:

> "For the court to make an order under section 15(1) it must consider it just to do so. In my judgment, before the court can consider it just to make an order depriving a divorced spouse of an opportunity to claim financial provision from the estate of the other spouse, it should be given some indication of what that estate is likely to consist of and some details of the persons whom the applicant considers to have a prior claim on his estate in the event of his decease. I am prepared to accept that the husband's capital asset is his interest in his present house and that this is likely to be the only asset of substance in his estate. It is a reasonable inference that he considers his present wife and, presumably his children, to have a prior claim on his estate in the event of his death, but nowhere in his evidence does he say so. The whole of his evidence is directed towards supporting his application for a discharge of the 1979 order, and he (or those advising him) appear to have assumed that his application under section 15 of the 1975 Act will stand or fall with that other application. In these circumstances it is hardly surprising that the judge made no mention of this limb of the husband's application. For my part, I would dismiss the appeal on the simple ground that the husband has not made out a case to support his application under section 15 of the 1975 Act. That is not to say that he may not be able to do so, and accordingly I would dismiss this part of the appeal without prejudice to the husband's right to renew the application under section 15."

It is submitted that, of the two decisions, that of Ormrod LJ in *Re Fullard* is to be preferred. The decision in *Whiting* fails to take account of social changes, including the increasing independence of women, the growing divorce rate and the fact that divorcing couples tend to be young and move on to form other relationships and have second families. It also disregards the concept of a final and clean break settlement on divorce. It is unrealistic, in the majority of cases, to expect divorcing couples to be able to give the details described in *Whiting*. To require an applicant under section 15 to provide details of those he considers would have a prior claim to his estate on his death some decades in the future is almost impossible to fulfil; if such a requirement were to be applied strictly, the provision would, in time, become redundant.

Practitioners should nevertheless ensure that there is full and frank disclosure where the court is considering financial provision, particularly where a clean break settlement is sought. If an order is made under section 15, and it is subsequently challenged on the basis that the court did not have the required information when it made the order; or if, in the absence of such an order, a claim is made under section 2, it does not follow that the claim under section 2 will necessarily succeed, because the claimant will still have to satisfy the court that the requirements under the Act are met. Where a former wife's claims under sections 23 and 24 of the Matrimonial Causes Act 1973 have been fully considered and a final order has been made, it is unlikely, save in exceptional circumstances, that a claim for an order under section 2 of the 1975 Act would succeed. (For an example of exceptional circumstances, see *Re Fullard* (above)).

This issue was raised in *Cameron v Treasury Solicitor* [1996] 2 FLR 716, [1997] 1 FCR 188, where, on the claimant's divorce, a clean break order was made by consent, requiring the deceased to pay the claimant a lump sum of £8,000. About twenty years later the husband died intestate. His estate, amounting to about £7,677, passed as *bona vacantia* to the Crown. The former wife applied for an order under section 2 of the 1975 Act. She was then suffering from ill-health and was in very straitened circumstances; there were no competing claims. At first instance it was held that the fact of the clean break did not preclude her from making the claim and she was awarded the whole of the net estate. On appeal it was held that the first task of the claimant in such cases is to make out a case that she is entitled to some relief under the Act. To do this she must satisfy the court that the disposition of the deceased's estate, effected by the law of intestacy in this case, was not such as to make a reasonable financial provision for her. In the present case, a clean break order had been obtained by consent some nineteen years before; the deceased had not since then offered any financial support to the claimant; there were no grounds to show that he owed her a moral obligation; nor were there any special circumstances to establish entitlement to an order. The court also expressed the view that it is now the practice of the court to include a section 15 direction in all clean break orders, and an order which did not include such a direction would suggest a fundamental error in drafting.

It is rare for the parties not to be legally represented in applications for financial relief following the breakdown of their marriage when final orders are made. There is provision for a full disclosure of information within those proceedings. Where there is a clean break order which includes a direction under section 15, then that order should be respected. Where such a direction is not included, there is usually a good reason for its absence from the order.

Where a section 15 direction is not made, it should not be assumed that its absence is an error. The court should consider any claim for an order under section 2 on its merits. Since the claimant has to establish that the disposition of the deceased's estate is not such as to make reasonable financial provision within the meaning of section 1(2)(b) of the 1975 Act, the circumstances at the time the ancillary relief order was made and the circumstances since then would have to be considered in the light of the factors the court is required to have regard to under section 3 of the Act. The claimant would have to jump over several hurdles to succeed. In some cases a trial of the preliminary issue may in the long run avoid delay and expense. Furthermore, although the decision in *Cameron v Treasury Solicitor* seems to suggest that a section 15 direction is inserted in all clean break orders as a matter of practice, the reality is that, although such a direction is usually considered seriously by practitioners who advise divorcing or separating couples, the court has to approve any settlement of the matrimonial proceedings which includes such an order. A claimant who seeks to challenge a section 15 order in a claim under the 1975 Act would need to establish some very exceptional circumstance in order to succeed.

It should also be noted that the provisions of section 15(3) and (4) and section 15A(2) and (3) of the 1975 Act are mandatory. It would therefore be open to the court, of its own motion, or on application by a defendant in a claim under the 1975 Act, to strike out the claim on the basis that the court does not have the power to entertain the claim by virtue of the aforesaid provisions.

The Civil Partnership Bill 2004 (see page 2) contains proposals to extend the provisions of section 15 to same-sex couples who have entered into civil partnerships.

Chapter 10

Personal Representatives and Trustees

Personal Representatives

General
The personal representatives of a deceased person are under a duty to collect and get in the real and personal estate of the deceased and administer it according to law. When required to so by the court, they must provide, on oath, a full inventory of the estate and, if required by the court, render an account of the administration of the estate to the court (Administration of Estates Act 1925, section 25).

The personal representatives are liable for any waste to the estate or the conversion of the real or personal estate of the deceased. Where it is apparent that a claim may be made under the Inheritance (Provision for Family and Dependants) Act 1975, the personal representatives must ensure that nothing is done by them to prejudice the claim.

The 1975 Act provides that any claim against the estate must be begun within six months from the date when the grant of representation was taken our. If the personal representatives have not, on the expiry of the time limit, received any notice of a claim, they are free to distribute the estate. Where distribution has taken place it is still possible for the court to direct the beneficiary/ies to meet any financial provision order it makes in favour of the claimant.

There are provisions in the 1975 Act which protect the personal representatives from liability in some circumstances.

Liabilities under the 1975 Act
The 1975 Act extends the categories of person to whom personal representatives owe a duty, but also provides certain protection from liability. A successful claimant is regarded in law as a person interested in the will or intestacy and is thus in the same position vis-à-vis the personal representatives as a beneficiary and has the same rights of action against them.

The personal representatives are liable to the beneficiaries and creditors for any loss of assets of the estate or breach of any trust contained in the will. Personal representatives may apply to the court for relief under section 61 of the Trustee Act 1925 where they have made an interim distribution of the estate without a court order. Personal representatives may be faced with the difficult situation that beneficiaries are suffering hardship because distribution has been delayed by the inheritance proceedings, while at the same time the personal representatives have a duty to the claimant to preserve property. In *Re Simson, Simson v National Provincial Bank Ltd* [1950] 2 All ER 826, Vaisey J expressed the view that it was the duty of executors faced with a claim for financial provision to make no distribution until the hearing of the claim, and to preserve the estate intact for the court to deal with. On the other hand, in *Re Ralphs, Ralphs v District Bank* [1968] 1 WLR 1522, [1968] 3 All ER 285, Cross J took a different view. He advocated that executors should:

> "form their own view, with the assistance of their legal advisers, as to payments which can properly be made, and if they are not prepared to make such payments on their own responsibility they should ask the parties who might conceivably be affected for their consent. If such consent was not forthcoming they could apply to the court for leave to make the payment in question. If the court finds that consent was unreasonably withheld it can penalise the party responsible in costs."

The protection afforded

Section 20 of the 1975 Act makes special provision in relation to the liabilities of personal representatives. It provides that a personal representative is not liable:

(a) for having distributed any part of the estate of the deceased, after the end of the period of six months from the date on which representation with respect to the estate of the deceased is first taken out, on the ground that he ought to have taken into account the possibility:
  (i) that the court might permit the making of an application for an order under section 2 of the Act after the end of that period (i.e. extend the time for making the application); or
  (ii) that, where an order has been made under section 2, the court might vary the order in exercise of the powers conferred on it by section 6. This provision, however, does not prejudice any power to recover, by reason of the making of an order under the Act, any part of the estate which has been distributed;

(b) for having made interim payments directed to be paid by an order under section 5 out of the net estate of the deceased, and thereby leaving the estate insufficient to make the payments, unless at the time of the making of the payments he has reasonable cause to believe that the estate is not sufficient;

(c) for postponing the payment of money or the transfer of property out of the estate of the deceased which the deceased had agreed by contract to leave by his will, until the expiration of six months from the date on which representation with respect to the estate of the deceased is first taken out or, if during that period, an application is made for an order under section 2 of the Act, until the determination of that application.

(section 20(3)).

These provisions protect the personal representative who distributes the assets after the period of six months from the grant of representation. He should, therefore, avoid any distribution which might prejudice the claim within six months from the grant. Where he has notice of a possible claim he should wait until the six months from the grant of representation have expired, and then give notice of his intention to distribute. He is also protected if he pays any sum directed to be paid by the court by way of interim payments under section 5 of the Act, unless, at the time of making the payments, he had reasonable grounds for believing that the estate was insolvent.

Protection is also provided where the personal representative makes a distribution under a contract which might be caught under section 11 of the Act, provided he did not make any payment of money or transfer any property until after the expiration of six months from the date on which representation was taken out. If a claim is pending, the personal representative must postpone any distribution until the final determination of the claim. Where he has notice of a possible claim, it would be desirable to give notice to the claimant or his/her legal advisers of the intention to distribute before doing so.

In relation to any application under section 10 (see Chapter 8), if the donee of an *inter vivos* disposition is dead, the court can proceed to make the appropriate order in like manner against the personal representative of the donee under section 10. The court does not, however, have the power to make any of the orders under section 10 in respect of any property which has been distributed by the personal representative. Further, a personal representative is not liable for having distributed any such property before he has notice of the making of an application under section 10 on the grounds that he ought to have taken into account the possibility that such an application would be made (section 12(4)).

Personal representatives do not have, in relation to claims under the 1975 Act, protection equivalent to that provided by section 27 of the Trustee Act 1925. Section 27 protects personal representatives from liability to any beneficiary who does not respond in time to an advertisement notifying the personal representatives' intention to distribute the estate. If there is any doubt about whether or not the estate may be distributed, an application should be made to the court for a direction.

A personal representative who is also a beneficiary must ensure that the two capacities are kept separate. In some circumstances it may be prudent for a claimant under the 1975 Act to apply to the court, under the Administration of Justice Act 1985, section 50, to replace that personal representative.

Where, on the death of the deceased, it appears that the person appointed executor might also be a possible claimant under the 1975 Act, it may be advisable that the grant is not taken out by that person unless that person is one of a number of personal representatives appointed.

Procedure

The procedure to be followed by personal representatives in cases under the 1975 Act is set out in CPR Part 57; see Chapter 12.

Trustees

Section 13 of the 1975 Act imposes limitations on the court's powers under sections 10 and 11. Section 13 applies where an application is made for:

(a) an order under section 10 of the Act in respect of a disposition made by the deceased to any person as a trustee;

(b) an order under section 11 of the Act in respect of any payment made or property transferred in accordance with a contract made by the deceased, to any person as a trustee.

In these cases, the powers of the court under sections 10 and 11, to order the trustee to provide a sum of money or other property from which the award to the claimant is to be met (see pages 122 and 126), are subject to limitation. The limitation is, in the case of an application under section 10, additional to any provision regarding the deduction of inheritance tax. The limitation is that the amount of any sum of money or the value of any property ordered to be provided:

(a) in the case of an application in respect of a disposition which consisted of the payment of money, or an application in respect of the payment of money in accordance with a contract, may not exceed the aggregate of so much of that money as is at the date of the order in the hands of the trustee and the value at that date of any property which represents that money, or is derived therefrom, and is at that date in the hands of the trustee;

(b) in the case of an application in respect of a disposition which consisted of the transfer of property (other than a sum of money) or an application in respect of the transfer of property (other than a sum of money) in accordance with a contract, shall not exceed the aggregate of the value at the date of the order of so much of that property as is at that date in the hands of the trustee and the value at that date of any property which represents the first mentioned property, or is derived therefrom, and is at that date in the hands of the trustee.

Where any application is made in respect of a disposition made to any person as a trustee, or in respect or any payment made or property transferred in pursuance of a contract to any person as a trustee, the trustee is not liable for having distributed any money or other property on the ground that he ought to have taken into account the possibility that such an application would be made (section 13(2)).

Where any such application is made in respect of a disposition made to any person as a trustee, or in respect of any payment made or property transferred in accordance with a contract to any person as a trustee, any reference in section 10 or 11 to the donee is to be construed as including a reference to the trustee or trustees for the time being in question, and any reference to a trustee is to be construed in the same way (section 13(3)).

Chapter 11

Forfeiture

The forfeiture rule is a common law rule of public policy which, in certain circumstances, precludes a person who has unlawfully killed another from acquiring a benefit in consequence of the killing. Such an offender may not take any benefit which would otherwise accrue to him under a disposition made in the victim's will, or on the victim's intestacy. The whole of any disposition in favour of the offender fails; nor are his successors entitled to benefit.

The Forfeiture Act 1982 has limited the operation of the rule in respect of claims made under the Inheritance (Provision for Family and Dependants) Act 1975 in cases where the claimant is convicted after 13 October 1982, the date the Forfeiture Act came into force. The 1982 Act enables a person who has unlawfully killed another to make a claim under any of the provisions of the 1975 Act for financial provision from the estate of the deceased (Forfeiture Act 1982, section 2(1) and (2)(a)).

Order Modifying the Effect of the Rule

The Forfeiture Act 1982, section 2(1), empowers the court, when determining a claim under section 2 of the 1975 Act, to make an order modifying the effect of the forfeiture rule. Section 2 of the Act provides as follows:

"(1)–Where a court determines that the forfeiture rule has precluded a person (in this section referred to as 'the offender') who has unlawfully killed another from acquiring any interest in property mentioned in subsection (4) below, the court may make an order under this section modifying the effect of that rule.

(2) The court shall not make an order under this section modifying the effect of the forfeiture rule in any case unless it is satisfied that, having regard to the conduct of the offender and of the deceased and to such other circumstances as appear to the court to be material, the justice of the case requires the effect of the rule to be so modified in that case.

(3) In any case where a person stands convicted of an offence of which unlawful killing is an element, the court shall not make an order under this section modifying the effect of the forfeiture rule in that case unless proceedings for the purpose are brought before the expiry of the

period of three months beginning with his conviction.

(4) The interests in property referred to in subsection (1) above are–

(a) any beneficial interest in property which (apart from the forfeiture rule) the offender would have acquired–

(i) under the deceased's will ... or the law relating to intestacy or by way of ius relicti, ius relictae or legitim;

(ii) on the nomination of the deceased in accordance with the provisions of any enactment;

(iii) as a donatio mortis causa made by the deceased; or

(iv) under a special destination (whether relating to heritable or moveable property); or

(b) any beneficial interest in property which (apart from the forfeiture rule) the offender would have acquired in consequence of the death of the deceased, being property which, before the death, was held on trust for any person.

(5) An order under this section may modify the effect of the forfeiture rule in respect of any interest in property to which the determination referred to in subsection (1) above relates and may do so in either or both of the following ways, that is–

(a) where there is more than one such interest, by excluding the application of the rule in respect of any (but not all) of those interests; and

(b) in the case of any such interest in property, by excluding the application of the rule in respect of part of the property.

(6) On the making of an order under this section, the forfeiture rule shall have effect for all purposes (including purposes relating to anything done before the order is made) subject to the modifications made by the order.

(7) The court shall not make an order under this section modifying the effect of the forfeiture rule in respect of any interest in property which, in consequence of the rule, has been acquired before the coming into force of this section by a person other than an offender or a person claiming through him.

(8) In this section–

'property' includes any chose in action or incorporeal moveable property; and

'will' includes codicil."

It will be observed that the court's powers are limited in the following respects:

(a) The court cannot make an order modifying the effect of the rule unless it is "satisfied, having regard to the conduct of the offender and of the deceased and to such other circumstances as appear to the court to be material, that the justice of the case requires the effect to be modified" in that case. The moral culpability of the offender and the justice of the case are matters which are relevant (section 2(2)).

(b) The court cannot make an order modifying the effect of the rule unless proceedings for the modification of the rule are commenced before the expiry of three months from the date of the offender's conviction. There is no power to extend the time limit (section 2(3)).

(c) The court cannot modify the rule in respect of any interest in property which, in consequence of the rule, has been acquired before the coming into force of section 2 by a person other than the offender or a person claiming through him (section 2(7)).

The Cases

In *Re Royse (Deceased), Royse v Royse* [1985] Fam 22, [1984] 3 WLR 784, [1984] 3 All ER 339, the claimant had been convicted of the manslaughter of her husband and committed to hospital under section 60 of the Mental Health Act 1959. On 31 March 1981 she was discharged from hospital and returned to live in the former matrimonial home, which was valued at £30,000, and which comprised the major part of the net estate of £32,000. The claimant was the sole beneficiary of the deceased's estate under his will. Letters of administration with the will annexed were first granted to the deceased's mother, and, on her death, to the brother and sister of the deceased. The claimant applied for financial provision to be made for her, because she was precluded from acquiring any benefit by reason of the forfeiture rule. In October 1982, after the claim had been made, the Forfeiture Act 1982 came into force. The application failed because the absence of reasonable financial provision was a consequence of a rule of public policy which precluded her from receiving any benefit under the will. The claimant's application under the Forfeiture Act 1982 also failed since the Act was not in force when she made the claim.

In *Re K (Deceased)* [1985] Ch 85, [1985] 2 WLR 262, [1985] 1 All ER 403, there had been a history of ill-treatment of the wife by the deceased during their marriage. On 30 September 1982, during an altercation, the deceased was killed at short range by a shot gun held by the wife. The wife was charged with murder but pleaded guilty to manslaughter. She was placed on probation. The deceased had bequeathed his residuary estate on trust to his widow for life and thereafter to four named beneficiaries. The estate was worth £412,000. The matrimonial home was held on a joint tenancy so the widow was entitled to the deceased's half share. The residuary beneficiaries contended that, notwithstanding the provisions of the Forfeiture Act 1982, section 7(4), which enabled the court to modify the operation of the forfeiture rule, and whether the killing occurred before or after the Act came into force, the court could not make an order under the Act in respect of an interest in property which had been acquired before the

Act came into force. Vinelott J held that, on the true construction of section 2(7) of the 1982 Act, an interest in property acquired before the coming into force of the Act denoted property which had actually been transferred to the person entitled to it by virtue of the operation of the forfeiture rule, or who had acquired an indefeasible right to have it transferred to him. It did not include property which, at the time the section came into force, was held by the personal representatives who had not completed the administration; such property could therefore be the subject of an order under the 1982 Act.

Although by reason of the wife's conduct the forfeiture rule applied, the purpose of the Act was to require the court to form a view of the culpability attending the killing, in order to see whether, in the particular case, the effect of the rule should be modified. On the facts, since the widow had been a loyal wife, who had been used with violence by the deceased, and since there were no other persons to whom the deceased owed a moral obligation, it was held that it would be unjust for the widow to be deprived of the benefits which the deceased had conferred on her by his will and those which had accrued to her by survivorship. The rule was modified and she was allowed to take under the will.

In *Re S (Deceased)* [1996] 1 WLR 325, [1996] 1 FLR 910, a husband, who had entered into a joint insurance endowment policy with his wife, was convicted of her manslaughter. They had one son. The wife died intestate and her estate therefore passed to the son. The husband sought an order under the Forfeiture Act 1982 in respect of the policy on the ground that it came within section 2(4)(b) of the 1982 Act, and was held on trust before the death of the wife pursuant to section 11 of the Married Women's Property Act 1882. The court held that the insurance policy could be treated as two separate policies for the husband and wife individually, for the benefit of each other. But for the application of the forfeiture rule, the beneficial interest under the policy would have passed to the husband. However, the policy constituted property held on contingent trust for him which had existed before the wife's death and thus came within section 2(4)(b) of the 1982 Act. In the circumstances it would be appropriate to apply the proceeds of the policy to a trust set up for the benefit of the son.

In *Re Jones, Jones v Midland Bank Trust Co Ltd* [1998] 1 FLR 246 (CA), the testatrix's will provided that her entire estate should pass to her son; if he predeceased her, her two nephews were to take in equal shares. The son killed his mother and was convicted of her manslaughter. He was sentenced to a community rehabilitation order. The son applied for relief under the Forfeiture Act. A preliminary issue was raised whether the residuary estate was to be held for those entitled on the deceased's intestacy, or for her two nephews. On appeal it was held that the estate should devolve as on the deceased's intestacy as the gift over could take effect only if the son had predeceased the testatrix.

In *Jones v Roberts* [1995] 2 FLR 422, the applicant was suffering from mental illness and killed both his parents. He pleaded guilty to manslaughter on the grounds of diminished responsibility. He was ordered to be detained under section 37 of the Mental Health Act 1983. The parents had died intestate. The claimant applied to the court for a determination whether, in view of his mental illness, he was precluded from taking on his father's intestacy. *Gray v Barr (Prudential Assurance Co Ltd third party)* [1971] 2 QB 554, [1971] 2 All ER 949, was relied on in support of a submission that the forfeiture rule did not apply automatically in every unlawful killing case, but only where the claimant had been guilty of deliberate and intentional manslaughter, violence or threats of violence. In rejecting the submission, the court distinguished the other cases cited. It found that the claimant's case was not one of insanity, nor of accident or recklessness. The defence of diminished responsibility reduced the charge of murder to manslaughter but the defendant was still criminally liable for his action. His application was refused.

The language of section 2(2) of the 1982 Act is in wide terms and the court is required to consider the justice of each case. In so doing, the intention of the offender, particularly of the survivor of a suicide pact, is a relevant factor. The wishes of the beneficiaries are also material and must be given weight (*Re K*, above). The court's duty is to consider what would be just in all the circumstances. In *Dunbar v Plant* [1998] Ch 412, [1997] 3 WLR 136, [1997] 4 All ER 289, which was a case of suicide, the claimant's son (the deceased) and the defendant were lovers. They had purchased a property in joint names with a collateral insurance policy. The son had a like policy for the benefit of the defendant. They had planned to marry. The defendant was then accused of fraud and decided to commit suicide. She told her fiancé (the deceased) of her decision. They agreed to commit suicide together. On the third attempt the claimant's son (the deceased) died and the defendant survived. It was held that the forfeiture rule applied to offences under the Suicide Act 1961, but the court had a discretion under the 1982 Act to modify the rule and had to consider section 2(2) when doing so. On the facts, the court directed that the forfeiture rule should not apply and granted the defendant full relief.

In *Dalton v Latham and Others* [2003] EWHC 796 (Ch), the claimant was sentenced to six years for the manslaughter of the deceased. The claimant was the sole residuary beneficiary of the deceased's estate. The claimant had a history of mental illness. On the facts, it was held that the claimant had taken advantage of the deceased, and the principle in *Jones v Roberts* applied; it was held that, by reason of the defence of diminished responsibility, the claimant's responsibility for his actions had been "reduced not extinguished", and that the interests of justice did not require that the rule should be modified.

Summary

(a) The Forfeiture Act 1982 does not apply to a claim made before the Act came into force.

(b) In applying the criteria set out in section 2(4) of the 1982 Act, the court, in exercising its discretion, has regard to the applicant's culpability, the deceased's conduct and any moral obligation the deceased owed to the applicant and any other beneficiaries. The wishes of the beneficiaries are a relevant factor.

(c) Where property is held on constructive trust, the court will give effect to the trust so as to provide a benefit to a third party, for example, a son of the deceased.

(d) The forfeiture rule will not be modified in cases where a charge of murder has been reduced to manslaughter by reason of diminished responsibility.

Chapter 12

Procedure

Introduction

Before 2 December 2002, all applications under the Inheritance (Provision for Family and Dependants) Act 1975 were made in the Chancery Division or the Family Division of the High Court, and were governed by Order 99 of the Rules of the Supreme Court 1965 (SI 1965 No 1776) as amended. Order 99 was revoked by the Civil Procedure (Amendment) Rules 2002 (SI 2002 No 2058), rule 35 and Schedule 10, with effect from 2 December 2002. Order 99 does not therefore apply to proceedings which were commenced before 2 December 2002 and still pending at that date. Order 99 has been replaced by Part 57 of the Civil Procedure Rules 1998 (SI 1998 No 3132, "CPR") as amended and the Practice Direction which supplements Part 57. The new rules are not dissimilar from the old rules, but now provide uniform practice and procedure in both the High Court and the county courts.

The county court's jurisdiction to entertain a claim under the 1975 Act was limited to estates not exceeding £30,000. This limit was removed by the Courts and Legal Services Act 1990, sections 1 and 120, and the High Court and County Courts Jurisdiction Order 1991 (SI 1991 No 724).

Venue

Proceedings may be commenced in the High Court or county court. Proceedings in the High Court are assigned to the Chancery Division and the Family Division of the High Court (CPR rule 57.15). The choice of division is a matter of discretion for the claimant. Where there have been matrimonial proceedings affecting the claimant or any of the parties to the proposed action, the court in which the matrimonial proceedings were heard would be the appropriate court in which to make the 1975 Act claim if the passage of time between the previous proceedings and the proceedings under the 1975 Act is not long. Where the claimant is seeking to bring the claim in the county court the claim may be started only in the county court for the district in which:

(a) the defendants or one of the defendants lives or carries on business; or
(b) the subject matter of the claim is situated.
(CPR Part 8B PD paragraph 6).

The decision on venue is made on the basis of the nature and complexity of the case. If there is an overseas aspect to the case, or if the claim or the estate is particularly large, it would be advisable to commence the proceedings in the High Court.

Since claims under the 1975 Act are commenced in accordance with CPR Part 8, the Master or the provincial Chancery District Registrars, or, in the Family Division, the district judge, has jurisdiction to hear them. Pursuant to *Practice Direction: Civil Procedure Rules: Allocation of Cases: Costs,* 22 April 1999 [1999] 1 FLR 1295, paragraph 3.2 of the (Civil Procedure) Practice Direction *Allocation of Cases to Level of Judiciary* (CPR PD 2b) applies to the Family Division district judges (including district judges of the Principal Registry), and they have jurisdiction to hear and dispose of proceedings under the 1975 Act.

The Claim Form

CPR rule 8.1(2) provides that the procedure under Part 8 ("alternative procedure for claims") may be used:

(a) where the court's decision on a question which is unlikely to involve a substantial dispute of fact is sought; or

(b) where a rule or practice direction in relation to a specified type of proceedings requires or permits the use of Part 8 procedure and disapplies or modifies any of the rules set out in Part 8 as they apply to those proceedings.

CPR rule 57.16 applies CPR Part 8 to claims under the 1975 Act. Part 8 and the Practice Directions under Parts 8 and 8B therefore also apply to a claim under the 1975 Act, as Part 8B, *inter alia,* provides that that practice direction applies to a claim if, before 26 April 1999, the action would have been commenced in the High Court by originating summons or in the county court by originating application.

Usually, where there is more than one claimant, the claimants agree to file a single claim form, but where this is not possible and separate claim forms are issued by each claimant, application should be made for the proceedings to be consolidated under CPR rule 3.1(2).

Contents

The claim form must be entitled "In the matter of [name] deceased" and "In the matter of the Inheritance (Family Provision and Dependants) Act 1975".

CPR rule 8.2 requires that the claim form must state:

(a) that Part 8 applies;

(b) the question which the claimant wants the court to decide; or the remedy or relief which the claimant is seeking and the legal basis for the claim to that remedy or relief;

(c) if the claim is being made under an enactment, what that enactment is;

(d) if the claimant is claiming in a representative capacity, what that capacity is; and

(e) if the defendant is sued in a representative capacity, what that capacity is.

If leave is required for an extension of the time limit under section 4 (see page 13), application to extend the time must be made in the claim form

CPR rule 8.5 provides that the claimant may rely on the matters set out in his claim form as evidence under the rule if the claim form is verified by a statement of truth, but see CPR rule 8.5(1), which states that if the claimant wishes to rely on written evidence, he should file it when his Part 8 claim form is issued (rule 8.8(1)), unless the evidence is contained in the claim form itself.

For examples of claims which might be included in the claim form, see page 230.

Time Limit

The claim must be issued within six months of the date on which representation is taken out, unless the court grants an extension of time (section 4 of the 1975 Act; see Chapter 2). Leave to extend the time limit must be made in the claim form.

Where it is intended to make an application under section 9 of the 1975 Act, to treat the deceased's severable share of a joint tenancy as part of the net estate (see page 114), the application must be made within six months of the date on which the grant of representation with respect of the deceased's estate was first taken out. There is no power to extend this time limit (section 9(1)).

Witness Statements and Affidavits

Evidence is normally in the form of a witness statement or an affidavit, but a claimant may rely on the matters set out in the claim form provided it has been verified by a statement of truth. Information about statements of truth is contained in CPR Part 22 and the practice direction which supplements it.

The written statement should contain the witness's own words so far as is practicable. The solicitor taking the statement must follow the Law Society's *Guide to the Professional Conduct of Solicitors*. The person taking the statement must not try to persuade the witness of what he should or should not say. See further *Aquarius Financial Enterprises Inc v Certain Underwriters at Lloyds* (2001) 151 NLJ 694.

The form of the witness statement must comply with the requirements of CPR Part 32 and the practice direction which supplements it.

In addition, rule 57.16(3) requires that the written statement filed and served by the claimant with the claim form must have exhibited to it an official copy of the grant of probate or letters of administration in respect of the deceased's estate, and of every testamentary document in respect of which probate or letters of administration were granted.

There is no other specific requirement in the rules relating to the contents of the claimant's witness statement or affidavit, but it is suggested that the statement or affidavit should contain the following matters in addition to those set out above:

(a) the name of the deceased, the date of his death and the country of his domicile at that date;

(b) a certified copy of the deceased's death certificate;

(c) the date on which representation with respect to the deceased's estate was taken out and the names and addresses of the personal representatives;

(d) the value of the net estate (to the best of the claimant's knowledge and belief). Where possible, brief details of the property comprised in the net estate, with an approximate value and any income received therefrom, and any known liabilities;

(e) the relationship of the claimant to the deceased, or other qualification of the claimant for making the claim (see section 1 and Chapter 3). In the case of a widow, the marriage certificate should be exhibited. In the case of a judicially separated spouse, the decree of judicial separation and a copy of any orders for ancillary relief made should be exhibited. In the case of a former spouse, a copy of the decree absolute and any order for ancillary relief made in those proceedings should be exhibited;

(f) particulars of any known proceedings relevant to the claim. Such material is particularly relevant to the question whether a claim which has been commenced in a county court ought to be transferred to the Chancery Division or the Family Division of the High Court;

(g) whether the disposition of the deceased's estate effected by his will or the law relating to intestacy was such as to make any provision for the claimant, and, if so, the nature of the provision;

(h) details of the persons or classes of person interested in the deceased's estate and the nature of their interests;

(i) full particulars of the claimant's present and foreseeable financial resources and financial needs, and any other information which the claimant relies on under section 3 of the 1975 Act (see Chapter 5, and *Re Smallwood*, page 79). The deceased's reasons, if known, for making or not making a provision should be included. In *Re Blanch, Blanch v Honhold* [1967] 1 WLR 987, [1967] 2 All ER 468, Buckley J said:

> "In certain cases there are likely to be respects in which the state of the deceased's mind may properly be regarded as relevant and material. For instance, the state of the deceased's mind may be very material to the weight to be attributed to any reasons which he may have given in his lifetime for failing to make provision for a

dependant or making such provision as he did make for such a dependant";

(j) where appropriate, a request for the court's permission to make the claim out of time and the grounds for the delay;

(k) the nature of the provision claimed.

Sample statements are set out at pages 231–236.

The Claimant

The claimant must fall within the classes of person listed under section 1(1) of the 1975 as amended (see page 23). If a claim it made jointly by two or more persons, and if it later appears that there is a conflict of interests between claimants:

(a) any claimant may choose to have separate representation or may appear in person;

(b) if the court considers that claimants should be separately represented, it may adjourn the action until they are.

(CPR Part 57 PD, paragraph 17).

Where a claimant is also a personal representative, provided that there is another personal representative, the action may proceed with the claimant continuing as personal representative. Where, however, it appears that there may be a conflict of interests it would be advisable for the claimant who is a personal representative to stand down.

Where a potential claimant dies before the claim is issued, the claim does not survive for the benefit of his or her estate, because the claim is personal to the claimant (*Re Bramwell* [1988] 2 FLR 263; *Whyte v Ticehurst,* page 4). Similarly, where a claim is issued but the claimant dies before an order is made, the claim dies with the claimant. Where an interim order was made, for example, for the payment of periodical payments, and arrears had accumulated before the claimant's death, the right to enforce those arrears survives.

Where the claimant is a bankrupt, provided the claim is limited to maintenance for the claimant, it seems that the claim can be pursued by the claimant personally, without the leave of the trustee in bankruptcy or permission from the court. Similarly, it seems that CPR rule 19.2(4) will not apply where the claimant becomes the subject of a bankruptcy order while the claim is pending and before a final order is made. It would seem that where the claim is not limited to provision for the maintenance of the claimant, but is for a capital sum or property, it could be argued that the trustee in bankruptcy should be brought in (see *Re Abrams* [1996] 2 FLR 379, where a discretionary/protective trust was created in order to avoid the benefits of the order being vested in a trustee in bankruptcy).

The Defendants

There are no rules on who should be made a party to the claim.

Personal representatives and beneficiaries under the deceased's will or intestacy are obvious defendants. Where there are numerous beneficiaries it may be desirable first to ascertain the extent of their beneficial interests. If they are entitled to receive small legacies or devises and their interest is not likely to be affected, it should be possible to reach agreement that they should not be made defendants. In any other case it may be desirable or appropriate to apply for a representation order under CPR rule 19.7, or apply for notice to be given to those who form members of a class, under rule 19.8A.

Where an order under section 8 of the 1975 Act (property to be treated as part of the net estate) is sought, the appropriate nominee or donee should be made a party.

Where an order under section 9 of the 1975 Act is sought (property held on a joint tenancy) the person beneficially entitled to the joint tenancy should be made a party.

Where it is sought to apply to set aside, under section 10, a disposition made by the deceased, the person in whose favour the disposition is made and against whom an order is sought should be made a party. The same applies where an order is sought under section 11.

Any other person who is alleged to be a constructive trustee of property belonging to the deceased or forming part of the estate should be joined in the claim.

Any other person directed by the court to be added as a defendant under the provisions of CPR rule 19.7 must be so added. For example, the court may order the appointment of a person to represent an unborn person, a person who cannot be found or a person who cannot easily be identified. Where the court exercises its powers under this rule, a judgment or order of the court given in the claim, or a settlement approved by the court, is binding on all persons who are interested in or may be affected (CPR rule 19.7(6) and (7)).

The Evidence

The personal representatives

Under rule 57.16 a personal representative of the deceased who is a defendant must file and serve written evidence within twenty-one days of service of the claim form. The evidence must state to the best of that person's ability:

(a) full details of the value of the deceased's net estate as defined by section 25(1) of the 1975 Act;
(b) the names and addresses of all living beneficiaries (unless they are claimants) and the value of their interests in the estate so far as known;

(c) whether any living beneficiary (and if so, naming him) is a child or patient within the meaning of rule 21.2; and
(d) any facts which might affect the exercise of the court's powers under the 1975 Act.

Unlike the old provisions of the Rules of the Supreme Court, Order 99.5(2)(d), which required a personal representative to state facts known to him to the best of his knowledge and belief, CPR rule 57.16(5) and Part 57 PD, paragraph 16, which are both mandatory, require that the evidence filed "must state to the best of the person's ability" the facts which might affect the court's decision. It would seem, therefore, that the rule, combined with the Practice Direction, imposes on the personal representatives a duty to make inquiries and to provide such facts as may be relevant and which may affect the exercise of the court's discretion.

Where a personal representative wishes to remain neutral in relation to the claim, and agrees to abide by any decision which the court may make, he should state this in section A of the acknowledgement of service form: Part 57 PD, paragraph 15.

Other defendants

It is no longer possible for defendants to a claim under the 1975 Act to wait until the first directions hearing to file their defence or their evidence. Under CPR rule 57.16(4), all defendants are required to file and serve an acknowledgement of service and any written evidence within twenty-one days after service of the claim form. Their statements must also comply with rule 8.5 unless the court otherwise directs under rule 8.6(1). It is essential to comply with the timescales in the rules (rules 8.5 and 57.16(4)). Where for some reason there may be difficulty in complying with the time limits, an application may be made for permission to file and serve the evidence out of time or for an extension of time under CPR Part 8 PD, paragraph 5.5. The parties may agree in writing to extend the time for filing and serving evidence under rule 8.5(3) or 8.5(5) (Part 8 PD, paragraph 5.6). However, an agreement extending time for a defendant to file his evidence under rule 8.5(3):

(a) must be filed by the defendant at the same time as he files his acknowledgement of service; and
(b) must not extend by more than fourteen days after the defendant files his acknowledgement of service.

(Practice Direction, paragraph 57.5(6.2)).

The claimant's reply

The claimant may, within fourteen days of service of the defendant's evidence on him, file and serve evidence in reply (rule 8.5(5) and (6)).

Party under Disability

Where a party, whether a claimant or defendant, is a child or a patient, CPR rule 21 must be considered. A child is defined as a person under eighteen. A patient means "a person who by reason of mental disorder within the meaning of the Mental Health Act 1983 is incapable of managing and administering his own affairs" (rule 21.1). Mental disorder is defined by section 1(2) of the Mental Health Act 1983 as "mental illness, arrested or incomplete development of mind, psychopathic disorder and any other disorder or disability of mind".

A child must have a litigation friend to conduct proceedings unless the court has made an order under rule 21.2(3) permitting the child to conduct proceedings without a litigation friend.

Where a claim is made by or on behalf of a child or patient, or against a child or patient, no settlement, compromise or payment and no acceptance of money paid into court will be regarded as valid unless it has been approved by the court (rule 21.10(1)). Where a settlement or compromise is reached for or on behalf of a child or patient, or against such a person before a claim is issued, the court procedure is for a claim to be made under Part 8 seeking the court's approval for the settlement or compromise (rule 21.10(2)). For this purpose it is advisable to prepare a case summary and submit a comprehensive opinion of counsel representing the child or patient setting out an analysis of the issues and the basis upon which it is suggested that the settlement is in the interest of the child or patient.

For a draft consent order setting out a compromise in favour of a claimant under disability, see page 238.

Interlocutory Matters, Directions and Case Management

The Civil Procedure Rules apply to claims under the 1975 Act. Where there is a risk of the assets being dissipated, particularly where it is sought to apply for an order under sections 8 to 11 of the 1975 Act, it is important to take steps to preserve the assets. This may be done by obtaining appropriate undertakings; registering the claim as a pending land action where appropriate; applying for an injunction forbidding any dealing with the property; and, in the case of liquid funds, seeking an order freezing such assets.

At the directions hearing it will be necessary to consider matters such as disclosure; the need for an expert's report, for example, a medical report; valuations; and accounts, as, for instance, in the case of a partnership or a private company.

A chronology, a summary of the facts, and a statement of issues should be provided to the court for the case management conference. It is always prudent to discuss beforehand the directions required and the reasons for them. Serious consideration should also be given to providing the court with a realistic time estimate. The availability of an interpreter, if needed, should be considered. When making a time estimate, account should be taken of the fact that the hearing takes longer when an interpreter is required or one of the parties is in person. Difficult issues, such as whether evidence by video link is necessary, where, say, a witness or a party is serving a long prison sentence or is violent, should be addressed. The question of whether the final hearing should take place in public or continue to remain private should also be considered (see below).

The Hearing

CPR rule 39.2 provides that in general a hearing is to be in public, but rule 39.2(3) makes provision for a hearing to be conducted in private in certain circumstances, including cases which involve confidential information (including information relating to personal financial matters) and where publicity would damage that confidentiality. CPR Part 39A PD, paragraph 1.5 also makes provision for proceedings under the 1975 Act to be listed in private in the first instance.

Endorsement of memorandum on grant

At the final hearing the personal representatives must produce to the court the original grant of representation to the deceased's estate (CPR Part 57 PD, paragraph 18.1). If an order is made under the 1975 Act, the original grant (together with a sealed copy of the order) must be sent to the Principal Registry of the Family Division for a memorandum of the order to be endorsed on or permanently annexed to the grant in accordance with section 19(3) of the Act (Part 57 PD, paragraph 18.2).

Subsequent Applications

Any subsequent applications under the 1975 Act, for example, for a variation of an order, must be made in the proceedings and must be supported by a written statement or affidavit setting out the grounds upon which it is made and the relief sought, as in the case of the original application.

Drawing up and Service of Orders.

Pursuant to CPR rule 57.15(2), the Family Proceedings Rules 1991 (SI 1991 No 1247) relating to the drawing up and service of orders apply to all orders made under the 1975 Act.

Procedural Table

Who may apply	– the spouse of the deceased; – the former spouse of the deceased who has not remarried; – a cohabitant of the deceased; – a child of the deceased; – any person who was treated as a child of the family; – any other person who, immediately before the death of the deceased, was being maintained by him.	1975 Act, s. 1
Venue	High Court (Chancery or Family Division) or county court. District judges (including district judges of the Principal Registry of the Family Division) have jurisdiction to hear applications.	CPR r. 57.15; PD, 22 April 1999
Claim	By Part 8 claim form, headed "In the Estate of .... deceased" and "In the matter of the Inheritance (Provision for Family and Dependants) Act 1975".	CPR rr. 57.16, 8.2; PD para. 8B
The time limit	The claim must be issued within six months of the date on which representation is taken out (unless extended by the court). Application to extend time must be made in the claim form. NB: There is no power to extend the time limit where a section 9 order is sought.	1975 Act, s. 4 1975 Act, s. 9(1)

Documents to be filed with the claim	A witness statement or affidavit in support, exhibiting an official copy of the grant of representation and of every testamentary document admitted to proof.	CPR rr. 57.16(3), 8.5(1), (2) and Chancery Guide 24.6
Defendants	– personal representatives; – beneficiaries; – other persons affected by the claim; – any other person directed by the court to be added.	CPR r. 19.7
	Defendants include: • a person beneficially entitled to a joint tenancy (where an order under section 9 is sought); • a beneficiary of a disposition in cases where section 10 applies; • the donee of nominated property under section 8(1); • a donee of *donatio mortis causa*	1975 Act, s. 8(2)
Service of claim	Acknowledgement of service must be filed with 21 days after service of the claim form and served on the claimant and other parties if served within the jurisdiction;	CPR rr. 57.16(4), 8.3(1), 10.3(1)
	otherwise in accordance with CPR r. 10.3(2) and Sch. 1, RSC Order 11, r 1A.	CPR r. 10.3(2)
Statement or affidavit in answer	Must be filed by the personal representatives within 21 days after service of the claim form; it should include the matters set out in PD 57, para 16.	CPR r. 57.16(4), (5); PD 57, para 16; Chancery Guide 24.8
	A statement or affidavit may be filed by other defendants within 21 days after service of the claim form.	CPR r. 57.16(4) Chancery Guide 24.7

Service of answer	Every defendant who files any written evidence within 21 days in answer must serve a copy on the claimant and every other defendant who is not represented by the same solicitor.	CPR r. 57.16(4)
Reply	A claimant may serve a statement in reply on all other parties within 14 days of service of the defendant's evidence on him.	CPR r. 8.5(5), (6)
Directions	At the same time as issuing the claim form, a directions hearing may be requested.	PD 8, para. 4.1
	The court will give directions after the defendant has filed the acknowledgement of service or after the time for filing it has expired.	PD 8, para. 4.2
Fee payable	High Court: £ 180	Supreme Court Fees Order 1999, as amended, Fee 1.2
	county court: £ 130	County Court Fees Order 1999, as amended, fee 1.3
Order	– periodical payments	1975 Act, s. 2(1)(a)
	– lump sum	1975 Act, s. 2(1)(b)
	– transfer of property	1975 Act, s. 2(1)(c)
	– settlement of property	1975 Act, s. 2(1)(d)
	– acquisition, transfer and settlement of property	1975 Act, s. 2(1)(e)
	– variation of ante- or post-nuptial settlement	1975 Act, s. 2(1)(f)
	– variation or discharge of secured periodical payments	1975 Act, s. 16
	– variation or revocation of maintenance agreement	1975 Act, s. 17
	– order relating to disposition intended to defeat a claim under the 1975 Act	1975 Act, ss. 10, 11

– treatment of deceased's former beneficial interest in joint property as part of his estate	1975 Act, s. 9

Chapter 13

Appeals

Introduction

Part 52 of the Civil Procedure Rules 1998 (SI 1998 No 3132 as amended, "CPR") applies to all appeals and provides a uniform procedure for appeals in the county courts, the High Court and the Court of Appeal. Part 52 does not, however, apply to proceedings which are defined as family business under the Matrimonial and Family Proceedings Act 1984. By section 32 of the 1984 Act "family business" means business of any description which in the High Court is assigned to the Family Division and to no other Division by or under section 61 of (and Schedule 1 to) the Supreme Court Act 1981. Appeals under the 1975 Act are therefore governed by Part 52.

Permission to Appeal

The Access to Justice Act 1999, section 54, provides that any right of appeal from the county court or the High Court and the Court of Appeal may be exercised only with permission.

By CPR rule 52.3(1), permission to appeal from the decision of a judge in the county court or the High Court is required in all cases.

An application for permission to appeal should be made orally to the trial judge at the hearing. If made subsequently it should be made to the appeal court. The appellant should not seek to apply for leave in the lower court (CPR Part 52 PD, paragraphs 4.6 and 4.7). When applying for permission to appeal, a reason or explanation for seeking permission to appeal is required.

Permission to appeal will be given only where:

(a) the court considers that the appeal would have a real prospect of success; or

(b) there is some other compelling reason why the appeal should be heard.

Grounds

An appeal will be allowed where the decision of the lower court was:

(a) wrong; or

(b) unjust because of a serious procedural or other irregularity in the proceedings in the lower court.

(CPR rule 52.11(3)).

The effect of (a) is that the appellant has to satisfy the appeal court that the decision of the lower court was:

(a) against the weight of evidence;

(b) wrong in law; or

(c) an error in the exercise of the court's discretion.

Where an appeal is based on the argument that the decision of the lower court was against the weight of the evidence, the decision on appeal depends on the judge's assessment of the evidence of witnesses, their reliability and credibility; and it is only in exceptional circumstances that such an appeal will succeed.

In an appeal based on a point of law, it must be shown that the judge was plainly wrong on a point of law which was crucial to the decision. For examples, see *Moody v Stevenson* [1992] Ch 486, [1992] 1 FLR 494 and *Re Besterman, Besterman v Grusin* [1984] Ch 458, [1984] 3 WLR 280, [1984] 2 All ER 656.

To succeed in an appeal based on an erroneous exercise of discretion, the appellant will have to show that the judge had misunderstood the facts; had taken account of irrelevant material; had failed to exercise his discretion; had made a decision that no reasonable judge could have made; or that there was no material before him to justify the decision he took. It has been stated that it must be shown that the decision was plainly wrong since it "was outside the ambit within which a reasonable disagreement is possible": *G v G (Minors)* [1985] 1 WLR 647, [1985] 2 All ER 225. See also *AEI Ltd v PPL* [1999] 1 WLR 1507, where it was stated:

> "Before the court can interfere it must be shown that the judge has either erred in principle in his approach or has left out of account or has taken into account some feature that he should, or should not, have considered, or that his decision was plainly wrong because the court is forced to the conclusion that he has not balanced the various factors fairly in the scale."

In cases under the 1975 Act, where the judge has clearly gone beyond the section 3 criteria or given it an interpretation which cannot be justified and re-written the deceased's will, it could be said that he has both erred in law and failed to exercise his discretion.

Route

CPR Part 52 PD, paragraph 2A.1 sets out the court to which an appeal should be made (subject to obtaining any necessary permission) as follows:

Decision of	*Appeal made to*
District judge of a county court	Circuit Judge
Master or district judge of the High Court	High Court
Circuit Judge	High Court
High Court	Court of Appeal

Time

The appellant must file his notice of appeal at the Court of Appeal within fourteen days after the date of the decision of the lower court unless such period has been extended by direction of the lower court. An application for an extension of time, if required, should be made at the final hearing, to the trial judge (CPR rule 52.4(2)).

Stay of Execution

Unless the appeal court or the lower court otherwise orders a stay, an appeal does not operate as a stay of any order made by the lower court. An application for a stay, if required, should be made at the conclusion of the final hearing, to the trial judge at the same time as the application for permission to appeal is made (CPR rule 52.7). If an application for a stay is not made at the conclusion of the hearing, or is made but refused, a separate application for a stay, supported by evidence, may be made to the appeal court. A court will not grant a stay unless it is satisfied by cogent, full and frank evidence that there is a real risk of injustice.

Procedure

For the procedure generally on appeal, see the CPR and the textbooks on the subject.

PART II

A SHORT INTRODUCTION TO CHALLENGING TESTAMENTARY DISPOSITIONS

Chapter 14

Introduction

Wills and Codicils

The document which, in general, is considered to govern the disposition of property on death is a will or testament, in a prescribed form, which sets out the wishes and intentions of the person making it regarding the disposition of his assets on his death. It comes into effect on the death of the person making the will (the testator). During the lifetime of the testator it has no legal effect; it merely stands as a declaration of the testator's intention. The testator may at any time revoke the will or vary it, but, to take effect, the revocation or variation must be made in accordance with the provisions relating to the making of a will. The revocable nature of a will may not be compromised by a declaration that it is irrevocable or by contract.

The will may be supplemented by a document known as a codicil, which is a document similar to a will but executed after a will has been made. The purpose of a codicil is to add to, vary or revoke the provisions of a will. To be valid and effective a codicil must comply with the formalities relating to a will. A codicil, however, exists independently of the will.

A will or a codicil may be challenged on the basis that it does not conform with the formal legal requirements.

A will, although valid, may be declared to be conditional on some contingency. Whether such a will may be challenged depends upon the construction of its terms and whether those terms make it clear that the will was conditional, or merely indicate the reason the testator chose to make the will. When construing the will the court applies the ordinary rules of construction. If the terms indicate a reason for making the will, the will is not regarded as conditional (*In the Goods of Spratt* [1897] P 28; *Halford v Halford* [1897] P 36). Much depends on the terms used. The words in the will must be clear, for example, if the will contains the words, "if I ...", or "should I die during my journey/expedition", it is regarded as conditional (*Re O'Connor* [1942] 1 All ER 546; *Re Gower (Deceased)* [1956] P 237). Extrinsic evidence will not be admitted to clarify the intention of the deceased. In *Corbett v Newey* [1998] Ch 57, [1996] 3 WLR 729, [1996] 2 All ER 914, it was stated that:

> "it would be against the weight of authority and contrary to the express terms of the Wills Act 1837 to allow extrinsic evidence as to the testator's

> intention to be used to write into the will, for probate purposes, a condition which the testator has neither stated in writing nor signed."

A conditional will is of no effect if the event which formed the basis on which it was made does not occur. To give effect to a conditional will the testator would need to re-execute it, or confirm it by codicil excluding the condition, after the conditional event has failed.

Other Testamentary Dispositions

In addition to making a disposition on his death by a will, a testator may also achieve the transfer of property on his death by means other than a will. He may do this by:

(a) an *inter vivos* disposition;
(b) transferring property into joint names so that, on the death of one of the parties, the property automatically passes to the survivor;
(c) *donatio mortis causa*;
(d) nominating the person who is, on his death, to receive property under a trust deed or the rules of a pension scheme.

Although it is not a direct challenge to the validity of the will, a person taking under such a transaction may make a claim against the estate to give effect to the transaction, which may in turn affect dispositions made in the will. Similarly, when such a claim is made, its validity can be challenged (see Chapter 21).

The Right to Challenge

The provisions of the Inheritance (Provision for Family and Dependants) Act 1975 ("the 1975 Act"), which give certain categories of claimant, who are considered as dependants of the deceased, the right to bring a claim for financial provision against the estate of the deceased, has sometimes been misunderstood as limiting a testator's freedom to dispose of his estate as he chooses; or as a means of challenging the validity of a will; or as giving the court jurisdiction to rewrite the deceased's will. The preamble to the 1975 Act, however, makes it clear that the objective of the Act is not to interfere with the testator's right, but "to make fresh provision for empowering the court to make orders for the making out of the estate of the deceased person of provision" for certain specified categories of person who fulfil the criteria set out in the Act. A claim for an order under section 2 of the Act may be made only on the ground that the disposition of the deceased's estate effected by his will or the law relating to intestacy, or the combination of his will and that law, is not such as to make reasonable financial provision for the claimant. When dealing with a claim under the Act it is not the function of the court to correct what may appear to be an injustice, or to make a fair or fairer division of the deceased's estate, but to give effect to the objective of the Act in cases which fall within its ambit. Where such a claim succeeds, the interests of those taking under the will may be adjusted, but only to the limited extent provided for in the Act. These provisions apply equally to dispositions of property made other than by will, subject to the provisions of the relevant sections of the Act (see Chapter 6), as the court has power to reduce or nullify the effect of any contract or to direct the donee to provide such funds or other property as may be necessary to make financial provision for a claimant under the Act. The court may direct the personal representatives of the deceased not to make any payments or transfer property under the contract, settlement or other transaction, other than as specified by the court.

Any interested party, whether or not qualified under the 1975 Act to make a claim, is entitled to challenge the validity of a deceased person's will on the ground that it fails to comply with the legal formalities, or on some other ground. It is also possible, in appropriate cases, while not seeking to challenge the validity of the will, to seek relief by way of a declaration that the will should take effect subject to the deceased's equitable obligations, for example, where there is an agreement to make mutually binding wills, or pursuant to the terms of a contract entered into by the deceased in his lifetime, or where the deceased's conduct raises issues of proprietary estoppel under the the doctrine of *donatio mortis causa*.

Formalities Relating to Wills

The form and manner in which a will should be made are set out in the Wills Act 1837, amended by the Administration of Justice Act 1982. The formal requirements are that:

(a) the will must be in writing;
(b) the will must be signed by the testator or by some other person in his presence and by his direction;
(c) it must appear that the testator intended by his signature to give effect to the will;
(d) the signature must be made or acknowledged in the presence of two witnesses present at the same time;
(e) each witness must attest and sign the will or acknowledge his signature in the presence of the testator.

Grounds for Challenge

The validity of a will may be challenged if any one or more of the above conditions is not satisfied. Generally, the grounds on which the validity of a will may be challenged include:

(a) that the will was not made in the form and manner required by law;
(b) that at the date of the will the testator did not have the mental capacity to make a will;
(c) that at the time of making the will the testator did not have the

intention to make the will so as to give effect to it on his death;

(d) that at the time of making the will the testator's mind was affected by fear, fraud, undue influence, want of knowledge and approval or by other matters which vitiated his intention;

(e) that the intention of the testator is not ascertainable or capable of being ascertained from the words used in the will;

(f) that the donee described in the will is not ascertainable or capable in law of taking the gift;

(g) that the subject matter of the gift is not ascertainable;

(h) that the will was revoked or altered or nullified by divorce.

As regards international wills, the Convention providing for a Uniform Law on the Formation of International Wills was concluded at Washington on 26 October 1973. An Annex to the Convention sets out requirements for the form of an international will; the Annex is set out in Schedule 2 to the Administration of Justice Act 1982, and, although not in force as yet, may be used as a guide.

It is proposed to consider some of the above grounds on which a will may be challenged. The purpose is to set out a basic guide and no more. It is not intended to provide a detailed and exhaustive study of the subject, nor would it be possible to do so within the framework of this work. Where it is intended to pursue a claim, reference should be made to the standard textbooks on the subject.

Chapter 15

Form and Content of a Will

Form of a Will

The form and manner in which a will is to be made is set out in the Wills Act 1837, as amended by the Administration of Justice Act 1982.

Every will, other than one that is privileged, must be in writing. A privileged will is one made by a soldier in actual military service, or by a mariner or seaman (including a member of the Royal Navy or marine forces) being either at sea or so circumstanced that, if he were a soldier, he would be in actual military service. Such a will is exempt from conforming to the provisions of the Wills Act 1937 as to writing and execution, and as to the age of the person making the will. Any form of words, whether written or spoken, by such a testator in the presence of a witness is sufficient, provided the testator clearly expressed his wish and it was evident that he intended it to have testamentary effect (*In the Estate of Knibbs, Flay v Truman* [1962] 1 WLR 852, [1962] 2 All ER 829).

There is no requirement as to the material upon which a will may be written. There is no requirement as regards the form of words that may be used as long as the testator's intention and his wishes appear clear from the language used. There is no requirement in law that a will should be dated. Where no date is included, or a wrong date has been inserted, it does not invalidate the will, but evidence of the date on which the will was executed will be called for before the will is admitted to proof. In *Corbett v Newey* [1998] Ch 57, [1996] 2 All ER 914, the testatrix and her solicitor were both under the mistaken belief that the dating of the will was essential to its validity and that the testatrix's signature would be ineffective until the will was dated. It was held that, in the absence of any indication in the body of the will that the will was conditional upon the happening of an event, the will could not be validly executed so as to have effect conditionally.

For the formal requirements relating to the execution of a will, see Chapter 16.

Uncertainty Relating to Intention, Subject Matter or Donee

When a will is drafted, the wishes and intentions of the testator should be expressed in clear terms. This is particularly important in relation to the donee of a gift or a class of person in whose favour a gift is made, and the subject matter of the gift. If the disposition is ambiguous or the words meaningless, the disposition may be challenged, and may fail on the ground of uncertainty.

On the other hand, courts are generally reluctant to hold a gift void for uncertainty, and generally do not do so if there is some evidence from which it is possible to discern the intention of the testator. Where possible, the court will adopt a construction which avoids finding the whole testamentary disposition invalid or void for uncertainty. The duty of the court is to give effect to the intentions of the testator by construing his language, however imperfect or inelegant it may be, robustly and in a common-sense way, seeking, as far as possible, to mould his language so as to do as little violence to it as possible: *Aitken's Trustees v Aitken* [1927] SC 374. In so doing, the court starts from the principle that the testator's intention should be ascertained by considering the whole will, together with any other evidence. If the intention of the testator can be ascertained, then the mode of expression and the form and language used in drafting are not important.

Under the Administration of Justice Act 1982, section 21(1)(a) and (2), extrinsic evidence is admissible to assist in the construction and interpretation of a will in order to ascertain the intention of the testator where the words in a testamentary document appear to be meaningless or ambiguous. Section 21 of the Administration of Justice Act 1982 applies to a will:

(a) in so far as any part of it is meaningless;
(b) in so far as the language used in any part of it is ambiguous on the face of it;
(c) in so far as evidence, other than evidence of the testator's intention, shows that the language used in any part of it is ambiguous in the light of the surrounding circumstances.

(section 21(1)).

Where the section applies, extrinsic evidence, including evidence of the testator's intention, may be admitted to assist in its interpretation (section 21(2)).

Where words are ambiguous, contradictory or obscure, or appear to be meaningless in the context in which they are used, or have more than one meaning, the court will look at all the circumstances to ascertain what the testator meant by the words used, and will adopt a construction which it considers the most likely to indicate what the testator meant. The court will not, however, give effect to an intention which is not expressed or cannot be implied from the language of the will. Where the words used in the will are clear and unambiguous, the court will not permit evidence to be introduced to show that the testator's intention was different from that which is evident from the language used in the will. In construing a will, the court is concerned with:

(a) examining the words used by the testator in the will to express his intention; and
(b) ascertaining how those words identify the donees and the subject matter of the disposition in question or clarify any other issues raised.

If the court is able to ascertain the intention of the testator, it will go on to consider whether there is anything which prevents that intention being put into effect; and, if not, how best it can be put into effect.

Re Doland's Will Trusts, Westminster Bank Ltd v Phillips [1970] Ch 267, [1969] 3 All ER 713, is an illustration of the application of this rule of construction in relation to wills. In *Re Doland*, the testator provided for his residuary estate to be disposed of in percentages, in some cases to named persons absolutely; and in other cases to named persons, but if they predeceased him, to their children. He gave two per cent to William Frederick Lewis absolutely, but he also got Lewis's wife to be one of the attesting witnesses. The testator then added a proviso:

> "Provided that if the trusts or any of the shares aforesaid of my residuary estate shall fail my trustees shall stand possessed of my residuary estate upon trust for [two named persons] in equal shares absolutely but should either of them predecease me then for the survivor of them absolutely or should they [the named persons] . . . both predecease me then for such of their children living at my death absolutely and if more than one in equal shares absolutely."

It was held that there was such a contradiction between what was set out in the proviso and the residuary disposition in the will that the conclusion could be drawn that the will was defective. The court, however, sought to ascertain the intention of the testator from the will as a whole, and found that there was a clear indication of a conflict between the intention which appeared to be expressed in the proviso and the intentions which were clearly expressed in other parts of the same clause. In those circumstances the view taken was that the court was entitled to remould the language or to read in additional words if, but only if, the true intention of the testator was clear, as was the case. It was held that the intention of the testator was that if a gift of a particular share of residue failed, then that share only was to be held in trust for the persons named in the proviso. The gift to Lewis failed because his wife had been an attesting witness and the court therefore treated the will as though it did not contain that disposition.

In *Re James's Will Trusts, Peard v James* [1962] Ch 226, [1960] 3 WLR 1031, [1960] 3 All ER 744, the issue was whether the testator had used the word "surviving" in the sense of being alive at and after the time of the event to be survived, or in some other secondary sense. The court held that the words should be given their natural meaning, although the testator, or the draftsman of his will, had shown himself to be somewhat careless; and that the testator had clearly used the words in their proper sense, without wholly appreciating the effect on the scheme of his disposition. (Buckley J also considered the previous case law.)

In *Re Harpur's Will Trusts, Haller v Attorney General* [1962] Ch 78, [1961] 3 WLR 924, [1961] 3 All ER 588, the testatrix provided that the residue of her estate should be accumulated for a period of ten years, and thereafter certain legacies should be paid to named charities. The gift was followed by a clause directing that the residue of her estate should be divided between "such institutions and associations having for their main object the assistance and care of soldiers, sailors, airmen and other members of HM Forces, who have been wounded or incapacitated during the recent world wars in such manner and in such proportions as my said executors and trustees may in their uncontrolled discretion select and deem appropriate". The issue before the court concerned the effect, if any, to be given to this clause. The gift failed for uncertainty of the object.

Extrinsic evidence, including evidence of the testator's intention, may be permitted in order to assist the court in construing a will (Administration of Justice Act 1982, section 21(1) and (2), above). Evidence may therefore be admitted for the purpose of identifying persons or things referred to in the will. Such evidence includes evidence to clarify an ambiguity, for example to show that there exists another person or subject matter to which the words in question refer or could refer. Where, even after admitting extrinsic evidence, the words used in a will are open to more than one meaning, or may be taken to apply to more than one person or subject matter, further evidence to clarify the matter will be admitted (*Re Ray, Cant v Johnstone* [1916] 1 Ch 461) to enable the court to put itself in the position of the testator at the time he made the will (*Perrin v Morgan* [1943] AC 399, [1943] 1 All ER 187). Thus, if the testator had a nickname for a person, or referred to that person by a name other than his true name, evidence may be called to show that the name or description given applies to that person and not to any other person.

When seeking to challenge the validity of a will on the basis of uncertainty, ambiguity or obscurity, careful consideration should be given to all the evidence which may be available to prove or disprove the issue(s) raised, and to assess and weigh the nature, quality and strength of that evidence and all the surrounding circumstances. It is only when there is overwhelming and convincing evidence of the interpretation sought that a challenge would be justified.

Chapter 16

Execution of a Will

Formal Requirements

A will may be challenged on the ground that it was not duly executed in accordance with the provisions of the Wills Act 1837 as amended by the Administration of Justice Act 1982. Section 9 of the Wills Act 1837 as amended provides that:

"No will shall be valid unless–

(a) it is in writing and signed by the testator, or by some person in his presence and by his direction; and

(b) it appears that the testator intended by his signature to give effect to the will; and

(c) the signature is made or acknowledged by the testator in the presence of two or more witnesses present at the same time; and

(d) each witness either–

(i) attests and signs the will; or

(ii) acknowledges his signature,

in the presence of the testator (but not necessarily in the presence of any other witness),

but no form of attestation shall be necessary."

Signature of the Testator

To be valid, therefore, the will must be signed by the testator or by some other person in his presence and at his direction, the testator intending, by the signature, to give effect to the will. Although it is usual for the testator to place his signature at the foot of the will, it does not invalidate a will if the signature appears elsewhere than at the end or foot. In *Wood v Smith* [1992] 3 All ER 556, the testator made a handwritten will starting with the words "My will by Percy Winterbone ...". He did not otherwise sign the will at the foot of the document or elsewhere. When the witnesses attested the will he told them that he had signed the will at the top and that it could be signed anywhere. It was contended that this will was not valid as it did not comply with the requirements of the Wills Act 1837, and that the purported signature, when made, was made on a document which was not a will containing any disposition. The Court of Appeal held that the writing of his name amounted to his signature as the testator had indicated in clear terms to the attesting witnesses that he regarded his name written by him as being his signature. Furthermore, the fact that the will was signed before the terms of the will were written did not invalidate the will, as the writing of the signature and the dispositive terms were all done in one operation. The signature did not necessarily have to be appended to the document after the substantive testamentary contents had been written out.

It must, however, be shown that the testator intended by his signature, wherever it appears, to give effect to his will. In *Re Bean's Estate* [1944] P 83, [1944] 2 All ER 348, probate was refused: the deceased did not sign the will but wrote his name and address on an envelope containing the will. In *The Goods of Mann* [1942] P 146, the testator had placed her signature on an envelope which contained the will, intending that the signature should be the signature of her will. Probate was granted on the ground that the envelope and the unsigned document together formed the will.

Where the testator signed the will before it is attested by the witnesses, the signature must be acknowledged expressly or by implication and the signature must be visible at the time it is acknowledged (*Re Groffman, Groffman and Block v Groffman* [1969] 1 WLR 733, [1969] 2 All ER 108).

Where the will, on the face of it, is regular and there is an attestation clause, the court will apply the presumption *omnia praesumnter rite esse acta* – all things are presumed to have been done rightly and regularly – and presume that the will was executed in compliance with the provisions of the Wills Act 1837.

For the will to be validly signed by the testator it is not necessary that the testator's full signature should appear on the document. A thumb print (*Re Finn (Deceased)* [1935] 154 LT) or a mark which signifies that it is intended to be regarded as a signature to give effect to the testamentary disposition suffices, particularly where the testator is disabled, for example if he is illiterate or blind. Initials may also suffice, as may a partial signature. In this regard, rule 13 of the Non-Contentious Probate Rules 1987 (SI 1987 No 2024) provides that:

> "Before admitting to proof a will which appears to have been signed by a blind or illiterate testator or by another person by direction of the testator, or which for any other reason raises doubt as to the testator having had knowledge of the contents of the will at the time of its execution, the district judge shall satisfy himself that the testator had such knowledge."

Evidence

The presumption that the will was duly executed may be rebutted by evidence to show the contrary. The court will, however, require strong evidence to displace the presumption, particularly where there is an appropriate and perfect attestation clause and all other matters appear to be regular. The evidence to rebut the presumption must be clear, positive and reliable (*Wyatt v Berry* [1893] P 5; *Pilkington v Gray* [1899] AC 401; *In the*

Goods of Moore [1901] P 44). Where the attestation clause is unclear or incomplete the presumption will be more readily displaced.

The evidence of the two witnesses who attested the signature of the testator is usually relied upon to prove that the will was duly executed. Where an issue relating to execution is raised, the court will prefer to hear the evidence of both witnesses if they are alive. If both witnesses give evidence on oath that the will was not duly executed, and there is no other evidence to the contrary, the court will be bound by that evidence (*Re Vere-Wardale, Vere-Wardale v Johnson* [1949] P 395, [1949] 2 All ER 250). Evidence other than that of, or in addition to that of, the attesting witnesses may be called to rebut or to support the presumption. Such evidence may take the form of calling other persons who were present when the will was executed. Where the witnesses are dead, the evidence of persons to whom an attesting witness made a statement may be relied on (*Re Yelland (Deceased), Broadbent v Francis* (1975) 119 SJ 562).

Where there is any doubt about due execution, the validity of the will is open to challenge. The burden of proving that the will was duly executed lies on the party who is seeking to prove the will. In most cases, the person who is challenging the will is content to allow the executors to seek to establish that the will was duly executed, requiring the executors to prove the will, and cross-examining any witnesses called to establish the validity of the will on behalf of the estate.

Rule 12 of the Non-Contentious Probate Rules 1987 is also relevant. It provides as follows:

"(1) Subject to paragraphs (2) and (3) below, where a will contains no attestation clause or the attestation clause is insufficient, or where it appears to the district judge or registrar that there is doubt about the due execution of the will, he shall before admitting it to proof require an affidavit as to due execution from one or more of the attesting witnesses or, if no attesting witness is conveniently available, from any other person who was present when the will was executed; and if the district judge, after considering the evidence, is satisfied the will was not duly executed, he shall refuse probate and mark the will accordingly.

(2) If no affidavit can be obtained in accordance with paragraph (1) above, the district judge or registrar may accept evidence on affidavit from any person he may think fit to show that the signature on the will is in the handwriting of the deceased, or of any other matter which may raise a presumption in favour of due execution of the will, and may if he thinks fit require that notice of the application be given to any person who may be prejudiced by the will.

(3) A district judge or registrar may accept a will for proof without evidence as aforesaid if he is satisfied that the distribution of the estate

is not thereby affected."

The will may be signed by someone else on behalf of the testator, provided that the third party signs the will in the presence of the testator and at his direction. The person attesting the will may sign in the testator's name or in his own name provided that the signature is expressly stated to be made for and on behalf of the testator. In such cases it will be necessary to satisfy the district judge that the testator had knowledge of the contents of the will at the time the will was executed (see Non-Contentious Probate Rules 1987, rule 13).

Attestation

A testator's signature must be made or acknowledged by him in the presence of two or more witnesses present at the same time. Each witness must then either attest and sign the will, or acknowledge his signature in the presence of the testator. There is thus no need for the testator to have observed and seen the witness sign the will as long as the attestation takes place in the presence of the testator and the testator is proved to have had the mental capacity to understand the nature of the transaction and what was being done: see *Re Chalcraft, Chalcraft v Giles and Rance* [1948] 1 All ER 700, where the testator became insensible before the witnesses signed the will, and it was held that the attestation was invalid. Although all the parties to the execution of a will are required to be concerned simultaneously in it, the evidencing of their joint activity can be made subsequently and separately.

In *Couser v Couser* [1996] 1 WLR 1301, [1996] 3 All ER 256, [1996] 2 FLR 46, the testator drafted his will and signed it. He then took it to his friends for attestation. When he arrived at their house only one of the witnesses, the wife, was present. She signed the will as a witness. A few minutes later her husband joined them. The wife told him what she had done but expressed doubts as to the validity of her attestation since the testator had signed the will in her absence. The testator nevertheless asked the husband to sign the will bearing the signatures of the testator and the female witness, and informed the husband that he had signed the will. The husband signed the will in the presence of his wife who continued to protest that what was being done was invalid. On the testator's death his son contended that the will had not been duly executed because the testator had not acknowledged his signature in the presence of two witnesses at the same time, and the female witness had not subscribed the will after the testator had acknowledged his signature on it. On the facts, it was held that the testator had not only acknowledged his signature to the female witness but had also subsequently done so in her presence and with her knowledge when her husband had attested the will. The testator had therefore acknowledged his signature in the presence of two witnesses, and by protesting about the invalidity of her signature, the female witness had acknowledged her signature at the time. The will was therefore validly executed.

The Competence of Witnesses

There is no statutory provision that disqualifies a person from witnessing a will. Witnesses should be of sound mind and capacity and of fixed abode; they should not be under a disability which prevents them from seeing or being aware of the act done. It is considered that a blind person is not capable of witnessing a will as he is not able to see what he is witnessing. In *Re Gibson (Deceased)* [1949] P 434, [1949] 2 All ER 90, the question whether a blind person could witness a will was left open.

Section 14 of the Wills Act provides that a will is not to be considered invalid because any person who attested its execution, either at the time of execution of the will or subsequently, is found to be incompetent to be admitted as a witness to prove execution. There is no rule which disqualifies a child from witnessing a will, but a will attested by a child witness may be challenged on the basis that his mental capacity at the time was such that he was unable to understand the nature of the act done. There is also the possibility that, at the time such a will is challenged, the child witness may not be competent to give evidence in support of the execution.

Section 15 of the Wills Act applies where a person attests the execution of a will and, under that will, any beneficial devise, legacy, estate, interest, gift or appointment, of or affecting any real or personal estate, is given or made to that person or to his or her wife or husband. Such a devise, legacy, estate interest, gift or appointment is, so far only as concerns the person attesting the execution of such will, or that person's wife or husband, or any person claiming under that person or that person's wife or husband, null and void. The person attesting the will may, however, be admitted as a witness to prove the execution of the will, or to prove its validity or invalidity, notwithstanding the devise, legacy, estate, interest, gift or appointment. In such cases, therefore, the gift fails but does not necessarily render the will invalid.

There are certain exceptions to the rule that a gift of this nature fails. These include gifts made in the following circumstances:

(a) where the beneficial interest is conferred on a witness under a secret trust and the witness is unaware of it at the time of attestation; see *Re Young, Young v Young* [1951] Ch 344, [1950] 2 All ER 1245;

(b) where the witness or his or her spouse does not witness an earlier will containing the gift, but witnesses a codicil to that will, even though the codicil confirms the will or it is clear from the circumstances that the testator does not intend to revoke the earlier gift and a second or subsequent will could be regarded as conditional on the gift's being valid. In *Re Finnemore (Deceased)* [1991] 1 WLR 793, [1992] 1 All ER 800, the testator made a will in which he left his house and its contents and the majority of the residuary estate to the first defendant. He bequeathed the remainder of his residuary estate to the second defendant and her husband. Two years later he executed two further wills. Under the first of these subsequent wills he made a bequest in favour of the first defendant in exactly the same terms as in the first will, but gave a legacy of only £500 to the second defendant and the remainder of his residuary estate to two charities. In the second of these two wills, made three weeks later, he made identical provisions save that the residuary estate was bequeathed to three charities. Both later wills expressed that all former wills were revoked. The last two wills made were attested by the first defendant's husband with the result that the gifts to her in both those wills were void under section 15 of the Wills Act 1837. The issue before the court was whether, the gift to the first defendant in the last will having failed, the property undisposed of by the will was held in trust for the (a) the first defendant on the basis that the revocation clause contained in the will was conditional or qualified so that she benefited under the earlier will giving her identical benefits; or (b) the next of kin on a partial intestacy. It was held that the clause in the will which revoked all previous wills could be read distributively so as to relate absolutely to some dispositions but only conditionally to others; and in an appropriate case the doctrine of conditional revocation could apply to save a gift from failing under section 15. It was also held in the alternative that, because of the testator's mistaken belief that the attestation of the last will by the first defendant's husband would not invalidate the gift to the wife, the will was qualified and conditional on the defectively attested will being a valid will and it was clear from all the surrounding circumstances that the testator had not intended to revoke the gift to the first defendant;

(c) where the donee marries an attesting witness after the attestation took place: *Thorpe v Bestwick* [1881] 6 QBD 311;
(d) if three or more people attest the will and at least two of them were people who, and whose spouses, did not take gifts under the will, no gift to any other witness or to his spouse is lost: Wills Act 1969;
(e) where a gift is made to an attesting witness or his spouse in a fiduciary capacity;
(f) where a donee under the will attests a codicil which increases the donee's share in the residue under the will; or where a codicil confirms a will containing a gift to an attesting witness to the will.

In summary, where, on the face of it, a will appears to be duly executed, the court applies the presumption that it has been executed in accordance with the requirements of the Wills Act. In the event of any challenge, the court requires strong, clear and reliable evidence to rebut the presumption.

Chapter 17

Testamentary Capacity

Introduction

For a will to be valid, the testator should be a person aged eighteen or over (except in the case of a privileged will; see page 167), and of sound mind, memory and understanding. The requisite mental capacity is regarded as higher than that required to enter into many other day-to-day transactions. In *Banks v Goodfellow* (1870) LR 5 QB 549, Cockburn CJ referred to the standard required in the following terms:

> "It is essential that a testator shall understand the nature of his act and its effects; the extent of the property of which he is disposing; shall be able to comprehend and appreciate the claims to which he ought to give effect, and, with a view to the latter object, that no disorder of mind shall poison his affections, pervert his sense of right, or prevent the exercise of his natural faculties, that no insane delusion shall influence his will in disposing of his property and bring about a disposal of it which, if his mind had been sound, would not have been made."

It was also stated, however, that a will could not be invalidated simply because the testator was moved "by capricious, frivolous, mean and even bad motives".

The test would seem to be that three criteria must be met at one and the same time:

(a) the testator must understand the nature of the act of making the will and its effect;

(b) he must understand the nature and extent of the property of which he is disposing; and

(c) he must be able to appreciate and understand the claims on his estate of those persons whom he is benefiting in his will, and of those whom he is not benefiting in his will.

In *Wood v Smith* [1993] Ch 90, [1992] 3 All ER 556 (see also page 171), the court was concerned to ascertain whether the testator had the capacity to comprehend the extent of the property being disposed of and the nature of the claims of those he was excluding. Both the court of first instance and the Court of Appeal applied and affirmed the test set out above. On the basis of the medical and professional evidence, and evidence from those who had cared for the deceased in a home, the court concluded that the testator did not have the required testamentary capacity to make a will.

The test is thus not the same as that applied in contractual and other transactions, such as marriage. In addition to having understanding, a testator must also have "memory" and sufficient "awareness" of his obligations. It should not, though, be assumed in every case where the testator has suffered mental disability or mental disorder (see below for the statutory definition) that he was incapable of making a will: it is presumed the testator had the mental capacity to make the will unless proved otherwise. The issue of the testator's mental capacity must be seriously and thoroughly considered before concluding that a will is invalid on the ground that the testator lacked mental capacity.

With the increase in the number of elderly people in the population, and in the numbers suffering mental disorder, there is likely to be greater scope to challenge the validity of a will on the grounds of lack of testamentary capacity. Such a challenge may be complicated where there is evidence that the testator's mental capacity varied from day to day, or from one moment to another. The nature and quality of the evidence available to prove or disprove capacity will therefore be significant. Medical or other professional evidence may not always suffice where it is known that the testator's condition fluctuated. The effect on the testator of medication may also be a relevant consideration. In some instances it could be proved to have had an adverse effect on capacity, but on other occasions to improve or restore it. The degree of mental incapacity may also vary. Each case must be considered on its merits having regard to all the circumstances. Some of the relevant considerations are reviewed below.

Mental Disorder

The Mental Health Act 1983, section 1(1), identifies four categories of disorder, as follows:

(a) "mental disorder" means mental illness, arrested or incomplete development of mind, psychopathic disorder and any other disorder or disability of the mind and "mentally disordered" shall be construed accordingly;

(b) "severe mental impairment" means a state of arrested or incomplete development of mind which includes severe impairment of intelligence and social functioning and is associated with abnormally aggressive or seriously irresponsible conduct on the part of the person concerned and "severely mentally impaired" shall be construed accordingly;

(c) "mental impairment" means a state of arrested or incomplete development or mind (not amounting to severe mental impairment) which includes significant impairment of intelligence and social functioning and is associated with abnormally aggressive or seriously irresponsible conduct on the part of the person concerned and "mentally impaired" shall be construed accordingly;

(d) "psychopathic disorder" means a persistent disorder or disability of mind (whether or not including significant impairment of intelligence) which results in abnormally aggressive or seriously irresponsible conduct on the part of the person concerned.

Delusions

The fact that a testator suffered from delusions with regard to a particular belief or matter does not necessarily lead to the conclusion that he was incompetent to make a will if, in other respects, he appeared to be rational. The test to be applied is whether the particular delusion is of such an extent and nature that no person in his senses, viewed objectively, could believe it: *Broughton v Knight* [1873] LR 3 PD 58. In *Banks v Goodfellow* (above, page 177) the test was stated as follows:

> "If the human instincts and affections, or the moral sense, become perverted by mental disease; if insane suspicion or aversion take the place of natural affection; if the reason and judgment are lost, and the mind becomes a prey for insane delusions calculated to interfere with and disturb its functions, and to lead to a testamentary disposition, due only to their baneful influence – in such a case it is obvious that the condition of the testamentary power fails, and that a will made under such circumstances ought not to stand."

In *Banks v Goodfellow,* the testator suffered from a delusion that he was being pursued and molested by a certain person who was already dead and in no way connected to the testator. The will was held to be valid as the delusions were not capable of influencing him in the provisions of his will. To invalidate the will, the delusion must have affected the testator's decision or influenced him in making the dispositions he made. It is not enough to show that the testator had formed an unjustified view of a child or some other person towards whom he had a moral obligation and or who was dependent on him. It is only when it can be shown that the view taken or feelings expressed by the testator, which influenced him to do as he did, emanated from mental disorder or defect and dominated his mind, that the court will set aside a disposition. In *Re Nightingale, Green v Nightingale (No 2)* (1974) 119 SJ 189, the testator was suffering from cancer. In his first will the main beneficiary was his son. Shortly before he died the testator made a second will in which he excluded his son because he was under an unjustified belief that his son was trying to kill him. The second will was held to be invalid.

Senility, Confusion and Lucid Intervals

The mere fact that a testator was of advancing years when the will was made does not suffice to invalidate a will for lack of testamentary capacity. The evidence must show that the testator's mental ability and understanding were reduced to such an extent that the testator did not understand and appreciate the act of making a will and its effect: *Banks v Goodfellow* (above). Where the evidence shows that the testator's condition varied, as in the case of someone suffering from senile dementia, it must be shown that the will was made during a lucid period when the testator was able to understand that he was making a will and the effect of it. In *Re Parsons* [2002] WTLR 237, the testator, who was elderly and incapacitated, instructed a licensed conveyancer to prepare a will for him. The licensed conveyancer drafted the will and engrossed it. Before the will was executed the testator was examined by a doctor to confirm that he had testamentary capacity. The testator signed his will by making a thumb print in the presence of the attesting witnesses, namely the doctor and the licensed conveyancer's secretary. On the same day the testator had a stroke. The beneficiaries under an earlier will sought to challenge the validity of the later will. On the evidence, the court was satisfied that the will was valid, but made the observation that where a would-be testator is elderly or incapacitated a solicitor with experience of wills should take instructions and supervise the execution of the will.

In *Richards v Allan* [2001] WTLR 1031, the testatrix was eighty-four years of age, prone to confusion and in poor health. At the suggestion of A she made a will. A approached her brother-in-law to prepare the will. The will appointed A as the sole executrix and beneficiary under the will. The will was challenged on the grounds of lack of testamentary capacity and lack of the requisite knowledge and approval, on the basis that the testatrix's condition meant that she had lucid intervals interspersed with periods of confusion. Evidence from her general practitioner confirmed that she had been confused earlier in the day on which she executed the will and she was subsequently admitted to hospital where it was noted that she was confused. The will was declared invalid. See also *Special Trustees for Great Ormond Street Hospital For Children v Rushin, sub nom Re Morris (Deceased)* [2001] WTLR 1137, where the court found that the deceased had been suffering from serious dementia in the form of Alzheimer's disease during the months prior to her death, and therefore lacked capacity to make any decision concerning her will and other transactions in favour of her housekeeper.

Drunkenness

The fact that a testator had been drinking when he signed his will is not sufficient to invalidate the will for lack of testamentary capacity. Where the evidence discloses that the testator was drunk, the issue arising is whether, at the time he gave his instructions and when the will was executed, he was clear in his mind how he wished to dispose of his property and why. A recent case where the matter was considered is *Chana (Gravinder) v Chana (Harjit Kaur)* [2001] WTLR 227, where the testator and one of the attesting witnesses had been drinking when the will was executed. The will had been drafted not by a solicitor, but by a friend, who was a business man and local councillor with some experience of drafting wills. The testator had indicated to him that he did not want to leave anything for his sons as they had physically and verbally assaulted him. One of his sons was severely physically disabled and the testator was aware of his disability. The testator was an alcoholic and died ten months later of alcoholism. On the evidence, and applying the test laid down in *Banks v Goodfellow,* it was found that the testator had a clear understanding of what he intended to do and its effect. Probate was granted.

Language and Literacy

A will may be challenged on the ground that the testator lacked an understanding of English or was illiterate. It is essential that those responsible for preparing a will ensure that language is not a barrier to obtaining instructions. In case of any doubt it would be prudent to engage an independent and qualified interpreter and to keep a full record, and perhaps also for the interpreter to sign the record as an accurate note of the instructions given. It would be advisable for the attestation clause to confirm that the will was translated to the testator before its execution and to contain a declaration by the interpreter to that effect. The test in *Banks v Goodfellow* applies to such a case. Where there is serious contest about the testator's capacity on this ground, much will depend on the evidence called to support his knowledge and understanding of the language, and/or confirmation that, although written in English, the will was interpreted to him. See *Chana (Gravinder) v Chana (Harjit Kaur)* (above), where the issue was raised but rejected.

Evidence and Proof

It is presumed that a testator was of sound mind, and where a will appears to be regular and its contents rational, then, unless it is contested, it will be admitted. But if the testator's capacity is challenged, it is for the person propounding the will to prove that the testator was of sound mind and had the appropriate understanding, both at the time of giving instructions and when executing the will.

The standard of proof is the civil standard, that is on the balance of probabilities.

All relevant oral and documentary evidence will be admitted to prove or disprove the issues raised. Evidence from witnesses regarding the testator's conduct before, at the time of, and after he made the will or gave instructions for the will to be made is relevant, but not conclusive if there is other evidence, particularly medical or professional evidence, or evidence from those who were closely involved with the testator and his care (see *Wood v Smith* (above)). Medical evidence may not, however, be sufficient if there is a break between the last observation of the testator by the witness and the time of making the will. Here, the evidence of those who were in daily constant touch with the testator and had him under observation may be more valuable in assessing the testator's condition. The evidence of the solicitor to whom instructions were given would be admissible and is usually relevant, as it is the duty of the solicitor to ensure that the test set out in *Banks v Goodfellow* is satisfied.

To support the validity of the will, the evidence must show that the testator was able to understand the nature of the act of making a will, that it would take effect on his death, and that he had the right to revoke or alter the will at any time before death. The evidence must show that the testator was able to understand the need to appoint an executor, and the duties and obligations which attach to the executor; and understand the implications of the dispositions he intended to make and deal with alternative options should the gift fail. There must be evidence to show that the testator was aware of the extent of all his property and its value (see *Wood v Smith* (above), where the testator believed that his portfolio of shares was worth just under £17,000 when in fact it was worth £105,000), including benefits payable on his death, such as insurance benefits. Finally, the evidence should establish that the testator was able to make a reasoned and rational decision about the dispositions he intended to make, and, where he sought to exclude obvious beneficiaries or sought to distinguish between them, that he was able to assess the position of the persons concerned and give reasons for his decision (*Chana (Gavinder) v Chana (Harjit Kaur),* above).

Duty to Establish Testamentary Capacity

The duty of a solicitor instructed to draw up a will is to advise and take instructions from the client. Where the circumstances raise doubt relating to the testamentary capacity of the client, or would have raised doubts in the mind of a competent solicitor, steps should be taken to allay those doubts before proceeding further. It is essential to keep a detailed record of all the steps taken in the drafting and execution of the will. Failure to do so may result in a claim for negligence against the solicitor (see *Public Trustee v Till* [2002] WTLR 1169).

If, when taking instructions to make a will, there appears to be any doubt or uncertainty about the testator's condition, it would be advisable to have the testator examined by a medical expert and to rely on the expert's opinion; where possible it may be helpful for the expert to witness the testator's signature so that there can be no doubt about the competency of the testator, both at the time he gave instructions and when he executed the will. It is always prudent to keep a written record of the circumstances at every step (see *Ross v Caunters* [1980] Ch 297, [1979] 3 WLR 605, [1979] 3 All ER 580) and for the medical expert to record the findings of his examination. It is recommended that when the doctor is asked to witness a testator's signature, the doctor ought not to sign unless he has assessed the testator's capacity; is satisfied on the balance of probabilities that the testator has the requisite capacity to make the will; and makes a formal record of his findings. Where a will is challenged, evidence on the basis of the above recommendation will go some way to assist the person propounding the will to discharge the burden of proof. In the absence of such evidence the will may be declared invalid.

In cases where there is any uncertainty about the testator's condition it may be appropriate to request the Court of Protection to consider the testator's status and, if necessary, to authorise the making of a will.

Chapter 18

Knowledge and Approval of Testator

Introduction

A person propounding a will must show that, at the time of execution, the testator knew, understood and approved the contents of the will. Problems in this context usually arise:

(a) where there was a mistake in the preparation of the will;
(b) where the testator suffered from some disability such as blindness, deafness or illiteracy; and
(c) where the circumstances surrounding the preparation and execution of the will are suspicious.

Since those who seek to challenge a will on the basis of lack of knowledge and approval do not always know the precise circumstances in which the will was made, it is not unusual for challenges made on this ground also to include allegations of undue influence, assertions that the testator lacked testamentary capacity and claims that there was want of due execution. Even where such allegations or claims are not raised in the pleadings as grounds for challenge, the persons who seek to challenge the will are permitted nevertheless to rely on those grounds where appropriate. But in so doing they expose themselves to having to pay costs if they fail to make out the case (see *Re Stott* [1980] 1 WLR 246, [1980] 1 All ER 259 and the Civil Procedure Rules 1998 (SI 1998 No 3132 as amended), rule 44.3).

Mistake

A mistake in the drafting of the will may arise as a result of the testator's own inadvertence or an error by the draftsman, or it may be caused by the deliberate act of another. A good example of a case where the mistake occurred as a result of the testator's inadvertence is *Re Phelan (Deceased)* [1971] 3 All ER 1256, where the testator used a printed will form to make his will in favour of his landlord and his wife, leaving them a legacy and his residuary estate. Subsequently he believed that his stocks and shares had to be dealt with by separate wills. He executed three further wills using printed will forms, leaving certain block units in certain trusts to his landlord and his wife, but he did not delete, from any one of those wills, the revocation clause, so that each will contained the revocation clause. There was no evidence to show which document was signed last. The beneficiaries sought to admit all four wills to probate. The court did so, omitting the revocation clause from the last three wills executed on the same day, on the basis that although the court cannot remake a will for a testator, "it can omit words which have come in by inadvertence or by misunderstanding if their omission gives effect to the true intention of the testator as found by the court".

Where the mistake is obvious and was made by the draftsman, whether a clerical error or a slip, and the mistake does not amount to a misunderstanding of the instructions given by the testator or of the legal effect of the words used, the court may permit the offending words to be omitted from the probate or rectify the will to give effect to the testator's wishes. Examples include an error in numbering the clauses of a will, or an error in an amount, as where the draftsman inserted "40" instead of "all my shares" (*Morell v Morell* (1882) 7 PD 68). In *Re Morris* [1971] P 62, [1970] 2 WLR 865, [1970] 1 All ER 1057, the testatrix executed her last will making provisions for her housekeeper in clause 3. In clause 7 she made a large number of pecuniary legacies, each of which was preceded by a roman numeral in brackets; this clause contained a legacy in favour of the housekeeper. Some two months later the testatrix wrote to her solicitors expressing her wish to alter the bequest to her housekeeper but in all other respects to retain the provisions of the will. The solicitor prepared a codicil in which, by an error in drafting, the words "I revoke clauses 3 and 7 of my said Will" were inserted instead of 'I revoke clauses 3 and 7(iv) of my said will". The codicil was executed as drafted, the testatrix not noticing the error. Clause 2 of the codicil made provisions in favour of the housekeeper in similar terms as before save that the amount of the pecuniary legacy was reduced. The codicil was admitted with the numeral clause 7 omitted. The court held that (a) although a testator might in some circumstances be bound by a mistake made by the draftsman, the testator would not be bound where the mind of the draftsman had never really been applied to the words introduced and never averted to their significance and effect and there was a mere clerical error on the part of the draftsman; and (b) although the fact that a testator had read and executed a will raised the inference that he knew and approved the contents there was no rule precluding the court from considering all the evidence to arrive at the truth and on the facts of the case there was obviously an error of which the testatrix could not have been aware and there was therefore no approval by her of it.

Similar principles apply where the draftsman, by a clerical error, omits words from the will contrary to the testator's instructions, for example where a number of words have been omitted by the typist when engrossing the will (*Re Reynette-James* [1976] 1 WLR 161, [1975] 3 All ER 1037). In such a case the court construes the will as if the words had been inserted in the will. Other examples include cases where the testator intended to give legacies to two named persons, but the draftsman inserted the same name twice (*In the Goods of Boehm* [1891] P 247).

To succeed on an application for rectification, it must be demonstrated that the will failed to carry out the instructions and/or intentions of the testator and what those instructions or intentions were. In *Bell v Georgiou* [2002] EWHC 1080, [2002] WTLR 1105, the son of the testatrix claimed that the fact that the legacy to him began with the expression "free of tax and duties" when no tax was payable on the estate indicated an error in the will, and that she had intended to make a further legacy to him equal to the nil rate band for inheritance tax. His application for rectification of the will failed because he was not able to prove that the will failed to carry out her instructions and what those instructions were; the evidence produced by him was not sufficiently convincing to displace the written evidence.

Where the mistake relates to the whole of the will, probate is generally refused, as it would be difficult to satisfy the court that the testator had known and approved of the contents of the will. In *The Goods of Hunt* [1875] 3 P&D 250, the testator, who lived with her sister, prepared two wills, one to be executed by each of them. By mistake, the testator executed the will prepared for her sister. The wills were in similar terms but the court refused probate because it was held that the testator did not know and approve of any part of the contents of the will she had executed. On the other hand, in *Re Vautier's Estate* (2000-01) 3 ITELR 566, a husband and wife, by mistake, executed each other's wills, which were in reciprocal terms. The mistake was not discovered until the wife had died. The court allowed rectification of the wife's will so as to alter the words to reflect her intention, as there was overwhelming evidence of the nature of the mistake.

Disability

Where the testator suffered from a disability which may have made it difficult for him to understand and approve the contents of his will, the court must be satisfied, by affirmative evidence, that the will sets out the testator's intentions. In *D'Eye v Avery* [2001] WTLR 227 the testator had suffered a severe stroke in 1986. In 1987 he was placed in the care of the Court of Protection because he was unable to manage his affairs in that he could not make himself understood, verbally or otherwise. In 1988 D took the testator to a bank, where instructions to draw up a will were given entirely by D and provided that everything should be left to D. The bank accepted the instructions. A second visit was made by the testator in the company of D when the will was executed. The will was not read over to the testator. Following the testator's death, the statutory next of kin challenged the will. The court refused to grant probate of the will on the ground that the testator did not understand the disposition he was making and lacked knowledge and approval.

In *Ewing v Bennett* [2001] 2 WTLR 249 the testatrix was elderly, very deaf and forgetful. On 29 October 1992 she gave her solicitors instructions to draw up a will leaving everything to her daughter E, to the exclusion of her daughter B, and gave reasons for her decision. To avoid problems in the future, however, the solicitor advised her to leave something for B. She accepted that advice and provided a legacy of £5,000 for B. She confirmed her instructions to the solicitors by signing the solicitor's record of her instructions to him. The draft was discussed at a second meeting with the solicitor, and at a third attendance at the solicitor's office the testatrix executed the will on 18 November 1992. In October 1992, however, a doctor had found difficulty communicating with the testatrix because of her deafness. There were also signs of dementia. In January 1993 she was described as having serious memory impairment. B's challenge on the grounds of want of execution, capacity and knowledge and approval was nevertheless rejected (see further below).

Suspicious Circumstances

If a will is prepared and executed under suspicious circumstances which suggest that the will, or any provision in it, did not express the intentions of the testator, it will not be admitted to probate unless the suspicion is removed by satisfactory evidence of the testator's knowledge and approval. A classic example is where a person prepares or causes the preparation of a will for the testator, and under that will the person himself is a substantial beneficiary. In such a case the suspicion will cause the court:

> "to be vigilant and jealous in examining the evidence in support of the instrument, in favour of which it ought not to pronounce unless the suspicion is removed and it is judicially satisfied that the paper propounded does express the true wish of the deceased." (*Barry v Butlin*; see below.)

The degree of suspicion varies according to the circumstances of each case. The burden of dispelling it may be slight so that it is easily dispelled, or the suspicion may be so "grave that it can hardly be removed". In *Wintle v Nye* [1959] 1 WLR 284, [1959] 1 All ER 552, the testator, who was sixty-six years of age, was being advised by her solicitor in the preparation of her will. In the first draft of the will the residuary estate was to be given to charities. Thereafter there were some twenty consultations between the testator and the solicitor regarding her will. The ultimate will that she executed was prepared by the solicitor and executed in his office. It appointed the solicitor as the sole executor and gave him the residuary estate, which was of substantial value. Subsequently, on the advice of the solicitor, the testatrix executed a codicil in which she revoked the provision she had made in respect of certain charities. The result was that the amount of the gifts to charities under earlier versions of the draft fell into the residue and for the benefit of the solicitor. The court found that the burden of dispelling the suspicion had not been discharged.

In *Re Ticehurst, Midland Bank Executor and Trustee Co v Hankinson* [1973] *The Times*, 6 March, where the will was prepared by correspondence with a solicitor through an amanuensis, who was the wife of one of the beneficiaries, the court refused to admit the will to probate, finding that the suspicion had not been dispelled. See also *Tyrell v Painton* [1894] P 151.

In a recent Privy Council case (*Ramcoomarsingh v The Administrator General* [2003] NLJ 123), the solicitor, who was the main beneficiary, was permitted to admit the will to probate. In that case the testator had been a law clerk. On his death in 1985 his sister sought probate of a will purported to have been made by the testator in 1984. That will was proved to be a forgery. The solicitor, for whom the testator had worked and who had been a close friend of the testator, sought to prove a will made in 1978 under which the sister was a life tenant and the solicitor was the remainderman. The sister challenged the will for lack of knowledge and approval. The evidence established that the testator had dictated the 1978 will to the solicitor's secretary while the solicitor was at lunch. The solicitor had known that the testator had intended to make him the main beneficiary of the will and had frequently tried to persuade the testator to make provision for his sister. On appeal it was found that there was sufficient evidence to find that the testator knew what he was doing; he had had many years of experience as a law clerk and he had dictated the will. The sister's argument that the solicitor had a conflict of interest and should have declined to act or allow his firm to act was rejected. The Privy Council held that the solicitor's duty to the testator was to carry out his testamentary wishes, and once undue influence was negatived, there was no conflict between the solicitor's interest and his duty.

A challenge for want of knowledge and approval also failed in *Minns v Foster* [2002] All ER (D) 225, [2003] NLJ 123, where the claimant, to whom the testator had gifted his house free of tax and who was seeking to admit the will, had helped the testator to organise meetings with the solicitor who had drafted the will, but had not attended the interview with the solicitor when instructions were given, nor when the will was executed. The testator had read the first draft of the will and corrected omissions within it, but there was no evidence as to whether the testator had read the will or had it read to him.

The Standard and Burden of Proof

The burden of proof lies upon the party propounding the will. This was laid down in *Barry v Butlin* [1838] II Moo PC 480, a Privy Council case giving rise to what is now know as the rule in *Barry v Butlin*. In the judgment delivered by Parke B it was stated:

"The rules of law according to which cases of this nature are to be decided do not admit of any dispute, so far as they are necessary to the determination of the present appeal .... These rules are two: the first that the *onus probandi* lies in every case upon the party propounding the Will; and he must satisfy the conscience of the Court that the instrument so propounded is the last Will of a free and capable Testator. The second is, that if a party writes or prepares a Will, under which he takes a benefit, that is a circumstance that ought generally to excite the suspicion of the Court, and calls upon it to be vigilant and jealous in examining the evidence in support of the instrument, in favour of which it ought not to pronounce unless the suspicion is removed, and it is judicially satisfied that the paper propounded does express the true Will of the deceased.

The strict meaning of the term *onus probandi* is this, that if no evidence is given by the party on whom the burden is cast, the issue must be found against him. In all cases the *onus* is imposed on the party propounding a Will, it is in general discharged by proof of capacity, and the fact of execution, from which the knowledge of and assent to the contents of the instrument are assumed, and it cannot be that the simple fact of the party who prepared the Will being himself a Legatee, is in every case, and under all circumstances, to create a contrary presumption, and to call upon the Court to pronounce against the Will, unless additional evidence is produced to prove the knowledge of its contents by the deceased. A single instance, of no infrequent occurrence, will test the truth of this proposition. A man of acknowledged competence and habits of business, worth £100,000, leaves the bulk of his property to his family, and a legacy of £50 to his confidential attorney, who prepared the will: would this fact throw the burden of proof of actual cognizance by the Testator, of the contents of the will, on the party propounding it, so that if such proof were not supplied, the will would be pronounced against? The answer is obvious, it would not. All that can truly be said is, that if a person, whether attorney or not, prepares a will with a legacy to himself, it is at most a suspicious circumstance, of more or less weight, according to the facts of the particular case: in some of no weight at all, as in the case suggested, varying according to the circumstances; for instance the *quantum* of the legacy, and the proportion it bears to the property disposed of, and numerous contingencies; but in no case amounting to more than a circumstance of suspicion, demanding the vigilant care and circumspection of the court in investigating the case and calling upon it not to grant probate without full and entire satisfaction that the instrument did express the real intentions of the deceased. Nor can it be necessary, that *in all such cases*, even if the testator's capacity is doubtful, the precise species of evidence of the deceased's knowledge of the will is to be in the shape of instructions for, or reading over the instrument. They form, no doubt, the *most* satisfactory, but they are not the *only* satisfactory description of proof, by which the cognizance of the contents of the will may be brought home to the deceased. The court would naturally look for such evidence; in some cases it might be impossible to establish a will without it, but it has no right in every case to require it."

This passage was approved in *Fulton v Andrew* (1875) LR 7 HL 448, and confirmed in *Wintle v Nye* [1959] 1 All ER 552 and in *Re Fuld (Deceased) (No 3), Hartley v Fuld (Fuld Intervening)* [1968] P 675, [1965] 3 All ER 776, and more recently in *Fuller v Strum* [2001] EWCA Civ 1879, [2002] 2 All ER 87. The nature of the evidence required therefore depends upon the degree of doubt and suspicion, and the circumstances surrounding the preparation of the will and its execution.

The test of whether the testator knew and approved his will is an objective one. The standard of proof is the civil standard – that is to say, the court must be satisfied, on the balance of probabilities, that the contents of the will truly represent the intentions of the testator. This standard nevertheless permits a degree of flexibility, so that where the allegations are serious, the burden is heavier than in cases where they are less serious or trivial: *Re H (Minors) (Sexual abuse: Standard of proof)* [1996] AC 563, [1996] 1 All ER 1.

Atter v Atkinson (1869) LR 1 P&D 665 may have given the impression that the standard of proof is that in criminal cases; in that case it was stated:

> "... if you have to deal with a will in which the person who made it himself takes a large benefit, you ought to be well satisfied, from evidence calculated to exclude all doubt, that the testator not only signed it, but that he knew and approved of its contents."

The recent case of *Fuller v Strum* (above) clearly indicates, however, that this is not the case. Longmore LJ, having reviewed the earlier authorities said:

> "I am satisfied that there is no basis for an approach that requires, in all cases, that a person propounding a will which he has prepared, and under which he takes a benefit, must satisfy the court by evidence which excludes all doubt – or by evidence which excludes all reasonable doubt (the standard of proof required in criminal proceedings) – that the testator knew and approved the contents of the will. The standard of proof required in probate proceedings (as in other non-criminal proceedings) is satisfaction on the preponderance (or balance) of probability. But the circumstances of the particular case may raise in the mind of the court a suspicion that the testator did not know and approve the contents of the document which he has executed which is so grave that, as Viscount Simmonds observed in *Wintle v Nye,* it can hardly be removed."

Where there are no unusual or suspicious circumstances, evidence which establishes that the will was read by, or read over to, the testator, who was at the time capable of understanding what he was reading or hearing and its effect, having regard to any moral or other obligations he may have had at the time to persons close to him, is generally sufficient to discharge the burden and standard of proof required. In *Hart v Dobbs, sub nom Re Dobbs (Lawrence Stanley) (Deceased)* [2001] WTLR 527, the testator had signed three identical copies of a new will prepared by the claimant, who was the major beneficiary under the will. The wills were executed by the testator in the presence of the two attesting witnesses. Five days later, he was admitted to hospital but discharged himself after six days. He was readmitted after being found in a coma. About a fortnight later he was discharged from hospital and on the same day was found dead. The coroner's inquest returned a verdict of unlawful killing. The claimant was a suspect but the Crown Prosecution Service eventually decided not to prosecute. He produced the will to the deceased's family and sought to admit it for probate. The deceased's brother challenged the validity of the will on the ground that the testator did not know that he was signing a will and had no knowledge of its contents. The claimant did not give evidence but the attesting witnesses did. They confirmed that the testator knew that the document was a will and knew of its contents when he signed it. Applying the test set out above, the court found, on the evidence, that the will was valid.

If the testator merely casts his eye over the will it may not be sufficient to establish knowledge and approval of the contents (*Re Morris* [1971] P 62, [1970] 2 WLR 865, [1970] 1 All ER 1057).

If the testator suffered from a physical disability, for example if he was deaf or dumb, and instructions were taken from him through sign language, evidence of the sign language used, and how and by whom it was interpreted, together with evidence of the testator's understanding and approval of the will, must be produced to discharge the burden of proof. Where the testator was blind or illiterate, evidence that the will was read over to him before execution must be provided. Rule 13 of the Non-Contentious Probate Rules 1987 provides that in such cases:

> "before admitting to proof a will which appears to have been signed by a blind or illiterate testator or by another person by direction of the testator, or which for any other reason raises doubt as to the testator having had knowledge of the contents of the will at the time of its execution, the district judge or registrar shall satisfy himself that the testator had such knowledge."

It is therefore essential that the attestation clause in the will of a blind or illiterate testator should include a statement that the testator signed the will after the will had been read over to him in the presence of the witnesses and that he appeared to approve and understand the contents in the presence of the witnesses. There may, however, be circumstances where this clause within an attestation clause may not suffice, and, depending on the degree of doubt or suspicion raised, other evidence may be required.

The Powers of the Court

It will be observed from the cases cited that where a challenge has been successful, the court has power to alter the words of the will so as to give effect to the testator's intention by:

(a) omitting from the will the words which were not known to and approved by the testator (*Re Morris,* above);

(b) directing rectification of the will (see Administration of Justice Act 1982, sections 73(6) and (11) and the Non-Contentious Probate Rules 1987, rule 55);

(c) construing the will so as to give effect to the intention of the testator by inserting, omitting or changing the words, provided there is clear evidence of the error made in drafting and of the true intention of the testator.

Rule 55 of the Non-Contentious Probate Rules 1987 provides that, if the application for rectification is not disputed:

(1) An application for an order that a will be rectified by virtue of section 20(1) of the Administration of Justice Act 1982 may be made to a district judge or registrar unless a probate action has been commenced.

(2) The application shall be supported by an affidavit setting out the grounds of the application, together with such evidence as can be adduced as to the testator's intentions and as to whichever of the following matters are in issue–

(a) in what respects the testator's intentions were not understood; or

(b) the nature of any alleged clerical error.

(3) Unless otherwise directed, notice of the application shall be given to every person having an interest under the will whose interest might be prejudiced or such other person who might be prejudiced by the rectification applied for and any comments in writing by any such person shall be exhibited to the affidavit in support of the application.

(4) If the district judge or registrar is satisfied that, subject to any direction to the contrary, notice has been given to every person mentioned in paragraph (3) above, and that the application is unopposed, he may order that the will be rectified accordingly.

The success or otherwise of a challenge on the ground of lack of knowledge and approval depends on the nature of the allegations made and on the weight and reliability of the evidence, particularly evidence of the surrounding circumstances.

Chapter 19

Undue Influence and Fraud

Undue Influence

A will made as a result of undue influence will not be admitted to probate. Where a will is challenged on the ground of undue influence, the party making the claim, in order to succeed, would have to show that the testator was coerced into making the will, or a disposition in the will, which he did not wish to make, and that the will or disposition was made not of his own volition but as a result of the influence of the third party who dominated the testator's mind:

> "It is only when the will of the person who becomes the testator is coerced into doing that which he does not desire to do that it is undue influence." (*Wingrove v Wingrove* [1885] 11 PD 81.)

Although there is no presumption of undue influence in the case of a testator who was weak or feeble, the challenge is more commonly raised in cases of testators who were of weak or impaired mental capacity, or suffering from ill-health. But such a challenge may also be raised in the case of a testator of sound mind and understanding and good health – undue influence may take many forms and physical force may even be used, as where the testator is assaulted (see, for example, *Chana (Gavinder) v Chana (Harjit Kaur)* [2001] 2 WTLR 205, where the testator was assaulted but it did not affect his capacity); or the undue influence may be mental, for example where extreme pressure is exerted on the testator to the extent that it breaks his will and he gives in to the pressure. Pressure or persuasion which does not affect the testator's mind so that the will of the testator becomes the will of the person exerting the pressure does not amount to undue influence.

The principle was stated in *Hall v Hall* (1868) LR 1 P&D 481 as follows:

> "Persuasion appeals to the affections or ties of kindred, to a sentiment of gratitude for past services, or pity for future destitution, or the like – these are all legitimate, and may be fairly pressed on a testator. On the other hand, pressure of whatever character, whether acting on fears or the hopes, if so exerted as to overpower the volition without which no valid will can be made ... In a word the testator may be led but not driven; and his will must be the offspring of his own volition and not the record of someone else's."

And:

> "Persuasion is not unlawful, but pressure of whatever character if so exercised as to overpower the volition without convincing the judgment of the testator will constitute undue influence, though no force is either used or threatened."

Mere influence exercised over the testator by another person does not constitute undue influence unless there is sufficient proof of coercion. Proof of motive and opportunity for the exercise of influence over the testator is relevant, but even if this has led the testator to make a disposition for the benefit of that person to the exclusion of others, that alone is not sufficient to establish undue influence; there must also be proof of coercion which overpowered the volition of the testator (*Craig v Lamoureux* [1920] AC 349).

In contractual and other transactions, if the parties are, at the time of the transaction, in a confidential relationship with each other, undue influence is presumed. In *Powell v Powell* [1900] 1 Ch 243, Farwell J said, "The mere existence of the fiduciary relation raises a presumption and must be rebutted by the donee".

These fiduciary relationships include those of a parent and child, husband and wife, and solicitor and client. Such a relationship does not. however, raise a presumption of undue influence to invalidate a will because in most cases such a relationship is the very reason the testator provides a benefit; to show undue influence the circumstances would have to be such as to demonstrate that the mind of the testator was dominated. See *Re Howell* [1955] OWN 85, where a will prepared by a parish priest, leaving nearly all the testator's estate to the parish church, was held to have been the result of undue influence. Recent cases where the issue has arisen to overturn lifetime gifts and transfers similarly illustrate the type of evidence that would be necessary to make a challenge on the ground of undue influence.

A gift made in the lifetime of the deceased, on the other hand, may be challenged on the basis of the presumption of undue influence where a fiduciary relationship exists; or where, in the absence of such a relationship, there has been coercion, domination or pressure to set aside a gift made by the deceased during his lifetime. The purpose of such a challenge would be to benefit the deceased's estate or for compensation to be paid to the estate. Recent cases where such gifts have been successfully challenged illustrate the scope for bringing claims in appropriate cases, applying the decision of the House of Lords in *Royal Bank of Scotland v Etridge (No. 2)* [2001] UKHL 44, [2002] AC 773.

In *Bradshaw v Hardcastle* [2003] NLJ 124, the testator, who was terminally ill, transferred his home into the joint names of himself and his wife, to whom he had been married for only three years. Three days before his death he executed a will leaving his estate to his daughter, and at the same time made a signed statement that he had made the transfer to the wife under duress. The daughter applied to set aside the transfer to the wife. Evidence was available which proved that the wife had, throughout the marriage, sought to have the property transferred into her name and that the testator had sought legal advice on the subject on several occasions. The court found, on the evidence, that the wife had conducted a campaign of harassment which was described as "nothing short of physical violence to break her husband's resistance".

In *Hammond v Osborn* [2002] EWCA Civ 885, the claim was brought by H, who was the cousin of P, the donor, against O, who was a neighbour of the donor and to whom P had made a gift of £297,005, which represented ninety per cent of his liquid assets and exposed him to a substantial tax liability. P was elderly and in poor health. P had not received any form of advice relating to the nature and effect of the gift. O's case was that, to rebut the presumption of undue influence, it was sufficient for her to show that her conduct was unimpeachable and that she had not done anything which raised any suspicion. It was held that the presumption could be rebutted only by the donee proving that the gift had been made after full, free and informed thought by the donor.

In *Jennings v Cairns* [2003] WTLR 959, the residual beneficiaries of their aunt's estate sought an order that their cousin C, the other residual beneficiary and executrix of the will, should make compensation to the estate on the ground that certain lifetime gifts made by the aunt to C had been procured by C's undue influence. C had assisted her aunt to manage her home and had provided practical assistance for many years. When the aunt suffered a stroke, C managed her affairs under an unregistered enduring power of attorney. At the time of the aunt's death very little remained of the capital of £300,000, which she had had when she made her will. The aunt had given £35,000 to C to enable her to buy out a share in a property. She had also benefited a trust set up for C's children by making a gift of £170,000. It was held that the aunt's vulnerability and dependence on C gave rise to a relationship of which C had the opportunity to take unfair advantage. Although the aunt's affection for C provided some explanation for her generosity towards C, the aunt had never been independently advised, particularly as to the conflict between her wish to be able to revoke the benefit under the settlement if necessary, and the aim of reducing liability to inheritance tax. C's husband had also misdirected her as to the nature of the trust established for the benefit of the children. The deceased had therefore not entered into the transaction after free and informed thought and C was directed to compensate the estate.

In *Pesticcio v Huet & Others* (2003) 73 BMLR 57, a deed of gift made by the donor in favour of her sister, in whom the donor had placed trust and confidence, was set aside even though the donor's solicitor gave evidence. It was found that the solicitor had failed to distinguish between the interests of the donor and those of the donee.

In *Williams v Williams* [2003] All ER (D) 403, the donor was under disability. He could not read, write or cope on his own. His brother and his wife persuaded the donor to relinquish one half share in his inherited house to them; they then moved out of their council accommodation and into the house to look after the donor. The discussion relating to the transaction was conducted by the solicitor in the presence of the donor's brother. The donor's disabilities were not brought to the attention of the solicitor, who had also failed to read his predecessor's file which contained information about the donor's disability. The correspondence between the donor and the solicitor was therefore being read to the donor by someone, and in the circumstances that could only have been the brother and his wife. The court found that the donee had not rebutted the presumption of undue influence.

In *Padgham v Rochelle* [2002] WTLR 1483, the beneficiaries under a will applied for an order setting aside an agreement that had been made between the deceased and the deceased's son; the son was also the deceased's executor and trustee. In the will, farm property had been left to the beneficiaries subject to a trust for sale, but five years after the deceased's death no steps had been taken to sell the property. The son claimed entitlement to an agricultural tenancy of part of the property pursuant to an agreement made by the deceased shortly before his death. The beneficiaries challenged the agreement on the ground of undue influence. The deceased had not had the benefit of independent advice and had not been given any explanation of the effect the transaction would have on the value of the property or on the dispositions he had made under his will. At the time the agreement was made the deceased was very old. As a result of the transaction the value of the land would have been substantially reduced, thereby reducing the value of the deceased's estate and the testamentary gifts to the beneficiaries under the will. As in the case of *Hammond v Osborn* (above) there was no evidence that the son had consciously sought to take advantage of the deceased, but the transaction was one which was highly advantageous to him and had no advantages at all for the deceased and could not otherwise be explained. Had the deceased sought advice, the agreement would have provided for a tenancy for a fixed term at a fixed rent with no provision for rent review. In the circumstances it was held that the son had not discharged the burden of showing that the agreement had been made as a result of free and independent advice and the exercise by the deceased of his free and independent will. The agreement was set aside and an order for sale was granted.

Fraud

As in the case of undue influence, a will, or a gift in a will, made as a result of fraud will not be admitted to probate. Where fraud is alleged it must be shown that the testator was misled into doing what he did. In probate proceedings fraud usually takes the form of false representations concerning a person's character or conduct with a view to inducing the testator to revoke a gift to that person, or securing the exclusion of that person from benefit under the will.

Burden of Proof

Unlike the other instances where a will may be challenged, the legal burden of proof of undue influence or fraud lies upon the party who makes the challenge (*Boyse v Rossborough, Boyse v Colclough* (1856) 6 HLC 2; *Tyrell v Painton* [1894] P 151; *Craig v Lamoureux* [1920] AC 349). The person who makes the allegation must prove that the will, or such part of it as is in issue, was made as a result of the undue influence and/or fraud of another person. The person who asserts that the will is valid must show that there was no force or coercion used which deprived the testator of his judgment and free will, and that what the testator did was what he desired to do of his own free will (*Wingrove v Wingrove* (1886) 11 PD 81; see also *Fuller v Strum*, page 190).

The burden of proof was recently considered in *Re Good (Deceased), Carapeto v Good* [2002] WTLR 801, where the testator had left the bulk of her estate to her housekeeper and her husband. The court held that where the circumstances of the making of a will raised suspicion, it would not be enough to show that the testator had knowledge of the contents of the will and approved it and in all other respects the testator had testamentary capacity. On the facts, however, it was found that the testatrix was an intelligent, strong-minded person who had sought advice before executing her will. She was aware of the contents of the will and its financial effect on her family, as these had been fully explained to her.

Where the testator may have been influenced by immoral considerations this does not amount to undue influence. An example is where a mistress uses her influence to induce a man to make a will in her favour, provided that the will expresses the man's wishes (*Wingrove v Wingrove,* above).

Where a testator is sick, weak or feeble, proof of a relatively small amount of pressure may be sufficient to discharge the burden of proving undue influence.

The necessary particulars of the acts alleged must be specifically pleaded and care should be taken to ensure that the allegations can be supported by evidence, or that such evidence can be obtained.

Where a person prepares a will for a testator, under which he takes a benefit, that may cause suspicion to arise. The degree of suspicion will vary according to the circumstances of each case; see page 187.

Undue Influence and Want of Knowledge and Approval Distinguished

Where the validity of a will is challenged on the grounds of undue influence or fraud, the burden of proof lies on the person making the allegation and thereby attacking the will. In the case of a challenge on the ground of lack of knowledge and approval, the burden rests on the person who is seeking to propound the will. By reason of the nature of the challenge in each instance, the person who seeks to put forward the challenge may have little if any, information about the precise circumstances in which the will was made. In a case based on lack of knowledge and approval, however, it is sufficient to submit a plea that the circumstances as known are such as to raise suspicion, and so should excite the vigilance of the court and place upon the person who seeks to propound the will the onus of proving that the testator had the necessary capacity and that he knew, understood and approved the contents of the will.

The standard of proof required is the civil standard of proof – on the balance of probabilities. However, the more serious the allegations, the stronger must be the evidence to discharge that burden (see pages 188–190).

Evidence

Before making a challenge on the ground of undue influence, it is necessary to examine all the surrounding circumstances and to ascertain what evidence is available to support the allegation, and the nature and strength of such evidence. Evidence as to the physical and mental condition of the deceased may be relevant. It is particularly important to take a careful overview of the case, as detailed particulars will have to be pleaded. Consideration should also be given to pleading the case on the basis of lack of knowledge and approval, as an additional or alternative ground.

Where gifts or transfers were made or transactions entered into during the lifetime of the deceased, the nature of such gifts and transactions and the circumstances surrounding them should be examined carefully to ascertain whether they raise any suspicion which could bring the case within the equitable doctrine of undue influence to set aside the transaction or to provide a basis to claim some other form of relief, such as compensation to the estate. Where an action is brought in relation to lifetime gifts and transactions, it is for the donee to rebut the presumption of undue influence.

Chapter 20

Revocation of a Will

Introduction

A will may be challenged on the ground that it has been revoked; and a will may be revoked in a number of ways.

A will can always be revoked by the testator as long as he has testamentary capacity to do so. By its very nature, a will is revocable at any time, even by a testator who has made an earlier will which he expressed to be his last will and to be regarded as irrevocable. In order to establish that a will was revoked it is necessary to prove that the testator had the capacity to know what he was doing and to understand the effect of his actions, as would be the case to prove the validity of the original will (*Re Sabatini* (1970) 114 SJ 35).

Section 20 of the Wills Act 1837 provides that a will may be revoked by:

> "burning tearing or otherwise destroying the same by the testator, or by some other person in his presence and by his direction, with the intention of revoking the same".

For a revocation to be effective, therefore, there must have been an intention to revoke the will or part of it. A will cannot be revoked simply by reason of a change of circumstances. There must be some evidence of the testator's actions from which it can be established that the testator intended to revoke the will. Conversely, the evidence may suggest that the testator did not have such an intention, but, for example, that the apparent revocation was in fact an act of inadvertence or a mistake, as occurred in *Re Phelan* [1971] 3 All ER 1256 (see page 184); or that the will was destroyed inadvertently or because of drunkenness at the time (*In the Goods of Brassington* [1902] P 1).

Where a testator mutilates or destroys a will with the intention of making a new will but fails to carry out that intention, it does not necessarily follow that the mutilation or destruction is ineffective to revoke the existing will. The revocation would be ineffective only where it appeared that, in mutilating or destroying the will, the testator's intention was that the revocation would take effect only when he executed a new will.

A testator may voluntarily revoke his will in three ways, namely by:

(a) a subsequent will;

(b) destruction;
(c) conditional revocation.

A will may also be revoked on marriage, or on the annulment or dissolution of marriage.

Revocation by a Subsequent Will or Codicil

To effect a valid and effective revocation, the instrument which purports to revoke an earlier will must be executed in the same manner as a will. A will may be revoked by executing a subsequent will or codicil which expressly revokes the earlier will or wills (Wills Act, section 20). It is usual to insert a revocation clause in a will, but the presence of such a clause is not conclusive evidence that the testator intended thereby to revoke his previous testamentary disposition (see *Re Phelan*, above, and *Re Wayland (Deceased)* [1951] WN 604, [1951] 2 All ER 1041).

The testator may, by a subsequent instrument, revoke the whole of a will, or part only of the will. The extent of the revocation depends on the intention expressed by the testator at the time of revocation (see *Re Finnemore*, page 175). In *Re Lawrence's Will Trusts, Public Trustee v Lawrence* [1972] Ch 418, [1971] 3 WLR 188, [1971] 3 All ER 433, the testator made a will in August 1934, in which he made provision for his employee, Helen Irene Humphreys. In July 1935 the testator executed a codicil in the following terms:

> "Whereas Helen Irene Humphreys in the said will mentioned has left my service I hereby revoke the bequests of a legacy and annuity and all other benefits given to her by the will and I direct that in all respects my said will shall be construed as if the bequests to Helen Irene Humphreys had not been made."

It was held that where a codicil contained not only words of revocation but also superadded words of construction susceptible of being read as relating to the same subject-matter, directing the will to be construed in a particular way, then *prima facie* those superadded words would be restrictively construed and the court would lean towards reading them as doing no more than reinforcing the words of revocation. The codicil directed that the will was to be construed as if certain bequests had not been made; the hypothesis was directed not to the will at large but to the bequests in particular, and this provided support for the view that the hypothesis should not be read as affecting anything save those bequests. The codicil should be read as if it did no more than remove from the will all provisions for the benefit of Helen Irene Humphreys without affecting the rest of the will.

Where it is suggested that a later will revoked an earlier one but the later will cannot be produced, the person making the assertion will have to prove, by evidence which is convincing and conclusive, that the later will contained a revocation clause.

Where a later will does not contain a revocation clause but makes dispositions in clear terms dealing with the testator's estate in its entirety, it may have the effect of revoking any earlier will. Where the later will does not deal with the testator's entire estate, the language used in the subsequent will determines whether it provides sufficient proof of the testator's intention concerning revocation. Where a will does not contain a revocation clause or any words to suggest revocation, and its provisions are inconsistent with an earlier will or a codicil, it is a matter of construction which, if any, of the wills should be admitted. In appropriate cases two or more wills may be read distributively in order to give effect to the intention of the testator (*Re Finnemore (Deceased)* (above); see also *Lemage v Goodban* (1865) LR 1 P&D 57).

Revocation by Destruction

Section 20 of the Wills Act 1837 provides that a will may be revoked by:

> "burning tearing or otherwise destroying the same by the testator, or by some other person in his presence and by his direction, with the intention of revoking the same".

The section refers to two specific ways in which a will may be destroyed, but provides for some other method to be used. Applying the *ejusdem generis* principle of construction, this must mean destruction by means similar to those referred to and therefore no other means, such as striking out the document, would suffice.

There are thus two elements to effect an effective revocation, namely the act of destruction and the mental element of intention to revoke. The intention of the testator may be proved by his act and anything expressed by him at the time, or it may be inferred from the surrounding circumstances. Statements or declarations made by the testator may be relied on to prove the case for or against revocation.

The destruction need not be complete as long as the evidence establishes that what was destroyed formed the material part of the disposition, or the evidence establishes that the testator could not have intended what remains to have any effect. In *Re Adams (Deceased)* [1990] Ch 601, [2000] 2 WLR 924, [1990] 2 All ER 97, the testatrix had made a will after obtaining advice from her solicitors. They retained the will. Subsequently she instructed them to destroy the will, but they returned it to her for destruction. On her death the will was found. It had been scribbled on with a ballpoint pen but the scribbling and the obliteration varied. The attestation clause and the signatures of the testatrix and the witnesses were so heavily obliterated that it was impossible to read them. The executors of the will, who were also the beneficiaries under the will, applied to admit the will for probate. The application was refused. It was held that where a material part of a will was obliterated to such an extent that that part of the will was not apparent to experts to decipher it without physically interfering with the document, the court would treat the document as having been revoked for the purposes of and within the meaning of section 20; since the signature had been destroyed, a material part of the will had been destroyed and it could not be admitted to probate.

Where a will has been partially destroyed, only that part which has been destroyed is revoked. In *Re Everest (Deceased)* [1975] Fam 44, [1975] 2 WLR 333, [1975] 1 All ER 672, the testator executed his will and deposited it at his bank. He later withdrew it to alter some of the provisions. Two days after his death his widow found the will. The lower half of the first page had been cut away. In the will the testator gave certain chattels to his widow for life, with directions that after her death they should form part of his residuary estate. He bequeathed his real estate and the residue of his personal estate to the bank on certain trusts. The trusts could not be identified because they had been set out in the part that had been cut away. In all other respects the will was complete and properly executed. It was held that the mutilation was not such as to give rise to an inference that the testator intended to revoke his will in its entirety. The inference was drawn that the testator had either intended his widow to inherit as on intestacy or that some other provision should be substituted for those which had been cut away. Although there was no evidence as to the nature of the trust which he set up, the court found that there was sufficient remaining of the will to indicate that he intended that what remained of the will should be effective. The court found that, in those circumstances, it would be wrong to refuse to give effect to his wishes in so far as they were determinable.

If a will cannot be found after the testator's death it is presumed that he destroyed it with the intention of revoking it, but the presumption may be rebutted by clear and convincing evidence (*Re Davies, Panton v Jones, The Times* 23 May 1978).

If a will has been destroyed, but the intention to revoke it cannot be proved, the will can be proved by producing a copy, or by some other evidence (*Sugden v Lord St. Leonards* (1876) 1 PD 154).

It is possible for a third party to revoke a testator's will by destruction, provided it is destroyed in the presence of the testator and by his direction. (Wills Act 1837, section 20). If the testator is not present at the time of destruction, the destruction is ineffective even though it takes place by the direction of the testator. Subsequent ratification by the testator of an unauthorised destruction does not revoke the will (*Gill v Gill* [1909] P 157).

Conditional Revocation

If a testator revokes his will conditionally, the will remains in effect until the condition has been satisfied. Where, however, the condition relates to another will of the testator and depends upon that will being valid, then even if that will is not valid, the revocation is not effective. This type of conditional revocation is known as "dependent relative revocation". The same doctrine applies where a testator destroys a will in the mistaken belief that its revocation will have the effect of reviving an earlier will; and where a testator destroys a will with the intention of making a new will but does not in fact make a new will, or makes an ineffective new will.

Where a testator has obliterated the amount of a legacy, or substituted a donee, or obliterated some words, it may be possible to infer that the testator did not intend to revoke the original, unless the substituted words were effective, in which case the doctrine applies and evidence would be admitted to show what the original words were (*Re Itter, Dedman v Godfrey* [1950] P 130, [1950] 1 All ER 68). Much depends on the circumstances and the evidence available as to the testator's intention. The court would need to be satisfied that the testator did not intend to revoke the original will except conditionally. See also *Re Finnemore*, page 175.

Revocation by Marriage

The Wills Act 1837, section 18, as amended, makes provisions relating to revocation of a will by reason of marriage. It provides:

"(1) Subject to subsection (2) and (4) below a will shall be revoked by the testator's marriage.

(2) A disposition in a will in exercise of a power of appointment shall take effect notwithstanding the testator's subsequent marriage unless the property so appointed would in default of appointment pass to his personal representatives.

(3) Where it appears from a will that at the time it was made the testator was expecting to be married to a particular person and that he intended that the will should not be revoked by the marriage, the will shall not be revoked by his marriage to that person.

(4) Where it appears from a will that at the time it was made the testator was expecting to be married to a particular person and that he intended that a disposition in the will should not be revoked by his marriage to that person–

(a) the disposition shall take effect notwithstanding the marriage;

(b) any other disposition in the will shall take effect also, unless it appears from the will that the testator intended the disposition to be revoked by the marriage."

A will is therefore revoked on the marriage of the testator unless any of the exceptions set out in the section applies. The section operates even if the marriage is voidable under the Matrimonial Causes Act 1973 (section 12) as amended. In *Re Roberts (Deceased)* [1978] 1 WLR 653, [1978] 3 All ER 225 (CA), the deceased made a will in March 1973 when he was aged sixty. John Herbert Roberts, the defendant ("D") was a beneficiary under the will.

In October 1974 the testator went through a ceremony of marriage with the claimant. After his death in March 1976, the claimant applied for letters of administration on the ground that the deceased had died intestate because, by going through the marriage the will was revoked by reason of the provision of section 18 of the Wills Act 1837. D alleged that the marriage was void as the deceased was suffering from senile dementia and other mental illness at the time of the marriage and did not have the necessary mental capacity to consent to it; since there was no valid marriage the section did not apply. It was held that the effect of the provisions of the Matrimonial Causes Act 1973 was to make the marriage voidable and not void. A voidable marriage had the effect of revoking an earlier will of the testator whether or not the marriage was annulled because the annulment was not retrospective in effect.

A will made in exercise of a power of appointment takes effect notwithstanding the testator's subsequent marriage, unless the property so appointed would, in default of appointment, pass to the testator's personal representatives.

Where a will was made on or after 1 January 1983 in contemplation of marriage to a particular person, and the testator intended that the will should not be revoked by that marriage, the will is not revoked by marriage to that person. Where the testator was expecting to be married to a particular person and intended that the disposition in the will should not be revoked by his marriage to that person, then the disposition takes effect notwithstanding the marriage. Any other disposition in the will takes effect unless it appears that the testator intended the disposition to be revoked by the marriage.

Wills made prior to I January 1983 are still governed by the Wills Act 1837 section 18 in its original form and the Law of Property Act 1925, section 177.

The Law Reform (Succession) Act 1995 amended the Wills Act 1837 by inserting section 18A in respect of testators dying on or after 1 January 1996. The amended section provides that where a testator's marriage is dissolved or annulled, any provision in his will which appoints his former spouse as an executor or trustee, or which confers a power of appointment upon him or her, takes effect as if the former spouse had died on the date on which the marriage is dissolved or annulled, unless the will shows a contrary intention. Any property, or interest in property, which is devised or bequeathed to the former spouse passes as if the former spouse had died on the date on which the marriage is dissolved or annulled, unless a contrary intention appears in the will (section 18A(1)(a) and (b)). Subsection (2) however, reserves the former spouse's right to apply for financial provision under the Inheritance (Provision for Family and Dependants) Act 1975 (see Chapter 3).

Chapter 21

Contracts Relating to Wills

Introduction

English law gives a testator the freedom to dispose of his assets as he wishes. The statutory inroads that have been made in relation to this freedom are discussed in Part I. Besides those statutory restrictions, the testator's freedom to dispose of his assets as he wishes may be restricted if he himself enters into a legally binding agreement. A testator may during his lifetime, by contract, personally bind himself and his personal representatives regarding the contents of his will or the devolution of his estate on his intestacy. Where a testator enters into such a contract and it is valid, his personal representatives are obliged to give effect to the agreement at the expense of the beneficiaries under the will or on the testator's intestacy, but there must be a binding agreement by the testator to dispose of his property in a certain way.

The only exception to this rule is in respect of a person who comes within the categories of person entitled to make a claim for an order for financial provision under section 2 of the Inheritance (Provision for Family and Dependants) Act 1975, who applies for an order under section 11 of the 1975 Act. See Chapter 3.

Binding Contract

Leaving aside the provisions of section 11 of the 1975 Act, a testamentary disposition made as a result of a contract may be challenged on the basis that it does not constitute a binding agreement under which the deceased agreed to dispose of property. For the agreement to be binding, certain preconditions must be met. Thus, a claimant pursuant to such an agreement must be able to prove, firstly, that there was a binding agreement in law and not a mere statement of intention or representation made by the deceased. Secondly he must be able to establish with certainty what the subject matter of the gift was to be, and that any formalities relating to the transfer of the property had been completed.

The agreement

For a binding contract to be created there must be an offer and acceptance, accompanied by consideration. The agreement may take the form of a covenant, that is, an agreement under seal. A mere statement or representation made by the deceased, indicating his intention to do something in the future, is not enough. There must be proof that, on the basis of the representation made, the claimant acted to his detriment with the knowledge of the deceased; or that as a result of the representation made and the consequent conduct of both a trust arose. Whether a binding agreement can be implied from conduct depends on the circumstances of the case. Vague statements will not suffice. For example, where a testator made a statement that he had made a will leaving his property equally among his children, this did not amount to a binding agreement (*Re Allen, Hincks v Allen* [1880] 49 LJ Ch 553).

The following are some of the cases where a contract was proved. In *Synge v Synge* (1894) 1 QB 466, the testator, in order to induce a woman to marry him, made a proposal to her that he would leave her his house and land.

In *Re Edwards, Macadam v Wright* [1958] Ch 168, [1957] 3 WLR 131, [1957] 2 All ER 465, the testatrix made a will in which she provided that a named property and the residue of her estate were to be divided between seven named relatives, including her sister. A few months later she entered into an agreement with her sister, the claimant, that if she gave up the tenancy of her accommodation to come and live with the deceased and look after her, the sister would live there rent-free during their joint lives and she would leave the house to her by her will. On the basis of the oral agreement the sister gave up her tenancy and went to live with and look after the testatrix. The testatrix did not vary her will to accord with the agreement. It was held that there was a binding agreement for which valuable consideration was given, and that the testatrix had held the property as bare trustee.

In *Schaefer v Schuhmann* [1972] AC 572, [1972] 2 WLR 481, [1972] 1 All ER 621, by his will the testator gave his four daughters legacies and left the residue of his estate to be shared equally between his three sons. In 1966 he purchased a house and, as he was in poor health, in May 1966 he engaged a housekeeper to keep house for him at a weekly wage of £12. In June 1966 he instructed his solicitors to prepare a codicil to his will providing for the house in which he was living and its contents to be devised to his housekeeper "if she should still be employed by me as a housekeeper at the date of my death". On 28 June he received the codicil and asked the housekeeper to read it to him as his eyesight was poor, and he then executed the codicil on the same day. Thereafter he did not pay any wages to the housekeeper and told her that he did not propose to pay her any wages as he had left the house to her. She was still employed by him when he died. The court found that there was a contract between the deceased and the housekeeper.

Where the agreement relates to land it must comply with the provisions of the Law of Property (Miscellaneous Provisions) Act 1989.

Where the deceased enters into an ante-nuptial agreement with a woman and subsequently marries her, but then makes a will otherwise than in accordance with the agreement, the agreement can be enforced; the will, in so far as it makes provisions otherwise than in accordance with the agreement, will be considered void (*Haque v Haque (No 2)* [1963] WALR 15).

In *Zamet v Hyman* [1961] 1 WLR 1442, [1961] 3 All ER 933, a woman was induced by her fiancé to execute a deed giving up her rights to make a claim against his estate on his death, in consideration of a covenant by him that he would give her £600 on his death. The couple were married and the husband died intestate. It was held that the deed was unenforceable, as the woman had executed it without having the benefit of any advice as to her rights, nor any knowledge of the extent of the deceased's estate or of what she was agreeing to give up.

Where a binding, enforceable agreement is established, the claimant's rights arise under the agreement independently of any will and can be enforced in the same way as any contract. Where the covenantor, by his actions during his lifetime, made it clear that he was in breach of the agreement, or it is clear that by his actions that he was making it impossible for him to carry out his part of the bargain, the covenantee can enforce the agreement in the lifetime of the covenantor. For example, where the agreement is to devise specific property which the covenantor then sells in his lifetime, the covenantee can treat this as a repudiation of the contract and enforce the agreement. Where the property has not yet been disposed of to a third party for valuable consideration, without notice, the covenantee can apply for a declaration of rights and an injunction forbidding the covenantor from disposing of, transferring or otherwise dealing with the property in any way during his lifetime. Another possible route for relief is to seek enforcement on the basis of the principle of "unjust enrichment".

Where the issue arises on the death of the covenantor, the agreement may be enforced against the estate on the same basis as if the claim had been made in the lifetime of the covenantor, requiring the personal representatives to convey the property so as to give effect to the agreement.

Subject matter

As in the case of a will, the subject matter of the agreement must be ascertainable by description or otherwise. Where a sum of money is in issue the amount must be clearly stated or be capable of calculation. Where the subject matter is specific real property it must be identified. Vague terms such as "to make ample provision" (*MacPhail v Torrance* (1909) 25 TLR 810) are unenforceable for uncertainty.

Proprietary Estoppel

The second way in which a testator's freedom to dispose of his assets may be restricted arises under the doctrine of proprietary estoppel. The doctrine is based on the equitable conduct of a party. As an equitable remedy it is both wide and flexible. For the doctrine to apply the claimant must show that:

(a) he has acted to his detriment;
(b) the defendant acquiesced in the conduct;
(c) the defendant encouraged the claimant in that conduct;
(d) the defendant promised or made representations as to his future conduct which led the claimant to believe that he would not insist on his legal rights;
(e) that, having regard to the above, the defendant's conduct is unconscionable.

The doctrine applies in situations where a person is encouraged to act to his detriment by representations made or encouragement given by another, so that it would be unconscionable for that other to insist on his strict legal rights. It can also arise where a person has acted to his detriment on the faith of a belief, which was known to and encouraged by the other person, that he either has or is going to be given rights over the other person's property. In such a case the second person cannot insist on his legal rights if to do so would be inconsistent with the first person's belief.

The doctrine applies to rights over land and other forms of property and assets.

The preconditions

Four conditions need to be satisfied for the doctrine to apply:

(1) The claimant must show that he has acted to his detriment either in money or money's worth or that he has otherwise acted so as to prejudice himself or to his detriment (*Greasley v Cooke* [1980] 1 WLR 1306; [1980] 3 All ER 710).

The most common cases are where the claimant has provided money, for example by paying the mortgage or carrying out repairs to property. The "detriment" is not, however, limited or restricted to monetary detriment. It can arise where the claimant worked for the third party without payment and became his mistress (*Pascoe v Turner* [1979] 1 WLR 431; *Greasley v Cooke*, above, and see the cases mentioned on pages 82–83).

(2) The claimant must have acted in the belief either that he already owned sufficient interest in the property to justify the expenditure, or that he would obtain such an interest.

In relation to a will, the facts will be scrutinised against the ordinary presumption that such an intention is subject to change. In *Gillett v Holt & Another*, Mr Gillett ("Gillet") began to work for Mr Holt ("Holt") on Holt's farm and continued in the employment until 1995. Holt had, over the years, indicated to Gillett that he intended to leave the bulk of his estate to Gillett. He had also made known that intention to Gillett and gave effect to it in wills executed by him. In 1995 their relationship broke down and Holt made a new will in favour of a Mr Wood. Gillett brought an action against Holt and Wood, claiming that Holt owed him an obligation based on the doctrine of proprietary estoppel to bequeath the bulk of his estate to him and that he had devoted his entire working life to Holt's service in the belief, fostered and encouraged by Holt, that he would inherit his estate including the farm business which he managed for Holt until 1995. In rejecting the claim, the court held that the overriding principle of the doctrine in the context of an alleged promise to make a will was that the testator should be held to his representation only if it would be unconscionable for him to go back on it. Although a binding contract in law was not necessary, an estoppel could be founded on an agreement in principle or:

> "a mere expectation created or encouraged by the party alleged to be bound, in reliance on which the other party had acted to his detriment … Further, in the application of the principle to statements about the intended contents of a will, the facts must be looked at against the ordinary presumption that such intentions are subject to change. It may be easier to infer a fixed intent when the subject matter is a particular property, which the plaintiff has been allowed to enjoy in return for services, than in relation to a whole estate. In any event, the plaintiff needs to show words or conduct by the prospective testator which go beyond mere statements of intention, and which, having regard to all the circumstances, he can reasonably claim to have regarded as amounting to an irrevocable promise by the prospective testator as to how his estate would be disposed of."
>
> (*per* Carnworth J.)

However, the Court of Appeal, in allowing Holt's appeal, held on the facts that:

- The doctrine of estoppel could not be treated as subdivided into three or four watertight compartments.
- The quality of assurances may influence the issue of reliance; that reliance and detriment are often intertwined; and that whether there is a distinct need for a "mutual understanding" may depend on how the other elements of the doctrine are formulated and understood.
- The overwhelming weight of authority shows that detriment is required, but they also show that detriment is not a narrow or technical concept. "Detriment need not consist of the expenditure of money or other quantifiable financial detriment so long as it is something substantial. Whether the detriment is sufficiently substantial must be approached as part of a broad enquiry as to whether repudiation of an assurance is or is

not unconscionable in all the circumstances and whether it would be unjust or inequitable to allow the assurance to be disregarded."

- There must be sufficient causal link between the assurance relied on and the detriment asserted.
- The issue of detriment must be judged at the moment when the person who given the assurance seeks to go back on it.
- The detriment alleged must be pleaded and proved

(*Gillett v Holt* [2001] Ch 210, [2000] 3 WLR 815, [2000] 2 All ER 289, in which the decision in *Taylor v Dickens* [1998] 1 FLR 806 was criticised).

In *Taylor v Dickens* the court had applied a stricter test – that the claimant had to show that the deceased had created a belief or expectation that the deceased would not withdraw from the agreement and that on the particular facts of the case there was no contract between the deceased and the claimant that she would not change her will. The claim was also refused because the agreement related to land and had not been made in writing. It is submitted that the court in *Taylor v Dickens* placed too much emphasis on procedural issues, at the expense of the substance and nature of the claim.

In *Jennings v Rice* [2002] EWCA Civ 159, [2002] WTLR 367, before her death, the deceased had been dependent on Jennings, who had worked as a gardener and handyman for her. From 1980 she had ceased paying him for his services, telling him that he would have her house and its contents, worth about £435,000, when she died. The deceased died intestate. Her estate was valued at £1.3 million. Jennings made a claim against the estate for the house and its contents on the basis of proprietary estoppel. Rice, the administrator of the estate, contended that the award should be proportionate to the detriment suffered by Jennings and his expectation. Jennings was awarded £200,000. He appealed. His appeal was dismissed. It was held that the duty of the court was neither to meet the claimant's expectations in full nor to award the minimum necessary. Proportionality between expectation and detriment was essential in deciding how to meet the claim based on equity and conscience.

(3) The claimant's belief must have been encouraged by the party who is alleged to be bound, as occurred in, for example, *Pascoe v Turner* [1979] 1 WLR 431, where a man assured his former mistress that the house in which they lived was hers.

Encouragement by the party alleged to be bound need not be active. It may be passive, for example, where the testator allows the person to act in the belief, thus encouraging him to continue in that belief (*Coombes v Smith* [1986] 1 WLR 808, [1987] 1 FLR 352).

Once it is shown that the defendant gave assurances or other encouragement to the claimant and the claimant suffers detriment, the court will infer that the detriment was suffered as a result of the encouragement. The burden of proof is on the defendant to show that the claimant's conduct was not induced by such assurances (*Greasley v Cooke* [1980] 1 WLR 1306).

(4) He who seeks equitable relief must come with clean hands, that is, the claimant can seek relief only if he has not himself acted unconscionably.

Effect of the doctrine

If the claimant is successful, the effect of the doctrine is only to place the claimant in the position he would have been in if the expectation encouraged by the defendant had been fulfilled.

The case of *Crabb v Arun District Council* [1976] Ch 179, [1975] 3 All ER 865 illustrates the application of the principles set out above. The case concerned the owner of five and a half acres of land near a public highway. He divided the land into two plots running from north to south, with two acres on the eastern side and three and a half on the western side. He developed the land adjoining the eastern boundary. Only the northern boundary of that plot had access to the highway. He made a new road on the developed two-acre plot connecting the back to the rear portions. After his death his executors obtained planning permission to develop the remaining land for housing which included a proposal to construct a new estate road running along the boundary between the two plots. It was thought at the time that one access would be sufficient because the two-acre plot was in one occupation. The road was the only access to the smaller plot as the previous access was to be closed. The executors then sold the two-acre plot to the claimant and agreed to erect a fence along the boundary line between the two plots which would allow access from the two-acre plot on to the proposed new road; gave a right of access at point A to the new road and a right of way along it to the highway. The executors sold the second plot of land three months later to the local authority, the defendants, but reserved the rights of access granted to the claimant. In the conveyance the local authority agreed to erect a fence along the boundary line save for a gap at point A. The claimant then decided to split his plot in two and sell them separately for separate use, but he recognised that he would need another access at point B. His plan was discussed with the defendant local authority and in particular at the meeting he explained that he would need access to the new road at another point (point B) to serve the southern portion. An agreement in principle was reached that the claimant would have access at points A and B so as to give access from the back portion on to the new estate road. In reaching the agreement the local authority's representative did not refer to any payment for the access. No formal agreement was drawn up, but the parties thereafter acted in the belief that the claimant had or would be granted such a right, because the local authority, when erecting a boundary fence, constructed gates at points A and B. The claimant sold the northern portion of his plot but, believing that he had access to the southern part at point B, he did not reserve any right of way over the northern plot. Three months later the local authority closed the access at point B and offered to grant access on payment of £3,000. Without any access to the southern part of his plot the land was useless.

The court found that the local authority was estopped from denying access by reason of the agreement reached at the meeting between the claimant and the local authority's representative, its subsequent conduct in erecting the boundary with a gate at point B at their expense, thus leading the claimant into the belief that he had the right of access, and its knowledge that the claimant intended to sell the two portions separately and would therefore need access at both points.

The judgment of Lord Cairns in *Hughes v Metropolitan Railway Co* (1877) 2 App Cas 439, referred to in the judgment of Lord Denning MR in *Crabb v Arun DC*, sets out the principles of the doctrine.

In cases against the estate of a testator, in giving effect to the doctrine of estoppel, the court will have regard to the rights of other beneficiaries (*Dodsworth v Dodsworth* (1973) 228 EG 115).

Mutual Wills

Where two persons, usually husband and wife, make an arrangement as to the disposal of their property after death, and that arrangement or agreement is intended to be binding, and they execute mutual wills in pursuance of that arrangement or agreement, then if one person dies having complied with the arrangement, the implied promise of the survivor will hold good as creating a trust for the beneficiaries named in the will. But it must be proved by independent evidence that an agreement had been reached by the deceased and the survivor, not merely to make identical wills, but to dispose of property in a particular way, thus giving rise to a contract between them.

If the survivor subsequently revokes or alters his will or testamentary disposition in breach of the arrangement or agreement, the survivor's personal representatives hold the property on constructive trust for the person(s) intended to benefit under the mutual agreement. The principle applies even where the agreement was to make wills leaving their respective properties to a third party, and not to each other.

This doctrine is illustrated in *Re Dale (Deceased), Proctor v Dale* [1994] Ch 31, [1993] 4 All ER 129, where Mr and Mrs Dale made identical wills which contained a bequest of all real and personal property in favour of their son and daughter in equal shares or the survivor of them, and appointed them as executors. Mr Dale died without altering his will. The value of his estate was £18,500. About two years after his death Mrs Dale made a new will in which she revoked all former wills and testamentary dispositions. She appointed her son executor of her will. She gave her daughter a legacy of £300 and gave her son all the remainder of her property. Just over four months later Mrs Dale died. Her net estate was valued at about £19,000. The daughter issued a claim alleging that there was an agreement between her parents as to the disposition of their estates; that it was intended by both to be binding and irrevocable; that they both made their original wills in pursuance of and in consideration of that agreement; that, on the death of Mr Dale, Mrs Dale became bound in equity to give effect to the agreement; and that the son therefore held the estate as trustee for her and himself in equal shares. It was held that the performance of the promise by Mr Dale was sufficient consideration for the agreement and sufficient detriment to constitute consideration. Failure by the survivor to carry out his or her part of the bargain amounts to a fraud, not only when the survivor has benefited under the deceased's will, but even if the beneficiaries are third parties and the personal representatives held the property on trust.

For the constructive trusts to arise:

(a) the arrangement between the parties must be more than an agreement to make wills in identical terms;
(b) there must be evidence to establish a contract not to revoke the will or to depart from the arrangements after the first of the parties dies (see *Birch v Curtis* [2002] EWHC 1158, [2002] WTLR 965; and *Edell v Sitzer* [2001-02] 4 ITELR 149;
(c) the will must clearly identify the extent to which the survivor's property, and the property passing from the deceased to the survivor, is bound by the mutual agreement (*Re Green, Lindner v Green* [1951] Ch 148, [1950] 2 All ER 913).

In some circumstances a "floating trust" may be created under which the intention is that the survivor, during his life, may deal as absolute owner with the deceased's property, and on his death bequeath the residue in accordance with the agreement.

Where parties have agreed to make mutual wills, they can by agreement release each other from the obligation. Either may revoke his will provided notice of revocation is given to the other party. See *Low v Perpetual Trustees Ltd* [1995] 14 WAR 35, where the wife suffered from senile dementia and the personal representatives of her husband, who was the first to die and who had made a new will, were found to hold his estate upon trust to perform the terms of the mutual wills.

It would seem that where the will of the first to die is not revoked, but is varied by a codicil, the survivor is not bound by the agreement (*Re Hobley (Deceased), The Times,* 16 June 1997).

The standard of proof required to establish the existence of mutual wills is the civil standard of proof, that is, on the balance of probabilities, but it has been held that such claims call for careful scrutiny by the court (*Lewis v Cotton* [2001] WTLR 1117, CA (NZ)). See also page 188 *et seq*.

Donatio Mortis Causa

In *Re Beaumont, Beaumont v Ewbank* [1902] 1 Ch 889 at 892, Buckley J described *donatio mortis causa* as a singular form of gift, which is of amphibious nature, being a gift which is neither entirely *inter vivos* nor testamentary. *Donatio mortis causa* is the delivery of property *inter vivos* to a donee, subject to the express or implied condition that the donee is to have an absolute right to the property only when the donor dies. The right to enforce the title lies against the executors of the estate.

For an effective *donatio mortis causa* to arise four conditions must be satisfied. These are discussed below.

Gift in contemplation of death

To be valid, the gift must have been made in contemplation of the donor's death. The donor must contemplate death in the near future or believe death to be impending (*Re Craven's Estate, Lloyds Bank Ltd v Cockburn (No 1)* [1937] Ch 423). It is immaterial that death occurs from a cause different from that which the deceased contemplated (*Wilkes v Allington* [1931] 2 Ch 104, where the donor contemplated death from cancer but died of pneumonia). A gift made in contemplation of death by suicide, however, was held not to be valid (*Dudman, Dudman v Dudman* [1925] Ch 553).

A gift *donatio mortis causa* is usually made when the donor is ill and is expecting to die. It seems that a gift made in contemplation of the risk of imminent air travel is not sufficient (*Thompson v Mechan* [1958] OR 357). The decision in *Thompson* was given when air travel was relatively safe. Having regard to the current risks from terrorists it is arguable that air travel now carries a real risk and different considerations should apply.

Gift to take effect on death

The gift must be made on condition, express or implied, that it is to take effect only on the donor's death. It must not be expressed to take effect in the future (*Treasury Solicitor v Lewis* [1900] 2 Ch 812; *Re Ward, Ward v Warwick* [1946] 2 All ER 206, (1946) 175 LT 284). The gift remains inchoate, and the donee's title incomplete, until the death of the donor. It is open to the donor to revoke a gift *donatio mortis causa* during his lifetime. Furthermore, when the contemplated risk ends, the gift is revoked automatically, as where the donor recovers from illness (*Agnew v Belfast Banking Co* [1896] 2 IR 204). The donor may revoke the gift by resuming control over the property or notifying the donee of revocation.

Delivery

Before death, the donor must make effective delivery of the subject matter of the gift (*Re Craven's Estate, Lloyds Bank Ltd v Cockburn,* above) or something representing it as in *Sen v Hedley* [1991] Ch 425, [1991] 2 WLR 1308, [1991] 2 All ER 636. In *Sen v Hedley,* the testator was the owner of a substantial property which was in a dilapidated condition. He was divorced and had no children. For many years he enjoyed a close relationship with the claimant and for ten years they cohabited, although at the time of his death they were living apart. Prior to his death he was admitted to hospital suffering from inoperable cancer of the pancreas. The claimant visited him and looked after his house. Three days before his death, and when they were alone, the claimant asked him what she should do with the house if anything should happen to him and he replied "the house is yours. You have the keys. They are in your bag. The deeds are in the steel box". He made similar remarks about the contents. The claimant found a bunch of keys in her bag after the deceased's death. The keys included the key for the steel box in which the title deeds to the house were kept. The deceased died intestate. The claimant succeeded because the conditions for a *donatio mortis causa* were satisfied; these included the indisputable evidence that the deceased had parted with dominion over the title deeds, thereby giving effective delivery. See also *Birch v Treasury Solicitor* [1951] Ch 298, [1950] 2 All ER 1198, where the handing over of a Post Office savings book was held to be sufficient delivery; and *Re Weston* [1902] 1 Ch 680, where the delivery was made two days after the donor had expressed his intention to make the gift.

There must be clear evidence that the donor intended to pass control over the property, and not mere physical possession of it. It is not enough that property is passed over for safe custody.

Delivery may be to the donee or his agent. Where the gift is intended for the benefit of two people, delivery may be to one donee personally and as agent for the second donee, as occurred in *Birch v Treasury Solicitor*, above. It is not necessary that delivery is made personally by the donor. It can be made by someone acting under his instructions (*Re Weston*, above and *Re Craven's Estate (No 1)*, above).

The following cases illustrate the nature of the acts which will be regarded as sufficient to make effective delivery. In *Re Lillingston, Pembery v Pembery* [1952] WN 338, [1952] 2 All ER 184, a testatrix wished to give to the donee her jewellery, some of which was in safe deposit. She handed over to the donee the key to one of the safe deposits, which contained the keys to the other safe deposits. It was held that the delivery of the one key was sufficient delivery.

In *Woodard v Woodard* [1995] 3 All ER 980, the claimant was the widow of the deceased and the sole beneficiary of his estate. Her claim against her son was for the proceeds of sale of a car owned by the deceased as an asset of the estate. The car had been sold shortly after the deceased's death. The son's defence was that the car had been given to him as an outright gift by the deceased a few days before he died. He was given leave to plead *donatio mortis causa* as an alternative. The son stated in evidence that had his father recovered from his illness he would have had the car back. Having regard to the circumstances in which the car keys had been delivered to the son, it was held that all the conditions for *donatio mortis causa* had been met and that the handing over of the keys was sufficient to indicate that the deceased had intended to part with control over the car to his son.

In *Re Wasserberg* [1915] 1 Ch 195, it was held that where the subject matter of the gift is a *chose in action*, delivery of a document which applies to the *chose* is sufficient delivery. Although in such cases the delivery of the document does not pass legal title the court will direct the personal representatives to perfect the gift.

Property capable of passing

The property must be capable of passing by *donatio mortis causa*. Anything which is transferable by delivery may be made the subject of a gift (see *Birch v Treasury Solicitor*, above; and *Re Beaumont*, above, where the delivery of a cheque was not regarded as sufficient, but, had the cheque been presented in the lifetime of the donor (*Rolls v Pearce* [1877] 5 Ch 730), or even after his death, there might have been a gift.

Where a claim is made for an order under section 2 of the Inheritance (Provision for Family and Dependants) Act 1975, any sum of money or property received by a person as *donatio mortis causa* is treated as part of the net estate of the deceased under section 8 of the 1975 Act; see page 113.

Chapter 22

Procedure

Introduction

In the vast majority of cases the validity of a will is not challenged in any way. In such cases the court's role is limited to issuing the grant of probate or letters of administration. This is know as non-contentious or common form probate. Where there are contentious matters relating to an application for a grant or the validity of a will, any claim made is known as a probate claim. In such cases any grant issued is a grant in solemn form.

Probate claims arise:

(a) where the validity of a will is challenged;
(b) in disputes relating to the interests of the parties;
(c) in actions for revocation.

Non-contentious probate matters are governed by the Non-Contentious Probate Rules 1987 (SI 1987 No 2024) as amended, and any application relating to such matters is assigned to the Family Division of the High Court.

Part 57 of the Civil Procedure Rules 1998 (SI 1998 No 3132 as amended, "CPR") and the Practice Directions thereunder apply to all contentious claims commenced after 15 October 2001. However, subject to Part 57 CPR, including the "overriding objective" of "enabling the court to deal with cases justly", the Pre-action Protocols apply generally to all contentious probate proceedings.

CPR rule 1.1(2) provides that dealing with a case justly includes, so far as practicable:

- ensuring that the parties are on an equal footing;
- saving expense;
- dealing with the case in ways which are proportionate to the amount of money involved, the importance of the case; the complexity of the issues, and the financial position of each party;
- ensuring that it is dealt with expeditiously and fairly;
- allotting to it an appropriate share of the court's resources, while taking into account the need to allot resources to other cases.

The court also has a duty to further the "overriding objective" by actively managing cases. Active management includes:

- encouraging the parties to co-operate with each other in the conduct

of the proceedings;
- identifying the issues at an early stage;
- deciding promptly which issues need full investigation and trial and accordingly disposing summarily of the others;
- deciding the order in which issues are to be resolved;
- encouraging the parties to use an alternative dispute resolution procedure if the court considers that appropriate, and facilitating the use of such procedure;
- helping the parties to settle the whole or part of the case;
- fixing timetables or otherwise controlling the progress of the case;
- considering whether the likely benefits of taking a particular step justify the cost of taking it;
- dealing with as many aspects of the case as it can on the same occasion;
- dealing with the case without the parties needing to attend at court;
- making use of technology; and
- giving directions to ensure that the trial of a case proceeds quickly and efficiently.

Probate claims are assigned to the Chancery Division of the High Court. If a claim under the Inheritance (Provision for Family and Dependants) Act 1975 is made, it can be dealt with in the same proceedings.

Although the county court has jurisdiction under the County Courts Act 1984, section 32, to deal with probate claims where the value of the net estate does not exceed £30,000 (County Courts Jurisdiction Order 1981, SI 1981 No 1123), very few claims are in practice brought in the county court. A probate claim may be brought in a county court only where there is a Chancery district registry, or in the Central London County Court.

All probate claims are allocated to the multi-track (CPR rule 57.2).

Caveats

Where there is any dispute as to the validity of a will or who is entitled to administer the estate, a caveat should be entered to ensure that the person lodging the caveat is informed of any application for the issue of a grant. A caveat should also be entered where time is required to obtain further information or evidence to:

(a) oppose proof of a will;
(b) obtain evidence to challenge the validity of a will;
(c) oppose the issue of the grant to the person entitled; or
(d) ascertain the eligibility of the person entitled under an intestacy.

Procedure

The Non-Contentious Probate Rules 1987, rule 44, set out the procedure to be followed. Any person wishing to enter a caveat, or a solicitor acting on his behalf, may enter a caveat by completing the prescribed form 3 in the appendix to the rules (see page 240). The caveat is entered by lodging the completed form, either personally or by post, in any registry or sub-registry, and paying the prescribed fee. An official acknowledgement of the entry of the caveat is provided by the registry. All caveats are entered into the registries' computer system.

Duration and renewal

Once entered, a caveat is effective for six months from the date of entry. This period may be extended by written application, which may be made by letter, to the registry or sub-registry where the caveat was entered, within the last month of the period of six months. The application should request an extension for six months and must be accompanied by the prescribed fee. Further extensions may be applied for in the same way for periods up to six months, until the caveat is removed or a probate claim is issued in the Chancery Division (rule 44(3)). A caveat is removed by an application made on notice to a district judge or by consent.

If a probate action is commenced, the caveat remains in force until the claim has been determined.

Warnings

Upon receipt of an application for a grant, the registry or sub-registry at which the application is made must cause to be made a search of the national electronically monitored index. If a caveat has been entered, the registry to which the application is being made is notified of the caveat. The applicant is likewise notified of the caveat and the application for the grant is stayed.

The applicant for the grant, or any person having an interest in the estate, may issue a warning, in form 4 (see page 240), against the caveat; it must be issued at the Leeds District Probate Registry. The person giving the warning must state his interest in the estate of the deceased and require the caveator to give particulars of his interest within eight days (inclusive of the day of service) of service of the warning. Service may be effected by post, DX or FAX.

On service of the warning, the caveator has two options:

(a) to enter an appearance within eight days of service; or

(b) if the caveator has no contrary interest, but wishes to show cause against the sealing of a grant to that person, he must issue and serve a summons for directions within eight days of the service of the warning. See page 243 for a specimen form.

Entering an appearance

If the caveator has a contrary interest, he must, within eight days of service of the warning, enter an appearance in form 5 (see page 241), by lodging the form at the Leeds District Probate Registry (rule 44(10)). The appearance must show that the caveator has an interest contrary to that of the person applying for the grant, otherwise the entry of appearance will be refused by the court. An appearance may be entered after the prescribed eight days provided that the person serving the warning has not filed an affidavit of service (rule 44(12)).

If an appearance is entered within the eight days, no grant may issue, except to the caveator, without an order of the court.

If the caveator neither enters an appearance nor issues a summons for directions within the prescribed eight days, the person serving the warning may file an affidavit of service of the warning, and the caveat thereupon ceases to have effect. See page 242 for a form of affidavit of service of warning and non-receipt of summons for directions.

If an appearance has been entered, a stamped copy must be served immediately on the person who lodged the warning. If an appearance has been lodged and an agreement has not been reached between the parties, one of the parties may commence proceedings in the Chancery Division for the issues to be determined by the court.

Summons for directions

If the caveator has no contrary interest, but objects to the issue of the grant, he must issue and serve a summons for directions within eight days of service of the warning upon him (inclusive of the day of service). The summons may be issued after the prescribed eight days provided that the person serving the warning has not filed an affidavit of service of the warning.

If a summons for directions is issued (see page 241 for a specimen form), it is listed for hearing by a district judge at the Principal Registry, or a registrar at the district probate registry where the application for a grant is pending. The summons must be supported by an affidavit. At the hearing, if the court is not satisfied that the caveator has shown sufficient reason for his objections to the issue of a grant, it will direct that the caveat shall cease to have effect and that the application for the grant should proceed. The court may give such other directions as may be necessary relating to any further proceedings or the application for the grant.

Summons for discontinuance

Where an appearance to the warning has been entered and subsequently an agreement is reached, a summons for discontinuance should be issued for hearing before a district judge or registrar, as the case may be. The caveat remains in force once the summons for directions is issued, until the matter is disposed of by the court

Withdrawal of caveat

A caveat may be withdrawn at any time by the caveator. When a warning is issued the caveator must give notice of his withdrawal to the person who issued the warning. The caveat is withdrawn at the registry at which it was entered, but notice of withdrawal must be accompanied by the acknowledgement of receipt of the caveat issued by that registry. The Leeds District Probate Registry is notified and the grant is then issued. No fee is payable on an application to withdraw the caveat.

Parties

The claimant in a probate claim must have an interest in the estate of the deceased. The claimant is usually the executor of a will, or a beneficiary or other person who has an interest in the estate and seeks to challenge the validity of the will.

Any person who may be adversely affected by the claim should be made a defendant, but in any event, such persons should be given notice of the proceedings so that they may apply to be joined as parties to the claim. In any case of doubt, application should be made to the court for a direction. CPR Part 19 and CPR PD 57, paragraph 4.1 provide for the court to consider the question of joinder of parties and to give the necessary directions. Under CPR rule 19.8A and CPR PD 57, paragraph 4.1 the court may direct that notice of a claim be given to any person who may be affected by it. An application for such a direction should be made in accordance with CPR Part 23.

In a probate claim for the revocation of a grant of probate or letters of administration, every person who is entitled, or claims to be entitled, to administer the estate under that grant must be made a party to the claim (CPR rule 57.6 (1)).

Any person who may be affected by the court's decision in the probate proceedings may apply to the court under CPR rule 19.4 to be joined as a defendant to the proceedings.

Starting a Probate Claim

Place of issue

A probate claim must be commenced in accordance with the procedure set out in CPR Part 7 and CPR PD 57, paragraphs 2.1 and 7.2. These rules provide that the claim should be commenced by using a Part 7 claim form. The claimant must provide additional copies of the claim form for the court and for each defendant.

The claim form may be issued personally or it may be posted. On issue the claimant must pay the issuing fee of £120 as at May 2004. The claim must be issued out of:

(a) Chancery Chambers at the Royal Courts of Justice;
(b) one of the Chancery district registries;
(c) if the claim is suitable to be heard in the county court:
  (i) a county court in a place where there is also a Chancery district registry; or
  (ii) the Central London County Court.

Section 32 of the County Courts Act 1984 identifies which probate claims may be heard in the county court. There are Chancery district registries at Birmingham, Bristol, Cardiff, Leeds, Liverpool, Manchester, Newcastle-upon-Tyne and Preston.

Contents of the claim form

A probate claim form and all subsequent court documents relating to the claim must be marked at the top "In the estate of [name], deceased (Probate)" (CPR PD 57, paragraph 2.1). It must set out the names of the parties.

The claim form must contain a statement of the nature of the interest of the claimant and of each defendant in the estate of the deceased (CPR rule 57.7). If the party disputes another party's interest in the estate this must be set out in the statement of claim, with reasons.

If it is alleged that at the time when a will was executed the testator did not know of and approve its contents, particulars of the facts and matters relied on must be set out.

Where it is alleged that the will was not duly executed; or that at the time of execution of the will the testator did not have testamentary capacity; or that the execution of the will was obtained by undue influence or fraud, the allegation made and the particulars of the facts and matters relied upon must be fully pleaded (CPR rule 57.7(3) and (4)). For a specimen particulars of claim asserting undue influence, see page 246.

The claimant must also file the testamentary documents of the deceased person and written evidence of the testamentary documents. Where the action is for the revocation of a grant of probate or letters of administration, the claimant, if the grant was made to him, must lodge the grant made to him when the claim form is issued. If the grant is not lodged at the time of issue it must be lodged within seven days of issue of the claim form.

The court office

On issue, the court stamps all the copies of the claim form, one of which is marked as the original. If the claim is issued in a district registry, the court sends a notice to the Principal Registry of the Family Division requesting that all testamentary and other relevant documents in the Principal Registry be sent to the relevant office. Notice of the proceedings is also sent to every caveator whose caveat is in force, and every caveator whose caveat is entered after the commencement of the claim, in accordance with the Non-Contentious Probate Rules 1987, rule 45(1) and (2).

Service

Service may be effected by the court or by the claimant personally, by post, document exchange or FAX, in accordance with the provisions of CPR Part 6. Where a defendant is outside the jurisdiction, CPR rules 6.17 to 6.31 apply and care should be taken that those provisions are complied with.

Acknowledgement of Service and Defence

A defendant within the jurisdiction must file the appropriate form of acknowledgement of service with the court within twenty-eight days after service of the claim form. If the particulars of claim are not served at the same time as the claim form, the acknowledgement of service must be filed within twenty-eight days of receipt of the particulars of claim (CPR rule 57.4(2)).

Where the defendant is outside the jurisdiction and the claim form is served on him out of England and Wales under CPR rule 16.9, the period for filing an acknowledgement of service is fourteen days longer than the period set out in rule 6.22 or the practice direction supplementing section 3 of Part 6 (CPR rule 57.4(3)).

When the defendant acknowledges service, the defendant must also lodge with the court any testamentary document of the deceased which is in his possession or control, and must, in written evidence, describe any testamentary document of the deceased of which he has knowledge. If he does not have any such document, he must state that fact.

If any testamentary document of which the defendant has knowledge is not his possession or control, the defendant must give the name and address of the person who has such possession or control. If the defendant does not know the identity and location of the person in whose possession or control the document is, the defendant must state that fact (CPR rule 57.5(3)). CPR Part 57 PD provides a specimen form for the written evidence about the testamentary documents, and that form should be used. The form *must* be signed by the defendant personally (CPR Part 57 PD, paragraph 3.2), or, in the case of a child or a person under disability, by the litigation friend.

See page 243 for a specimen form of witness statement concerning testamentary documents. See pages 244–245 for sample forms of limited defence.

Inspection of Testamentary Documents

Except with the permission of the court, a party to a claim is not permitted to inspect the testamentary documents or the written evidence lodged or filed with the court by any other party until he himself has lodged his testamentary documents and filed his evidence. Where access to the documents is required, an application must be made to the court setting out the reason, for example that the documents are required for forensic examination.

Counterclaim

A defendant who wishes to make a claim or seek any remedy relating to the grant of probate or letters of administration must serve a counterclaim (a Part 20 claim) with his defence (CPR rule 57.8).

If the claimant fails to serve his particulars of claim, the defendant may, with the permission of the court, serve a counterclaim. In this event the action continues as if the counterclaim were the particulars of claim, and the defendant is then regarded as the claimant. If the defendant does not wish to raise any claim or seek any remedy, but simply wishes to exercise his right to test the validity of a will by cross-examining the attesting witnesses, he may give notice in his defence that he does not wish to raise any positive case (CPR rule 57.7(5)).

Particulars of Claim/Defence

The particulars of claim/defence and counterclaim must comply with CPR rule 16.4. which provides that the particulars of claim must include a concise statement of the facts on which the claimant relies. The defence must state which of the allegations in the particulars of case are admitted or denied by him, or that he is unable to admit or deny, and put the claimant to proof of them. Where any allegation is denied, reasons for so doing must be set out in the defence. The defendant must put forward his own version of events if it differs from that pleaded by the claimant (CPR rule 16.5(1) and (2)). Where undue influence and/or fraud is alleged, it is essential to plead the case as fully as is possible, with detailed particulars of all facts and matters relied on, with dates. The more serious the allegations, the higher the burden of proof. Where valuations are disputed the defence must state the reason for disputing them and, if he is able, he must give his own statement of the value (CPR rule 16.5(6)).

Failure to Acknowledge Service or File a Defence

Where any of several defendants does not file an acknowledgement of service or a defence, the claimant cannot, in a probate action, apply for default judgment (CPR rule 57.10(1)). In such a case, the claimant, provided the time for filing the acknowledgement has expired, may file written evidence of service on the defendant of the claim form and of the particulars of case, and seek to proceed with the claim as if the defendant had acknowledged service (CPR rule 57.10(2)).

Where no defendant acknowledges service or files a defence, the claimant may, after the time for filing the acknowledgement of service and defence has expired, apply to the court for an order either that the claim should be discontinued, or that the claim should proceed to trial (CPR rule 57.10(3)). The claimant must support such an application with written evidence of service of the claim form and the particulars of claim. Where such an application is made, the court may direct that the claim should proceed and that the hearing should take place on written evidence only. This allows the court to continue its supervisory role, including its role in approving any compromise and ensuring that every person who may be affected by the claim has had notice and consents to the proposals.

Discontinuance or Dismissal of a Claim

Under the provisions of CPR rule 57.11, the court has power to allow the claim to be discontinued or dismissed, on terms as to costs or otherwise, and to grant probate of the will or letters of administration to the person entitled to the grant. CPR Part 57 PD, paragraph 6.1 also provides that where the parties have agreed to settle a probate claim the court may:

(a) order the trial of the claim on written evidence, which will lead to a grant in solemn form;
(b) order that a claim be discontinued or dismissed under rule 57.11, which will lead to a grant in common form;
(c) pronounce for or against the validity of one or more will(s) under section 49 of the Administration of Justice Act 1985.

Extension of Time Limits

CPR rule 2.11 provides that the time limits specified by a rule or by the court may be varied by the written agreement of the parties, unless the rules or practice direction provide otherwise or the court orders otherwise. Where the court has listed a case management conference or a pre-trial directions hearing, or listed a case for a final hearing, the parties cannot agree to adjourn the hearing. Where it is sought to adjourn a listed hearing, the parties will have to apply to the court under CPR rule 28.4. Such an application must be supported by written evidence setting out good reasons for the application. The court may accede to the application subject to further directions and the listing of a review hearing.

Disclosure

Pre-action disclosure

As in other civil actions, in probate claims advantage can be taken of CPR rule 31.16 which provides for pre-action disclosure. The rule permits an application for disclosure to be made to the court. The application must be supported by written evidence, which should address the matters which the court is likely to take into consideration when determining the application. These include the following:

(a) whether the party against whom the disclosure is sought is likely to be a party to the subsequent proceedings;
(b) whether the applicant is also likely to be a party in those proceedings;
(c) whether the documents of which disclosure is sought are of a nature which, if the proceedings had been commenced, the respondent would be under a duty to disclose by way of standard disclosure;
(d) whether disclosure is desirable in order to dispose fairly of the anticipated proceedings, or to assist in resolving the dispute without

resort to proceedings and to save costs.

The application should specify the documents or class of documents of which disclosure is sought, and request a direction that the respondent should be required, when making the disclosure, to specify which documents are no longer in his control; to indicate what has happened to those documents; and for the respondent to provide inspection.

Disclosure under the Supreme Court Act 1981

Sections 122 and 123 of the Supreme Court Act 1981 make provision for a person who is interested in the estate of a deceased to apply to the court for an order that a document in the possession of another, which may be relevant to any issue in question, should be brought to court for examination, and for a *subpoena* to be issued against the person. Section 122 provides that:

(1) Where it appears that there are reasonable grounds for believing that any person has knowledge of any document which is or purports to be a testamentary document, the High Court may, whether or not any legal proceedings are pending, order him to attend for the purposes of being examined in open court.

(2) The court may–

(a) require any person who is before it in compliance with an order under subsection (b) to answer any question relating to the document concerned; and

(b) if appropriate, order him to bring in the document in such manner as the court may direct."

Any person who, having been required by the court to do so under this section, fails to attend for examination, answer any question or bring in any document, is guilty of contempt of court.

Where it appears that any person has in his possession, custody or power any document which is or purports to be a testamentary document, the High Court may, whether or not any legal proceedings are pending, issue a *subpoena* requiring him to bring in the document in such manner as the court may in the *subpoena* direct (section 123, Supreme Court Act 1981).

Standard disclosure

CPR rule 31.10 applies to standard disclosure which every party is obliged to give. Where specific disclosure is sought, a request should initially be made in writing within a reasonable time scale. If such disclosure is not forthcoming, an application may be made for disclosure to be ordered. The application should be supported by evidence setting out the reasons the disclosure is sought; why the documents are relevant; and why it is reasonable for the court to direct such disclosure.

Disclosure pursuant to CPR Part 18

By its very nature a probate claim concerns a situation where the party seeking to pursue or defend the claim may not have all the relevant information; the particulars of claim may leave many questions unanswered. In such instances the facility to seek further information under CPR Part 18 is useful. A written request for such information should always be made before making any application to the court. It is only when the information is not forthcoming, or such information as is given is inadequate, that an application for an order should be made.

Finally it must be stressed that the General Pre-Action Protocol and the Chancery Guide 2002 must be consulted and followed at every step of the proceedings. These documents may be downloaded from www.courtservice.gov.uk. Chapter 24 of the Chancery Guide, on probate and inheritance claims, is reproduced in Appendix D to this book.

Appendix A

Forms and Precedents

Contents

APPENDIX A

Application for a Standing Search

The Non-Contentious Probate Rules 1987, Schedule 1, Form 2

In the High Court of Justice
Family Division
[Principal] [...................... District Probate] Registry
In the Estate of ...., Deceased

I apply for the entry of a standing search so that there shall be sent to me an office copy of every grant of representation in England and Wales in the estate of:

Full name of the deceased:
Full address:
Alternative or alias name:
Exact date of death:

which either has issued not more than twelve months before the entry of this application or issues within six months thereafter.

Signed:
Name in block letters:
Address:
Reference (if any):

Example Claims to be Included in the Part 8 Claim form

The claimant claims:

1. An order that such reasonable financial provision may be made for the claimant from the estate of [*name*] deceased as the court thinks just.
2. An order be made for the claimant for such periodical payments and for such term out of the estate of the deceased as may be just.
3. An order for the payment to the claimant of such lump sum[s] out of the estate of the deceased as may be just.
4. The property at [*address*] or such other property forming part of the estate of the deceased as the court may specify be transferred to the claimant.
5. An order for the settlement for the benefit of the claimant of such property comprised in the estate of [*name*] the deceased as may be specified by the court and on such terms as the court thinks just.
6. An order for the acquisition out of the property forming part of the net estate of the deceased, of such property as may be specified and for the transfer of the property so acquired to the claimant or for the settlement thereof for the benefit of the claimant.
7. An order for the variation of the ante-nuptial settlement [*give details of the settlement*] for the benefit of the claimant [*who must be the surviving spouse of the marriage to whom the settlement related*] or [*name*] the child of the deceased and the claimant.
8. An order pursuant to section 9 of the Inheritance (Provision for Family and Dependants) Act 1975 that the severable share of [*name*] the deceased at the date of [his] [her] death in the property at [*insert address*] be treated as forming part of the net estate of the deceased.
9. An order pursuant to section 10 of the Inheritance (Provision for Family and

Dependants) Act 1975 that [*identify the donee of the disposition*] do provide such sum or sums of money or other property for the making of reasonable financial provision for the claimant.

10. An order pursuant to section 11 of the Inheritance (Provision for Family and Dependants) Act 1975 that [*name*] do provide the following sums of money and property for the purposes of making an order for reasonable financial provision for the claimant:
    (a) the sum of £ ...... contracted to be paid by the deceased to [*name*];
    (b) [*identify any property which was the subject of the contract*].
11. An order pursuant to section 11 of the Inheritance (Provision for Family and Dependants) Act 1975 directing the personal representatives of the deceased not to [make any payment] [transfer any property under the contract] [make any further payment] [transfer any further property].
12. An order for the variation of [*set out the details of the orders under the Matrimonial Causes Act 1973 of which variation is sought; see sections 16 to 18 of the 1975 Act*].
13. An order giving permission to issue the claim notwithstanding that more than six months have elapsed from the date on which representation with respect to the estate of the deceased was granted namely since [*date*] on the grounds set out in the statement of the claimant served with this claim.
14. [*Set out details of any injunctive relief sought, for example, a restraining order or a freezing order.*]
15. An order that the claimant's cost of this claim be paid out of the deceased's estate.

Statement by Claimant (A Surviving Spouse)

In the High Court of Justice Claim no.......
Family Division
[Principal Registry] [................................ District Registry]

In the Matter of the Estate of ...., Deceased
And in the Matter of the Inheritance (Provision for Family and Dependants) Act 1975

BETWEEN

[*Name*] Claimant
and
[*Name*] First Defendant (the personal representative of the deceased)
and
[*Name*] Second Defendant

[*All interested parties should be made defendants; see Chapter 12.*]

WITNESS STATEMENT OF THE CLAIMANT

I, [*name*] the above named claimant of [*address*] unemployed will say as follows:

1. I am the widow of ...., deceased. The deceased and I were married on 10 March 1970. A copy of our marriage certificate is attached to this statement and marked "...". We had three children, a daughter and two sons.

2. The deceased died on 21 June 2003. A certified copy of his death certificate is attached to this statement marked "…". The deceased was domiciled in England and Wales.
3. A grant of probate with respect to the deceased's estate was taken out on 15 August 2003 by [*names*] his executors from the Principal Registry. An official copy of the grant with his last will dated 10 January 2003 is marked "…".
4. To the best of my knowledge and belief the net estate is valued at approximately £ [*give the value*] and consists of:
   [*Set out the details, or if a schedule has been prepared by the executors and is available, refer to the schedule and exhibit it to the statement.*]
5. [*Set out the history of the marriage and such of the section 3 factors as may be relevant (see Chapter 5); if possible set out a schedule of income from all sources, details of capital and property and a list of expenditure. The information should also include the relevant factors which apply under section 24 of the Matrimonial Causes Act 1973.*]
6. [*If an order under section 9 to 11 is sought, set out details of the reasons for seeking such an order.*]
7. [*Set out details of and reasons for the orders sought.*]

Statement of truth [*see CPR, Practice Direction, paragraph 32.20.*]

I believe that the facts set out in this statement are true.

Signed:

Witness Statement of the Personal Representative

In the High Court of Justice Claim no…….
Family Division
[Principal Registry] [................................ District Registry]

In the Matter of the Estate of ...., Deceased
And in the Matter of the Inheritance (Provision for Family and Dependants) Act 1975

BETWEEN

[*Name*] Claimant
and
[*Name*] First Defendant (the personal representative of the deceased)
and
[*Name*] Second Defendant

[*All interested parties should be made defendants; see Chapter 12.*]

WITNESS STATEMENT OF THE FIRST DEFENDANT

I [*name*] of [*address*] solicitor will say as follows:

1. I am a solicitor of the Supreme Court and partner in the firm of Messrs ....
2. I am one of two executors of the will of the deceased. I have personal and professional knowledge of the deceased and his estate and knowledge derived from my involvement as an executor of the estate.

3. The grant of probate was granted to me and [*name*] out of the District Registry at .... on 15 August 2003. A true copy of the grant is attached to my statement marked "…".
4. The gross value of the deceased's estate was accounted for probate at £ ...... and the net estate at £ ...... The estate consists of:

The property at [*address*] valued at	£ 350,000
Premium Bonds:	£ 5,000
National Savings Certificates:	£ 2,000
Cash at................................Bank:	£ 300
Total	£ 357,300

[*Set out all identifiable assets and values and give the total.*]
5. The deceased was entitled to receive a death benefit from his employers under the terms of his employer's pension scheme. The deceased nominated [*name*] his cohabitee to receive the said benefit. The death benefit amounted to £ ...... and the said sum was paid to [*name*] on [*date*].
6. The liabilities of the deceased at the date of his death were as follows:
[*Set these out, including, for example, credit card debts, utility bills, loans, sums due under HP agreements.*]
7. The funeral expenses of the deceased amounted to £ ......
8. The whole of the estate was liable to inheritance tax subject to exemptions. Full details of the property comprised in the estate are set out in the Schedule attached to this statement marked "…".
9. The estate has not yet been administered.
10. [*If there has been delay in making the claim and the application for an extension is opposed, set out the reasons for the objection to the application.*]
11. [*If an order under section 9 is sought by the claimant, set out details of the assets and any other information which may be of assistance to the court; similarly if the claim includes a claim for orders under section 10 and 11.*]
12. The persons beneficially entitled to the deceased's estate are: [*set out the names and addresses of all beneficiaries, and if any of the beneficiaries is a child or under a disability, give details.*]
13. [*If there are matters to which the court's attention needs to be drawn these should be dealt with in addition to answering any matter set out in the claimant's statement.*]

APPENDIX A

Statement by a Cohabitant of the Deceased

In the High Court of Justice Claim no…….
Family Division
[Principal Registry] [................................ District Registry]

In the Matter of the Estate of ...., Deceased
And in the Matter of the Inheritance (Provision for Family and Dependants) Act 1975

BETWEEN

[*Name*] Claimant
and
[*Name*] First Defendant (the personal representative of the deceased)
and
[*Name*] Second Defendant

[*All interested parties should be made defendants; see Chapter 12.*]

WITNESS STATEMENT OF [*Name*]

I [*name*] of [*address*] will say:

1. The deceased was married to [*name*] on [*date*]. They had no children.
2. I met the deceased in January 1990 and shortly thereafter he left his wife [*name*] and came to live with me. I was then working and had lived in a flat at [*address*] which was owned by me. The deceased purchased the property at [*address*] in which I now live. I sold my flat and the net proceeds of sale were used to pay the deposit on the property. The property was purchased in the sole name of the deceased as I trusted him. The mortgage was also in his sole name. Thereafter we lived in the property as husband and wife.
3. We have two children, a son, Thomas, born on 1 January 1991 and a daughter, Samantha, born on 25 December 1993.
4. When I met the deceased I was working full time as a manager of the local supermarket store. The deceased did not like me working and when I became pregnant he asked me to give up work and be a full time carer of our child. Since then I and my children have been fully dependent on him.
5. Both children have attended public schools and the fees were paid for by the deceased. The deceased provided us with a high standard of living. We had two holidays a year with the children in Europe and sometimes further afield.
6. When the deceased began suffering from ill health I considered taking up employment to help with the finances but he assured me that there was no need for me to do so and that he would ensure that I and the children would be provided for if anything should happen to him. He also assured me that he would arrange for the property to be transferred into my name so that I would not have to worry if anything should happen to him.
7. Before the deceased could attend his solicitor to make a will he died. He was domiciled in England and Wales. A copy of his death certificate is attached to this statement marked "…".
8. As a result of his failure to make a new will I and the children have been left without support and his widow is the main beneficiary under the will. I produce a copy of the grant taken out by his executors marked "…".
9. Since the death of the deceased I have had to rely on state benefits. I have been

unable to discharge the school fees. I have no other income. [*Set out details of the claimant's earning capacity if any.*]

10. I have the following outgoings: [*List the outgoings or produce a schedule.*]
11. I am informed that the deceased's widow has insisted that the property in which I live with my children should be sold. If I have to vacate the home I and the children will become homeless. My solicitors have given to the executors and the solicitors acting for the widow all the relevant information and have been trying to negotiate a settlement. Negotiations had been progressing well. My solicitors were urged not to issue proceedings with a view to saving costs particularly as the negotiations had reached the final stages and the agreement was in the process of being drafted. Unfortunately the widow has withdrawn from the negotiations. I was obliged to apply for public funding to issue proceedings and this caused some delay. The delay, however, has been minimal. Proceedings were not issued immediately as there appeared to be a realistic hope of reaching an agreement without recourse to litigation. The estate has not yet been administered. No prejudice has been caused to any beneficiary. I therefore request that I be granted permission to pursue my claim notwithstanding the fact that the proceedings were not issued within six months from the date when the grant was taken out.
12. If permission to make the claim is refused I and my children will suffer extreme hardship and an injustice.
13. [*Set out in detail the orders sought and the reasons.*]

Witness Statement of an Adult Person Treated as a Child of the Family

In the High Court of Justice Claim no.......
Family Division
[Principal Registry] [................................ District Registry]

In the Matter of the Estate of ...., Deceased
And in the Matter of the Inheritance (Provision for Family and Dependants) Act 1975

BETWEEN

[*Name*] Claimant
and
[*Name*] First Defendant (the personal representative of the deceased)
and
[*Name*] Second Defendant

[*All interested parties should be made defendants; see Chapter 12.*]

I [*name*] of [*address*] will say as follows:

1. I am the deceased's step-son. My mother married the deceased on [*date*]. A copy of my mother's marriage certificate is attached to this statement marked "..." and a copy of my birth certificate is attached marked "...".
2. I was fourteen years of age when my mother married the deceased. I lived with them and the deceased treated me as his son. My mother and the deceased had two children from their marriage. They are Solomon born on [*date*] and Jacob born on [*date*]. The deceased did not treat me any differently after the birth of

my step-brothers. We all went to public schools. The deceased encouraged me to take up medicine. He paid all my college tuition fees and paid all my other expenses.

3. The deceased died domiciled in England and Wales on [*date*]. Copies of his death certificate and of his will and the grant of representation of the deceased's estate are attached to this statement marked "...", "..." and "..." respectively.
4. I believe that the deceased's estate is valued at £ 2.5 million. There is no provision made for me in his will although he has made provision for my step-brothers who are also adults and in full-time education.
5. My father has never seen me or maintained me. I am informed by my mother that he had a brief relationship with her when he was serving in the USA forces and was stationed here. When he discovered that she was pregnant he terminated the relationship and returned to the USA. His whereabouts are not known. I always regarded the deceased as my father.
6. [*Set out the claimant's financial circumstances and any other matter of relevance under section 3, see Chapter 5.*]

Draft Orders

The precedents below are intended to be a guide only. The orders made by the court vary depending on the circumstances of each individual case.

In the High Court of Justice Claim no.......
Family Division
[Principal Registry] [................................ District Registry]

In the Matter of the Estate of ...., Deceased
And in the Matter of the Inheritance (Provision for Family and Dependants) Act 1975

BETWEEN

[*Name*] Claimant
and
[*Name*] First Defendant (the personal representative of the deceased)
and
[*Name*] Second Defendant

[*All interested parties should be made defendants; see Chapter 12.*]

UPON HEARING [counsel] [solicitor] for the Claimant and [counsel] [solicitor] for the Defendant[s] and the Third Defendant appearing in person [*set out the representations or otherwise of the parties before the court.*]
AND UPON READING the documents in the court file and the agreed bundle of documents
AND UPON THE COURT being satisfied that the disposition of the estate of the deceased [*name*] effected by his [will] [intestacy] is not such as to make reasonable financial provision for the Claimant
IT IS ORDERED pursuant to section 2 of the Inheritance (Provision for Family and Dependants) Act 1975 that:

Periodical payments
There be paid out of the estate of the Deceased [*name*] to the Claimant [*name*] periodical payments to the Claimant at the rate of £ ...... per annum payable monthly from 1 February 2004 and thereafter on the first day of each calendar month until [the claimant shall remarry] [the claimant shall cease his/her full time education etc] [*if the payments relate to the income from assets, set out the rate which is equal to whole of the income*] [*or as the case may be*] of the estate comprised by ....

Lump sum
There be paid to the Claimant the lump sum of £ ...... out of the net estate of the Deceased within ...... days from the date of this order; or
There be paid to the Claimant the lump sum of £ ...... out of the estate of the Deceased in four instalments of £ ...... payable on 31 March 2004, 30 June 2004, 30 September 2004 and 30 December 2004 [*if the payments are to be made in, e.g., twelve equal monthly instalments, state the same or as the case may be*.]

Transfer of property
There be transferred to the Claimant from the estate of the Deceased within three months from the date of this order the property at [*address*].

Settlement of property
The property at [*address*] forming part of the net estate of the Deceased be settled for the benefit of the Claimant [*set out the settlement ordered, e.g. for life*] and that the form of the deed of settlement be agreed between the Claimant and the Defendants or in default of agreement be referred to conveyancing Counsel to settle.

Acquisition of assets
From the net estate of the Deceased there be purchased the property at [*address*] and that [the same be transferred into the name of the Claimant absolutely] [such property be settled for the benefit of the Claimant to the effect that [*set out the terms of the settlement*]] and that the form of deed of settlement be agreed and in default of agreement be referred to conveyancing Counsel to settle.

Variation of ante-nuptial/post nuptial settlement
The [ante-] [post-] nuptial settlement made between [*name*] and the Deceased etc be varied so as to provide as follows: [*set out the variation(s)*].

Order under section 9
The severable share of the Deceased in the property at [*address*] be treated as part of the estate of the Deceased in [*set out the proportions directed*] for the purposes of facilitating the making of the financial provision set out in this Order.

Order under section 10 or 11
That pursuant to section [10] [11] of the Inheritance (Provision for Family and Dependants) Act 1975 [*name*] is directed to provide the sum of £ ...... to the Claimant [or transfer to the Claimant the property at [*address*] [within ...... days of the making of this order] or [within ...... days of the receipt of this order by him/her].

Order under section 4
Pursuant to Section 4 of the Inheritance (Provision for Family and Dependants) Act 1975, IT IS ORDERED THAT the period of six months prescribed by section 4 of the 1975 Act be extended until ....

Draft Consent Order Setting out Compromise of Claim and Declaration of Trust on Behalf of Claimant under Disability

UPON HEARING Counsel for the parties and reading the consents of the defendants

AND UPON READING the evidence filed and documents recorded in the court file

AND UPON THE COURT being of the opinion that the disposition of the estate of [*name*] the Testator effected by his will is not such as to make reasonable financial provision for the maintenance of [*name*] the Claimant, the Testator' son.

AND UPON THE COURT being satisfied that the terms of compromise reached between the parties are for the benefit of the Claimant

THE COURT DOES APPROVE THE SAID TERMS OF COMPROMISE AND IT IT IS ORDERED THAT:

1. The first defendant [*name*] as personal representative of the Testator be at liberty to and so carry the said terms of compromise into effect.
2. Pursuant to section 2(1)(d) of the Inheritance (Provision for Family and Dependants) Act 1975 that the residue of the estate of the said Testator including all accumulations of income [*or otherwise identify the property to be settled*] shall be settled upon the trusts named in the will for the benefit of the claimant in accordance with the terms set out in the Schedule hereto.
3. [*Set out details of any adjustments which need to be made to any clauses in the will relating to any legacies or bequests.*]
4. The costs of the Claimant and the Defendants be referred to a district judge for detailed assessment and paid out of the residuary estate of the Testator [*or set out details of the agreement if any on costs.*]

Dated this..........day of 2004

SCHEDULE

That the Testator's estate shall henceforth be administered as if:

1. The Testator had omitted from his Will Clause 3 and Clause 6(j) therein contained
2. The Testator had included in his Will the following clause in substitution of Clause 2 as therein contained:
   (a) My trustees shall hold the remainder of the trust fund after payment of the foregoing legacies (hereinafter called "the discretionary fund") upon the following trusts and with and subject to the following powers:
   (b) (i) During the life of my son [*name*] (hereinafter "my said son") my trustees shall have power in their absolute discretion to pay or apply the whole or any part or proportion of the income of the discretionary fund as they think fit to or for the maintenance care or benefit of my said son with power to pay such income to any person or persons responsible for his care without seeing to the application thereof.
   (ii) After expiration of the period of [twelve years] [*or insert appropriate term*] from my death my trustees shall have the further power in their absolute discretion to pay any income then arising which in their opinion is surplus to the present and future needs of my said son to the persons who would be entitled thereto if he were dead and in equal shares.

(iii) During the period of [eighteen years] [*or insert appropriate term*] from my death while my said son is living my trustees shall accumulate the income of the discretionary fund which shall not be paid or applied as aforesaid as an accretion to the capital thereof but shall have power to pay or apply such accumulations to or for the maintenance care or benefit of my said son during his life as if the same were income of the then current year.

(iv) If my said son is still living at the expiration of the said period of [eighteen years] my trustees shall thereafter during the remainder of his life pay all income then arising which shall not be paid or applied under the foregoing powers to the persons who would be entitled thereto if he were dead and in equal shares.

(c) My trustees being at least two in number or a trust corporation shall have the following powers in addition to those set out in Clause 9 of the Will and the following provisions shall apply [*set out the powers, for example*:]

(i) power to sell exchange convey lease mortgage charge agree to let licence or otherwise conduct the management of any land of any tenure that may at any time be subject to the trusts hereof as if my trustees were the sole beneficial owners thereof;

(ii) power to change or vary any property or investments for the time being subject to the trusts hereof;

(iii) power to invest [*set out details*];

(iv) power to permit my son to have use and enjoyment of any chattel forming part of the discretionary fund in such manner and subject to such conditions (if any) as my trustees may consider reasonable and without being liable to account for any consequential loss;

(v) power to invest the whole or any part of the discretionary fund in the purchase or improvement any dwellinghouse or flat and to permit the same to be used as a residence for my son whether alone or jointly with another person without being required to insist upon the payment by any other person whether or not a joint occupier thereof of a market rent;

(vi) power to apply any part of the capital or income of the discretionary fund towards meeting the cost of–

A altering or adapting any residential accommodation in the ownership of any person or body for the more convenient occupation thereof by my said son as a home;

B purchasing domestic appliances or procuring domestic assistance for my said son;

C holidays for my said son or the expenses incurred by any person with whom he resides to enable such person to accompany him on holiday or to make provision for a carer to care for him.

(d) After the death of my said son my trustees shall stand possessed of the discretionary fund and the income thereof (or so much thereof as may not have been paid or applied under any trust or power affecting the same) in trust for the residuary beneficiaries (that is to say [*naming them*]) in equal shares PROVIDED THAT for the avoidance of doubt should any of those persons entitled to the discretionary fund predecease my said son their share of the discretionary fund shall accrue to their estates AND PROVIDED FURTHER that (notwithstanding the aforementioned trusts) my trustees may pay out of the capital of the discretionary fund such funeral expenses in respect of my said son as they may consider appropriate and reasonable.

(e) Any of my trustees may join in exercising any of the powers under this clause notwithstanding that he or she is one of the beneficiaries and will or may benefit from any such exercise.

(f) Any of my trustees being a solicitor, accountant or other person engaged in any profession or business shall be entitled to be paid all usual professional or proper charges for business transacted time expended acts done by him/her or any partner of his/her in connection with the trusts hereof including acts which a trustee not being in any profession or business could have done personally.

Caveat

The Non-Contentious Probate Rules 1987, Schedule 1, Form 3

In the High Court of Justice
Family Division
[Principal] [...................... District Probate] Registry
In the Estate of ...., Deceased

Let no grant be sealed in the estate of [*name and address of deceased*] deceased, who died on the ...... day of .... 20.. without notice to [*name of caveator*].

Dated the ...... day of .... 20..
Signed ....
whose address for service is ....
[Solicitor for the said ....]

Warning to Caveator

The Non-Contentious Probate Rules 1987, Schedule 1, Form 4

In the High Court of Justice
Family Division
The Leeds District Probate Registry
In the Estate of ...., Deceased

To [*name*] of [*address*] a party who has entered a caveat in the estate of [*name*] deceased.

You have eight days (starting with the day on which this warning was served on you):

(i) to enter an appearance either in person or by your solicitor or probate practitioner at the Leeds District Probate Registry, Third Floor, Coronet House, Queen Street, Leeds LS1 2BA setting out what interest you have in the estate of the above-named [*name*] of [*address*] deceased contrary to that of the party at whose instance this warning is issued; or

(ii) if you have no contrary interest but wish to show cause against the sealing of a grant to such party, to issue and serve a summons for directions by a District Judge of the Principal Registry or a Registrar of a District Probate Registry.

If you fail to do either of these the court may proceed to issue a grant of probate or administration in the said estate notwithstanding your caveat.

Dated the ...... day of .... 20..
Issued at the instance of [*set out the name and interest of the party warning, the name of his solicitor and the address for service.*]

Appearance to Warning
The Non-Contentious Probate Rules 1987, Schedule 1, Form 5

In the High Court of Justice
Family Division
The Leeds District Probate Registry
In the Estate of ...., Deceased

Caveat number .... dated the ...... day of .... 20..
Full name and address of deceased: ....
Full name and address of person warning: ....
Full name and address of caveator: ....
Enter an appearance for the above-named caveator in this matter.

Dated the ...... day of .... 20..
Signed .... [Solicitor for the said ....][.................. in person]
whose address for service is ....

Summons For Directions

Summons No
In the High Court of Justice
Family Division
[Principal] [....................... District Probate] Registry
In the Estate of ...., Deceased

BETWEEN

[*name*] Applicant
and
[*name*] Respondent

LET ALL PARTIES attend before the [District Judge sitting in Court No. ..... at the Principal Registry of the Family Division, First Avenue House, 42 – 49 High Holborn, London WC1V 6NP] [Registrar of the .... District Probate Registry] at …am/pm on ..... day the ..... day of ..... 2004 on the hearing of an application on the part of the Applicant for an order that:
[*Set out the directions applied for*].
[The Caveat No ..... lodged by the Respondent be struck out.]
[Probate be granted to the Applicant.]
[The Respondent be ordered to pay the Applicant's costs.]

Dated the ..... day of 2004
The estimated duration of this application is 30 minutes.

Counsel will [not] be appearing on behalf of the Applicant.

This summons was taken out by [*name*] of [*address*], Solicitors for the Applicant.

To Messrs [*name*] of [*address*], Solicitors for the Respondent

Affidavit of Service of Warning and of non-Receipt of Summons for Directions

In the High Court of Justice
Family Division
[Principal] [Leeds District Probate] Registry
In the Estate of ...., Deceased

BETWEEN

[*name*] Applicant
and
[*name*] Respondent

I [*name*] of [*address*], Solicitor for the Applicant make oath and say that:

1. On [*date*] I duly served Messrs [*name*] of [*address*], solicitors acting for [*name*], a true copy of the warning now produced and marked "..." by delivering to and leaving the said copy with [*set out the name of the person and his status, e.g. a legal executive of Messrs Clever Cloggs*] at their offices at [*address*] at [*time*] or by sending by prepaid special delivery/registered post to Messrs [*name*] at [*address*] the address for service of [*name*] the Caveator herein, or by leaving the same at the ...... DX for box No ..... at ..... Exchange or by leaving the same at the ..... Document Exchange for transmission to the ..... Document Exchange No ..... set out in the address for service given by [*name*] in the Caveat [*delete or adjust as appropriate*].
2. No summons for directions under Rule 44 of the Non-Contentious Probate Rules 1987 has been received by my firm.

Sworn by [*name*]
at [*address*] [*date*]
Before me [*signature*], A solicitor or Commissioner for Oaths.

Summons for Directions by Caveator to Show Cause

In the High Court of Justice
Family Division
[Principal] [...................... District Probate] Registry
In the Estate of ...., Deceased

BETWEEN

[*name*] Applicant
and
[*name*] Respondent

Let [*name*] the person warning, or his Solicitor, attend [one of the District Judges at the Principal Registry of the Family Division, First Avenue House, 42 – 49 High Holborn, London WC1V 6NP] [the registrar of the .... District Probate Registry] at ..... am/pm on ..... day the ..... day of ..... 2004 on the hearing of an application on the part of [*name*] the Caveator for the following orders:
for directions under Rule 44(6) of the Non-Contentious Probate Rules 1987; and [*set out any other directions or order sought e.g. for pre-action disclosure or inspection.*]
This summons was taken by [*name*] of [*address*] Solicitors for [*name*]
To [*name*] Solicitors for AB

Note: It may be more appropriate to use Form N244.

Witness Statement About Testamentary Documents
(CPR rule 57.5)

In the High Court of Justice
Chancery Division
[Principal] [...................... District Probate] Registry
In the Estate of ...., Deceased

BETWEEN
[*name*] Applicant
and
[*name*] Respondent

I [*name*] the [claimant] [defendant] [*or as the case may be*] state that:
I have the following document relating to [*name*] the deceased whose estate is the subject of this claim [*identify the document(s)*]:
I have no knowledge of any other document being or having the effect of a will or codicil of [*name*] the deceased nor of any other document purporting to be his instructions or request of or under the instructions or directions of the deceased. [*Set out details of any relevant material. See CPR 57.1 for the definition of "testamentary document".*]
I believe that [*set out the name of any relevant person*] of [*give his address if known, or if not known, state that*] has in his possession or control the following documents which may be relevant [*set these out; see CPR rule 57.1.*]:

The facts stated in this witness statement are true.

Defence Limited to Putting the Personal Representatives to Proof of the Will

In the High Court of Justice
Chancery Division
[Principal] [....................... District Probate] Registry
In the Estate of ...., Deceased

BETWEEN

[*name*] Applicant
and
[*name*] Respondent

DEFENCE

It is admitted that the deceased died on [*date*)].
The Defendant puts the Claimant to proof that;
(a) the Will alleged in the claim was duly executed;
(b) the deceased was of testamentary capacity when it was made; and
(c) the deceased knew and approved the contents of the said will.

[Date]
Signed, etc.

Notice of Intention to Cross-Examine

In the High Court of Justice
Chancery Division
[Principal] [....................... District Probate] Registry
In the Estate of ...., Deceased

BETWEEN

[*name*] Applicant
and
[*name*] Respondent

DEFENCE

TAKE NOTICE that at the trial of this probate claim the Defendant intends merely that the Will be proved in solemn form and intends only to cross examine the witnesses produced in support of the Will.

[Date]
Signed, etc.

Defence Alleging Want of Due Execution: Lack of Testamentary Capacity

In the High Court of Justice
Chancery Division
[Principal] [....................... District Probate] Registry
In the Estate of ...., Deceased

BETWEEN

[*name*] Applicant
and
[*name*] Respondent

DEFENCE

1. It is admitted that the deceased died on .... (date).
2. It is admitted that the Claimant is named in the deceased's Will as the executor of the Deceased's Will.
3. It is denied that at the time of the execution of the Will the Deceased had testamentary capacity.

PARTICULARS

At the time of execution of the will the deceased was ninety years of age and was suffering from Alzheimer's disease and senile dementia. His mental capacity was impaired in that:

(1) He suffered from acute loss of memory [*set out examples*].
(2) He was known to be confused at all times over all matters and had lost all power of recall and was unable to identify his children members of his extended family and even his closest friends.
(3) He was totally confused about his whereabouts, his finances and his property. He believed, for instance, that he was homeless and that his home had been burned down [*give details*].
(4) Further or in the alternative, at the time of execution of the will the deceased did not know or approve of the contents of the will by reason of:
    (a) the matters set out in paragraph 3 hereof;
    (b) the fact that the will was prepared by the claimant and not a solicitor;
    (c) the fact that the will bequeaths the entire estate to the claimant whom the deceased had met only a few months before he was taken into the nursing home [*set out any other matters of relevance*].

[Date]
Signed, etc.

APPENDIX A

Particulars of Claim: Undue Influence

In the High Court of Justice
Chancery Division
In the Estate of ...., Deceased
BETWEEN

[*name*] Applicant
and
[*name*] Respondent

PARTICULARS OF CLAIM

1. [*Name*] the deceased died on [*date*]
2. On [*date*] he had executed a will ("the first will") in which he had named the claimant as his executor and had divided his net estate between his four children in equal shares. The claimant is the deceased's son.
3. The defendant [*name*] has sought to obtain probate of a later will ("the disputed will") which allegedly was executed by the deceased on [*date*].
4. Under the terms of the disputed will the defendant is the sole executor and beneficiary of the net estate.
5. The disputed will was procured by the undue influence of the defendant.
6. At the time of the disputed will the deceased was ninety years of age and extremely frail. The defendant had been his next door neighbour and about three months prior to the deceased's death she had moved into the deceased's home purportedly to take care of him although the family had arranged for professional carers to attend to the deceased's needs.
7. The defendant was known to be extremely domineering towards the deceased, and had repeatedly threatened to have him removed to a home unless he made a will leaving his estate to her. The deceased was fearful of her and believed that he would be removed and had constantly asked the carers not to take him to a home.
8. Despite the assurances given to the deceased by the carers the defendant had continually told the deceased that she was making arrangements for his removal.
9. On [*date*] she presented the disputed will to the deceased with her sons and told him that if he did not sign the will they would take him away. He was so afraid of what the defendant might do that he executed the disputed will prepared by the defendant and the defendant's two sons signed it as witnesses.
10. The next day when the carers arrived they found the deceased in a collapsed state, distraught, visibly shaking, fearful and having difficulty in breathing. They were able to elicit from him what had happened.
11. Although steps were taken to prevent the defendant staying with the deceased unfortunately his condition deteriorated and he died on [*date*].

The Claimant claims:

1. That the defendant be refused a grant of probate in respect of the disputed will.
2. That the court pronounce a grant in solemn form for the first will dated [*date*].
3. Costs

[*date*]
Signed, etc.

Appendix B

The Inheritance (Provision for Family and Dependants) Act 1975

The text of the Act, as amended by the Administration of Justice Act 1982, the Matrimonial and Family Proceedings Act 1984, and the Law Reform (Succession) Act 1995, is set out below.

The Inheritance (Provision for Family and Dependants) Act 1975

An Act to make fresh provision for empowering the court to make orders for the making out of the estate of a deceased person of provision for the spouse, former spouse, child, child of the family or dependant of that person; and for matters connected therewith.

[12th November 1975]

Application for financial provision from deceased's estate

1.–(1) Where after the commencement of this Act a person dies domiciled in England and Wales and is survived by any of the following persons–

(a) the wife or husband of the deceased;

(b) a former wife or former husband of the deceased who has not remarried;

(ba) any person (not being a person included in paragraph (a) or (b) above) to whom subsection (1A) below applies;

(c) a child of the deceased;

(d) any person (not being a child of the deceased) who, in the case of any marriage to which the deceased was at any time a party, was treated by the deceased as a child of the family in relation to that marriage;

(e) any person (not being a person included in the foregoing paragraphs of this subsection) who immediately before the death of the deceased was being maintained, either wholly or partly, by the deceased;

that person may apply to the court for an order under section 2 of this Act on the ground that the disposition of the deceased's estate effected by his will or the law relating to intestacy, or the combination of his will and that law, is not such as to make reasonable financial provision for the applicant.

(1A) This subsection applies to a person if the deceased died on or after 1st January 1996 and, during the whole of the period of two years ending immediately before the date when the deceased died, the person was living–

(a) in the same household as the deceased, and

(b) as the husband or wife of the deceased.

(2) In this Act "reasonable financial provision"–

(a) in the case of an application made by virtue of subsection (1)(a) above by the husband or wife of the deceased (except where the marriage with the deceased was the subject of a decree of judicial separation and at the date of death the decree was in force and the separation was continuing), means such financial provision as it would be reasonable in all the circumstances of the case for a husband or wife to receive, whether or not that provision is required for his or her maintenance;

(b) in the case of any other application made by virtue of subsection (1) above, means such financial provision as it would be reasonable in all the circumstances of the case for the applicant to receive for his maintenance.

(3) For the purposes of subsection (1)(e) above, a person shall be treated as being maintained by the deceased, either wholly or partly, as the case may be, if the deceased, otherwise than for full valuable consideration, was making a substantial contribution in money or money's worth towards the reasonable needs of that person.

Powers of court to make orders

2.–(1) Subject to the provisions of this Act, where an application is made for an order under this section, the court may, if it is satisfied that the disposition of the deceased's estate effected by his will or the law relating to intestacy, or the combination of his will and that law, is not such as to make reasonable financial provision for the applicant, make any one or more of the following orders–

(a) an order for the making to the applicant out of the net estate of the deceased of such periodical payments and for such term as may be specified in the order;

(b) an order for the payment to the applicant out of that estate of a lump sum of such amount as may be so specified;

(c) an order for the transfer to the applicant of such property comprised in that estate as may be so specified;

(d) an order for the settlement for the benefit of the applicant of such property comprised in that estate as may be so specified;

(e) an order for the acquisition out of property comprised in that estate of such property as may be so specified and for the transfer of the property so acquired to the applicant or for the settlement thereof for his benefit;

(f) an order varying any ante-nuptial or post-nuptial settlement (including such a settlement made by will) made on the parties to a marriage to which the deceased was one of the parties, the variation being for the benefit of the surviving party to that marriage, or any child of that marriage, or any person who was treated by the deceased as a child of the family in relation to that marriage.

(2) An order under subsection (1)(a) above providing for the making out of the net estate of the deceased of periodical payments may provide for–

(a) payments of such amounts as may be specified in the order,

(b) payments equal to the whole of the income of the net estate or of such portion thereof as may be so specified,

(c) payments equal to the whole of the income of such part of the net estate as the court may direct to be set aside or appropriated for the making out of the income thereof of payments under this section,

or may provide for the amount of the payments or any of them to be determined in any other ways the court thinks fit.

(3) Where an order under subsection (1)(a) above provides for the making of payments of an amount specified in the order, the order may direct that such part of

the net estate as may be so specified shall be set aside or appropriated for the making out of the income thereof of those payments; but no larger part of the net estate shall be so set aside or appropriated than is sufficient, at the date of the order, to produce by the income thereof the amount required for the making of those payments.

(4) An order under this section may contain such consequential and supplemental provisions as the court thinks necessary or expedient for the purpose of giving effect to the order or for the purpose of securing that the order operates fairly as between one beneficiary of the estate of the deceased and another and may, in particular, but without prejudice to the generality of this subsection–

(a) order any person who holds any property which forms part of the net estate of the deceased to make such payment or transfer such property as may be specified in the order;

(b) vary the disposition of the deceased's estate effected by the will or the law relating to intestacy, or by both the will and the law relating to intestacy, in such manner as the court thinks fair and reasonable having regard to the provisions of the order and all the circumstances of the case;

(c) confer on the trustees of any property which is the subject of an order under this section such powers as appear to the court to be necessary or expedient.

Matters to which court is to have regard in exercising powers under section 2

3.–(1) Where an application is made for an order under section 2 of this Act, the court shall, in determining whether the disposition of the deceased's estate effected by his will or the law relating to intestacy, or the combination of his will and that law, is such as to make reasonable financial provision for the applicant and, if the court considers that reasonable financial provision has not been made, in determining whether and in what manner it shall exercise its powers under that section, have regard to the following matters, that is to say–

(a) the financial resources and financial needs which the applicant has or is likely to have in the foreseeable future;

(b) the financial resources and financial needs which any other applicant for an order under section 2 of this Act has or is likely to have in the foreseeable future;

(c) the financial resources and financial needs which any beneficiary of the estate of the deceased has or is likely to have in the foreseeable future;

(d) any obligations and responsibilities which the deceased had towards any applicant for an order under the said section 2 or towards any beneficiary of the estate of the deceased;

(e) the size and nature of the net estate of the deceased;

(f) any physical or mental disability of any applicant for an order under the said section 2 or any beneficiary of the estate of the deceased;

(g) any other matter, including the conduct of the applicant or any other person, which in the circumstances of the case the court may consider relevant.

(2) Without prejudice to the generality of paragraph (g) of subsection (1) above, where an application for an order under section 2 of this Act is made by virtue of section 1(1)(a) or 1(1)(b) of this Act, the court shall, in addition to the matters specifically mentioned in paragraphs (a) to (f) of that subsection, have regard to–

(a) the age of the applicant and the duration of the marriage;

(b) the contribution made by the applicant to the welfare of the family of the deceased, including any contribution made by looking after the home or caring for the family;

and, in the case of an application by the wife or husband of the deceased, the court shall also, unless at the date of death a decree of judicial separation was in force and the separation was continuing, have regard to the provision which the applicant might reasonably have expected to receive if on the day on which the deceased died the marriage, instead of being terminated by death, had been terminated by a decree of divorce.

(2A) Without prejudice to the generality of paragraph (g) of subsection (1) above, where an application for an order under section 2 of this Act is made by virtue of section 1(1)(ba) of this Act, the court shall, in addition to the matters specifically mentioned in paragraphs (a) to (f) of that subsection, have regard to–

(a) the age of the applicant and the length of period during which the applicant lived as the husband or wife of the deceased and in the same household as the deceased;

(b) the contribution made by the applicant to the welfare of the family of the deceased, including any contribution made by looking after the home or caring for the family.

(3) Without prejudice to the generality of paragraph (g) of subsection (1) above, where an application for an order under section 2 of this Act is made by virtue of section 1(1)(c) or 1(1)(d) of this Act, the court shall, in addition to the matters specifically mentioned in paragraphs (a) to (f) of that subsection, have regard to the manner in which the applicant was being or in which he might expect to be educated or trained, and where the application is made by virtue of section 1(1)(d) the court shall also have regard–

(a) to whether the deceased had assumed any responsibility for the applicant's maintenance and, if so, to the extent to which and the basis upon which the deceased assumed that responsibility and to the length of time for which the deceased discharged that responsibility;

(b) to whether in assuming and discharging that responsibility the deceased did so knowing that the applicant was not his own child;

(c) to the liability of any other person to maintain the applicant.

(4) Without prejudice to the generality of paragraph (g) of subsection (1) above, where an application for an order under section 2 of this Act is made by virtue of section 1(1)(e) of this Act, the court shall, in addition to the matters specifically mentioned in paragraphs (a) to (f) of that subsection, have regard to the extent to which and the basis upon which the deceased assumed responsibility for the maintenance of the applicant and to the length of time for which the deceased discharged that responsibility.

(5) In considering the matters to which the court is required to have regard under this section, the court shall take into account the facts as known to the court at the date of the hearing.

(6) In considering the financial resources of any person for the purposes of this section the court shall take into account his earning capacity and in considering the financial needs of any person for the purposes of this section the court shall take into account his financial obligations and responsibilities.

Time-limit for applications

4. An application for an order under section 2 of this Act shall not, except with the permission of the court, be made after the end of the period of six months from the date on which representation with respect to the estate of the deceased is first taken out.

Interim orders

5.–(1) Where on an application for an order under section 2 of this Act it appears to the court–

(a) that the applicant is in immediate need of financial assistance, but it is not yet possible to determine what order (if any) should be made under that section; and

(b) that property forming part of the net estate of the deceased is or can be made available to meet the need of the applicant;

the court may order that, subject to such conditions or restrictions, if any, as the court may impose and to any further order of the court, there shall be paid to the applicant out of the net estate of the deceased such sum or sums and (if more than one) at such intervals as the court thinks reasonable; and the court may order that, subject to the provisions of this Act, such payments are to be made until such date as the court may specify, not being later than the date on which the court either makes an order under the said section 2 or decides not to exercise its powers under that section.

(2) Subsections (2), (3) and (4) of section 2 of this Act shall apply in relation to an order under this section as they apply in relation to an order under that section.

(3) In determining what order, if any, should be made under this section the court shall, so far as the urgency of the case admits, have regard to the same matters as those to which the court is required to have regard under section 3 of this Act.

(4) An order made under section 2 of this Act may provide that any sum paid to the applicant by virtue of this section shall be treated to such an extent and in such manner as may be provided by that order as having been paid on account of any payment provided for by that order.

Variation, discharge etc of orders for periodical payments

6.–(1) Subject to the provisions of this Act, where the court has made an order under section 2(1)(a) of this Act (in this section referred to as "the original order") for the making of periodical payments to any person (in this section referred to as "the original recipient"), the court, on an application under this section, shall have power by order to vary or discharge the original order or to suspend any provision of it temporarily and to revive the operation of any provision so suspended.

(2) Without prejudice to the generality of subsection (1) above, an order made on an application for the variation of the original order may–

(a) provide for the making out of any relevant property of such periodical payments and for such term as may be specified in the order to any person who has applied, or would but for section 4 of this Act be entitled to apply, for an order under section 2 of this Act (whether or not, in the case of any application, an order was made in favour of the applicant);

(b) provide for the payment out of any relevant property of a lump sum of such amount as may be so specified to the original recipient or to any such person as is mentioned in paragraph (a) above;

(c) provide for the transfer of the relevant property, or such part thereof as may be so specified, to the original recipient or to any such person as is so mentioned.

(3) Where the original order provides that any periodical payments payable thereunder to the original recipient are to cease on the occurrence of an event specified in the order (other than the remarriage of a former wife or former husband) or on the expiration of a period so specified, then, if, before the end of the period of six months from the date of the occurrence of that event or of the expiration of that period, an application is made for an order under this section, the court shall have power to make any order which it would have had power to make if the application had been made before that date (whether in favour of the original recipient or any such person as is mentioned in subsection (2)(a) above and whether having effect from that date or from such later date as the court may specify).

(4) Any reference in this section to the original order shall include a reference to an order made under this section and any reference in this section to the original recipient shall include a reference to any person to whom periodical payments are required to be made by virtue of an order under this section.

(5) An application under this section may be made by any of the following persons, that is to say–

(a) any person who by virtue of section 1(1) of this Act has applied, or would but for section 4 of this Act be entitled to apply, for an order under section 2 of this Act,

(b) the personal representatives of the deceased,

(c) the trustees of any relevant property, and

(d) any beneficiary of the estate of the deceased.

(6) An order under this section may only affect–

(a) property the income of which is at the date of the order applicable wholly or in part for the making of periodical payments to any person who has applied for an order under this Act, or

(b) in the case of an application under subsection (3) above in respect of payments which have ceased to be payable on the occurrence of an event or the expiration of a period, property the income of which was so applicable immediately before the occurrence of that event or the expiration of that period, as the case may be,

and any such property as is mentioned in paragraph (a) or (b) above is in subsections (2) and (5) above referred to as "relevant property".

(7) In exercising the powers conferred by this section the court shall have regard to all the circumstances of the case, including any change in any of the matters to which the court was required to have regard when making the order to which the application relates.

(8) Where the court makes an order under this section, it may give such consequential directions as it thinks necessary or expedient having regard to the provisions of the order.

(9) No such order as is mentioned in sections 2(1)(d), (e) or (f), 9, 10 or 11 of this Act shall be made on an application under this section.

(10) For the avoidance of doubt it is hereby declared that, in relation to an order which provides for the making of periodical payments which are to cease on the occurrence of an event specified in the order (other than the remarriage of a former

wife or former husband) or on the expiration of a period so specified, the power to vary an order includes power to provide for the making of periodical payments after the expiration of that period or the occurrence of that event.

Payment of lump sums by instalments

7.–(1) An order under section 2(1)(b) or 6(2)(b) of this Act for the payment of a lump sum may provide for the payment of that sum by instalments of such amount as may be specified in the order.

(2) Where an order is made by virtue of subsection (1) above, the court shall have power, on an application made by the person to whom the lump sum is payable, by the personal representatives of the deceased or by the trustees of the property out of which the lump sum is payable, to vary that order by varying the number of instalments payable, the amount of any instalment and the date on which any instalment becomes payable.

Property available for financial provision

Property treated as part of "net estate"

8.–(1) Where a deceased person has in accordance with the provisions of any enactment nominated any person to receive any sum of money or other property on his death and that nomination is in force at the time of his death, that sum of money, after deducting therefrom any inheritance tax payable in respect thereof, or that other property, to the extent of the value thereof at the date of the death of the deceased after deducting therefrom any inheritance tax so payable, shall be treated for the purposes of this Act as part of the net estate of the deceased; but this subsection shall not render any person liable for having paid that sum or transferred that other property to the person named in the nomination in accordance with the directions given in the nomination.

(2) Where any sum of money or other property is received by any person as a donatio mortis causa made by a deceased person, that sum of money, after deducting therefrom any inheritance tax payable thereon, or that other property, to the extent of the value thereof at the date of the death of the deceased after deducting therefrom any inheritance tax so payable, shall be treated for the purposes of this Act as part of the net estate of the deceased; but this subsection shall not render any person liable for having paid that sum or transferred that other property in order to give effect to that donatio mortis causa.

(3) The amount of inheritance tax to be deducted for the purposes of this section shall not exceed the amount of that tax which has been borne by the person nominated by the deceased or, as the case may be, the person who has received a sum of money or other property as a donatio mortis causa.

Property held on a joint tenancy

9.–(1) Where a deceased person was immediately before his death beneficially entitled to a joint tenancy of any property, then, if, before the end of the period of six months from the date on which representation with respect to the estate of the deceased was first taken out, an application is made for an order under section 2 of this Act, the court for the purpose of facilitating the making of financial provision for the applicant under this Act may order that the deceased's severable share of that property, at the value thereof immediately before this death, shall, to such extent as appears to the court to be just in all the circumstances of the case, be treated for the purposes of this Act as part of the net estate of the deceased.

(2) In determining the extent to which any severable share is to be treated as part of the net estate of the deceased by virtue of an order under subsection (1) above, the court shall have regard to any inheritance tax payable in respect of that severable share.

(3) Where an order is made under subsection (1) above, the provisions of this section shall not render any person liable for anything done by him before the order was made.

(4) For the avoidance of doubt it is hereby declared that for the purposes of this section there may be a joint tenancy of a chose in action.

Powers of court in relation to transactions intended to defeat applications for financial provision

Dispositions intended to defeat applications for financial provision

10.–(1) Where an application is made to the court for an order under section 2 of this Act, the applicant may, in the proceedings on that application, apply to the court for an order under subsection (2) below.

(2) Where on an application under subsection (1) above the court is satisfied–

(a) that, less than six years before the date of the death of the deceased, the deceased with the intention of defeating an application for financial provision under this Act made a disposition, and

(b) that full valuable consideration for that disposition was not given by the person to whom or for the benefit of whom the disposition was made (in this section referred to as "the donee") or by any other person, and

(c) that the exercise of the powers conferred by this section would facilitate the making of financial provision for the applicant under this Act,

then, subject to the provisions of this section and of sections 12 and 13 of this Act, the court may order the donee (whether or not at the date of the order he holds any interest in the property disposed of to him or for his benefit by the deceased) to provide, for the purpose of the making of that financial provision, such sum of money or other property as may be specified in the order.

(3) Where an order is made under subsection (2) above as respects any disposition made by the deceased which consisted of the payment of money to or for the benefit of the donee, the amount of any sum of money or the value of any property ordered to be provided under that subsection shall not exceed the amount of the payment made by the deceased after deducting therefrom any inheritance tax borne by the donee in respect of that payment.

(4) Where an order is made under subsection (2) above as respects any disposition made by the deceased which consisted of the transfer of property (other than a sum of money) to or for the benefit of the donee, the amount of any sum of money or the value of any property ordered to be provided under that subsection shall not exceed the value at the date of the death of the deceased of the property disposed of by him to or for the benefit of the donee (or if that property has been disposed of by the person to whom it was transferred by the deceased, the value at the date of that disposal thereof) after deducting therefrom any inheritance tax borne by the donee in respect of the transfer of that property by the deceased.

(5) Where an application (in this subsection referred to as "the original application") is made for an order under subsection (2) above in relation to any

disposition, then, if on an application under this subsection by the donee or by any applicant for an order under section 2 of this Act the court is satisfied–

(a) that, less than six years before the date of the death of the deceased, the deceased with the intention of defeating an application for financial provision under this Act made a disposition other than the disposition which is the subject of the original application, and

(b) that full valuable consideration for that other disposition was not given by the person to whom or for the benefit of whom that other disposition was made or by any other person,

the court may exercise in relation to the person to whom of for the benefit of whom that other disposition was made the powers which the court would have had under subsection (2) above if the original application had been made in respect of that other disposition and the court had been satisfied as to the matters set out in paragraphs (a), (b) and (c) of that subsection; and where any application is made under this subsection, any reference in this section (except in subsection (2)(b)) to the donee shall include a reference to the person to whom or for the benefit of whom that other disposition was made.

(6) In determining whether and in what manner to exercise its powers under this section, the court shall have regard to the circumstances in which any disposition was made and any valuable consideration which was given therefor, the relationship, if any, of the donee to the deceased, the conduct and financial resources of the donee and all the other circumstances of the case.

(7) In this section "disposition" does not include–

(a) any provision in a will, any such nomination as is mentioned in section 8(1) of this Act or any donatio mortis causa, or

(b) any appointment of property made, otherwise than by will, in the exercise of a special power of appointment,

but, subject to these exceptions, includes any payment of money (including the payment of a premium under a policy of assurance) and any conveyance, assurance, appointment or gift of property of any description, whether made by an instrument or otherwise.

(8) The provisions of this section do not apply to any disposition made before the commencement of this Act.

Contracts to leave property by will

11.–(1) Where an application is made to a court for an order under section 2 of this Act, the applicant may, in the proceedings on that application, apply to the court for an order under this section.

(2) Where on an application under subsection (1) above the court is satisfied–

(a) that the deceased made a contract by which he agreed to leave by his will a sum of money or other property to any person or by which he agreed that a sum of money or other property would be paid or transferred to any person out of his estate, and

(b) that the deceased made that contract with the intention of defeating an application for financial provision under this Act, and

(c) that when the contract was made full valuable consideration for that contract was not given or promised by the person with whom or for the benefit of whom the contract was made (in this section referred to as "the donee") or by any other person, and

(d) that the exercise of the powers conferred by this section would facilitate the making of financial provision for the applicant under this Act,

then, subject to the provisions of this section and of sections 12 and 13 of this Act, the court may make any one or more of the following orders, that is to say–

(i) if any money has been paid or any other property has been transferred to or for the benefit of the donee in accordance with the contract, an order directing the donee to provide, for the purpose of the making of that financial provision, such sum of money or other property as may be specified in the order;

(ii) if the money or all the money has not been paid or the property or all the property has not been transferred in accordance with the contract, an order directing the personal representatives not to make any payment or transfer any property, or not to make any further payment or transfer any further property, as the case may be, in accordance therewith or directing the personal representatives only to make such payment or transfer such property as may be specified in the order.

(3) Notwithstanding anything in subsection (2) above, the court may exercise its powers thereunder in relation to any contract made by the deceased only to the extent that the court considers that the amount of any sum of money paid or to be paid or the value of any property transferred or to be transferred in accordance with the contract exceeds the value of any valuable consideration given or to be given for that contract, and for this purpose the court shall have regard to the value of property at the date of the hearing.

(4) In determining whether and in what manner to exercise its powers under this section, the court shall have regard to the circumstances in which the contract was made, the relationship, if any, of the donee to the deceased, the conduct and financial resources of the donee and all the other circumstances of the case.

(5) Where an order has been made under subsection (2) above in relation to any contract, the rights of any person to enforce that contract or to recover damages or to obtain other relief for the breach thereof shall be subject to any adjustment made by the court under section 12(3) of this Act and shall survive to such extent only as is consistent with giving effect to the terms of that order.

(6) The provisions of this section do not apply to a contract made before the commencement of this Act.

Provisions supplementary to sections 10 and 11

12.–(1) Where the exercise of any of the powers conferred by section 10 or 11 of this Act is conditional on the court being satisfied that a disposition or contract was made by a deceased person with the intention of defeating an application for financial provision under this Act, that condition shall be fulfilled if the court is of the opinion that, on a balance of probabilities, the intention of the deceased (though not necessarily his sole intention) in making the disposition or contract was to prevent an order for financial provision being made under this Act or to reduce the amount of the provision which might otherwise be granted by an order thereunder.

(2) Where an application is made under section 11 of this Act with respect to any contract made by the deceased and no valuable consideration was given or promised

by any person for that contract then, notwithstanding anything in subsection (1) above, it shall be presumed, unless the contrary is shown, that the deceased made that contract with the intention of defeating an application for financial provision under this Act.

(3) Where the court makes an order under section 10 or 11 of this Act it may give such consequential directions as it thinks fit (including directions requiring the making of any payment or the transfer of any property) for giving effect to the order or for securing a fair adjustment of the rights of the persons affected thereby.

(4) Any power conferred on the court by the said section 10 or 11 to order the donee, in relation to any disposition or contract, to provide any sum of money or other property shall be exercisable in like manner in relation to the personal representative of the donee, and–

(a) any reference in section 10(4) to the disposal of property by the donee shall include a reference to disposal by the personal representative of the donee, and
(b) any reference in section 10(5) to an application by the donee under that subsection shall include a reference to an application by the personal representative of the donee;

but the court shall not have power under the said section 10 or 11 to make an order in respect of any property forming part of the estate of the donee which has been distributed by the personal representative; and the personal representative shall not be liable for having distributed any such property before he has notice of the making of an application under the said section 10 or 11 on the ground that he ought to have taken into account the possibility that such an application would be made.

Provisions as to trustees in relation to sections 10 and 11

13.–(1) Where an application is made for–

(a) an order under section 10 of this Act in respect of a disposition made by the deceased to any person as a trustee, or
(b) an order under section 11 of this Act in respect of any payment made or property transferred, in accordance with a contract made by the deceased, to any person as a trustee,

the powers of the court under the said section 10 or 11 to order that trustee to provide a sum of money or other property shall be subject to the following limitation (in addition, in a case of an application under section 10, to any provisions regarding the deduction of inheritance tax) namely, that the amount of any sum of money or the value of any property ordered to be provided–

(i) in the case of an application in respect of a disposition which consisted of the payment of money or an application in respect of the payment of money in accordance with a contract, shall not exceed the aggregate of so much of that money as is at the date of the order in the hands of the trustee and the value at that date of any property which represents that money or is derived therefrom and is at that date in the hands of the trustee;
(ii) in the case of an application in respect of a disposition which consisted of the transfer of property (other than a sum of money) or an application in respect of the transfer of property (other than a sum of money) in accordance with a contract, shall not exceed the aggregate of the value at the date of the order of so much of that property as is at that date in the hands of the trustee and the value at that date of any property which represents the first-mentioned

property or is derived therefrom and is at that date in the hands of the trustee.

(2) Where any such application is made in respect of a disposition made to any person as a trustee or in respect of any payment made or property transferred in pursuance of a contract to any person as a trustee, the trustee shall not be liable for having distributed any money or other property on the ground that he ought to have taken into account the possibility that such an application would be made.

(3) Where any such application is made in respect of a disposition made to any person as a trustee or in respect of any payment made or property transferred in accordance with a contract to any person as a trustee, any reference in the said section 10 or 11 to the donee shall be construed as including a reference to the trustee or trustees for the time being of the trust in question and any reference in subsection (1) or (2) above to a trustee shall be construed in the same way.

Special provisions relating to cases of divorce, separation etc.

Provision as to cases where no financial relief was granted in divorce proceedings etc.

14.–(1) Where, within twelve months from the date on which a decree of divorce or nullity of marriage has been made absolute or a decree of judicial separation has been granted, a party to the marriage dies and–

(a) an application for a financial provision order under section 23 of the Matrimonial Causes Act 1973 or a property adjustment order under section 24 of that Act has not been made by the other party to that marriage, or

(b) such an application has been made but the proceedings thereon have not been determined at the time of the death of the deceased,

then, if an application for an order under section 2 of this Act is made by that other party, the court shall, notwithstanding anything in section 1 or section 3 of this Act, have power, if it thinks it just to do so, to treat that party for the purposes of that application as if the decree of divorce or nullity of marriage had not been made absolute or the decree of judicial separation had not been granted, as the case may be.

(2) This section shall not apply in relation to a decree of judicial separation unless at the date of the death of the deceased the decree was in force and the separation was continuing.

Restriction imposed in divorce proceedings etc on application under this Act

15.–(1) On the grant of a decree of divorce, a decree of nullity of marriage or a decree of judicial separation or at any time thereafter the court, if it considers it just to do so, may, on the application of either party to the marriage, order that the other party to the marriage shall not on the death of the applicant be entitled to apply for an order under section 2 of this Act.

In this subsection "the court" means the High Court or, where a county court has jurisdiction by virtue of Part V of the Matrimonial and Family Proceedings Act 1984, a county court.

(2) In the case of a decree of divorce or nullity of marriage an order may be made under subsection (1) above before or after the decree is made absolute, but if it is made before the decree is made absolute it shall not take effect unless the decree is made absolute.

(3) Where an order made under subsection (1) above on the grant of a decree of

divorce or nullity of marriage has come into force with respect to a party to a marriage, then, on the death of the other party to that marriage, the court shall not entertain any application for an order under section 2 of this Act made by the first-mentioned party.

(4) Where an order made under subsection (1) above on the grant of a decree of judicial separation has come into force with respect to any party to a marriage, then, if the other party to that marriage dies while the decree is in force and the separation is continuing, the court shall not entertain any application for an order under section 2 of this Act made by the first-mentioned party.

Restriction imposed in proceedings under the Matrimonial and Family Proceedings Act 1984 on application under this Act

15A.–(1) On making an order under section 17 of the Matrimonial and Family Proceedings Act 1984 (orders for financial provision and property adjustment following overseas divorces, etc), the court, if it considers it just to do so, may, on the application of either party to the marriage, order that the other party to the marriage shall not on the death of the applicant be entitled to apply for an order under section 2 of this Act.

In this subsection "the court" means the High Court or, where a county court has jurisdiction by virtue of Part V of the Matrimonial and Family Proceedings Act 1984, a county court.

(2) Where an order under subsection (1) above has been made with respect to a party to a marriage which has been dissolved or annulled, the court shall not entertain an application under section 2 of this Act made by the first-mentioned party.

(3) Where an order under subsection (1) above has been made with respect to a party to a marriage the parties to which have been legally separated, then, if the other party to the marriage dies while the legal separation is in force, the court shall not entertain an application under section 2 of this Act made by the first-mentioned party.

Variation and discharge of secured periodical payments orders made under Matrimonial Causes Act 1973

16.–(1) Where an application for an order under section 2 of this Act is made to the court by any person who was at the time of the death of the deceased entitled to payments from the deceased under a secured periodical payments order made under the Matrimonial Causes Act 1973, then, in the proceedings on that application, the court shall have power, if an application is made under this section by that person or by the personal representative of the deceased, to vary or discharge that periodical payments order or to revive the operation of any provision thereof which has been suspended under section 31 of that Act.

(2) In exercising the powers conferred by this section the court shall have regard to all the circumstances of the case, including any order which the court proposes to make under section 2 or section 5 of this Act and any change (whether resulting from the death of the deceased or otherwise) in any of the matters to which the court was required to have regard when making the secured periodical payments order.

(3) The powers exercisable by the court under this section in relation to an order shall be exercisable also in relation to any instrument executed in pursuance of the

order.

Variation and revocation of maintenance agreements
17.–(1) Where an application for an order under section 2 of this Act is made to the court by any person who was at the time of the death of the deceased entitled to payments from the deceased under a maintenance agreement which provided for the continuation of payments under the agreement after the death of the deceased, then, in the proceedings on that application, the court shall have power, if an application is made under this section by that person or by the personal representative of the deceased, to vary or revoke that agreement.

(2) In exercising the powers conferred by this section the court shall have regard to all the circumstances of the case, including any order which the court proposes to make under section 2 or section 5 of this Act and any change (whether resulting from the death of the deceased or otherwise) in any of the circumstances in the light of which the agreement was made.

(3) If a maintenance agreement is varied by the court under this section the like consequences shall ensue as if the variation had been made immediately before the death of the deceased by agreement between the parties and for valuable consideration.

(4) In this section "maintenance agreement", in relation to a deceased person, means any agreement made, whether in writing or not and whether before or after the commencement of this Act, by the deceased with any person with whom he entered into a marriage, being an agreement which contained provisions governing the rights and liabilities towards one another when living separately of the parties to that marriage (whether or not the marriage has been dissolved or annulled) in respect of the making or securing of payments or the disposition or use of any property, including such rights and liabilities with respect to the maintenance or education of any child, whether or not a child of the deceased or a person who was treated by the deceased as a child of the family in relation to that marriage.

Availability of court's powers under this Act in applications under sections 31 and 36 of the Matrimonial Causes Act 1973
18.–(1) Where–

(a) a person against whom a secured periodical payments order was made under the Matrimonial Causes Act 1973 has died and an application is made under section 31(6) of that Act for the variation or discharge of that order or for the revival of the operation of any provision thereof which has been suspended, or

(b) a party to a maintenance agreement within the meaning of section 34 of that Act has died, the agreement being one which provides for the continuation of payments thereunder after the death of one of the parties, and an application is made under section 36(1) of that Act for the alteration of the agreement under section 35 thereof,

the court shall have power to direct that the application made under the said section 31(6) or 36(1) shall be deemed to have been accompanied by an application for an order under section 2 of this Act.

(2) Where the court gives a direction under subsection (1) above it shall have power, in the proceedings on the application under the said section 31(6) or 36(1), to make an order which the court would have had power to make under the provisions

of this Act if the application under the said section 31(6) or 36(1), as the case may be, had been made jointly with an application for an order under the said section 2; and the court shall have power to give such consequential directions as may be necessary for enabling the court to exercise any of the powers available to the court under this Act in the case of an application for an order under section 2.

(3) Where an order made under section 15(1) of this Act is in force with respect to a party to a marriage, the court shall not give a direction under subsection (1) above with respect to any application made under the said section 31(6) or 36(1) by that party on the death of the other party.

Miscellaneous and supplementary provisions

Effect, duration and form of orders

19.–(1) Where an order is made under section 2 of this Act then for all purposes, including the purposes of the enactments relating to inheritance tax, the will or the law relating to intestacy, or both the will and the law relating to intestacy, as the case may be, shall have effect and be deemed to have had effect as from the deceased's death subject to the provisions of the order.

(2) Any order made under section 2 or 5 of this Act in favour of–

(a) an applicant who was the former husband or former wife of the deceased, or

(b) an applicant who was the husband or wife of the deceased in a case where the marriage with the deceased was the subject of a decree of judicial separation and at the date of death the decree was in force and the separation was continuing,

shall, in so far as it provides for the making of periodical payments, cease to have effect on the remarriage of the applicant, except in relation to any arrears due under the order on the date of the remarriage.

(3) A copy of every order made under this Act other than an order made under section 15(1) of this Act shall be sent to the Principal Registry of the Family Division for entry and filing, and a memorandum of the order shall be endorsed on, or permanently annexed to, the probate or letters of administration under which the estate is being administered.

Provisions as to personal representatives

20.–(1) The provisions of this Act shall not render the personal representative of a deceased person liable for having distributed any part of the estate of the deceased, after the end of the period of six months from the date on which representation with respect to the estate of the deceased is first taken out, on the ground that he ought to have taken into account the possibility–

(a) that the court might permit the making of an application for an order under section 2 of this Act after the end of that period, or

(b) that, where an order has been made under the said section 2, the court might exercise in relation thereto the powers conferred on it by section 6 of this Act,

but this subsection shall not prejudice any power to recover, by reason of the making of an order under this Act, any part of the estate so distributed.

(2) Where the personal representative of a deceased person pays any sum directed by an order under section 5 of this Act to be paid out of the deceased's net estate, he shall not be under any liability by reason of that estate not being sufficient to make the payment, unless at the time of making the payment he has reasonable cause to

believe that the estate is not sufficient.

(3) Where a deceased person entered into a contract by which he agreed to leave by his will any sum of money or other property to any person or by which he agreed that a sum of money or other property would be paid or transferred to any person out of his estate, then, if the personal representative of the deceased has reason to believe that the deceased entered into the contract with the intention of defeating an application for financial provision under this Act, he may, notwithstanding anything in that contract, postpone the payment of that sum of money or the transfer of that property until the expiration of the period of six months from the date on which representation with respect to the estate of the deceased is first taken out or, if during that period an application is made for an order under section 2 of this Act, until the determination of the proceedings on that application.

[Sections 21 and 22 have been repealed.]

Determination of date on which representation was first taken out
23. In considering for the purposes of this Act when representation with respect to the estate of a deceased person was first taken out, a grant limited to settled land or to trust property shall be left out of account, and a grant limited to real estate or to personal estate shall be left out of account unless a grant limited to the remainder of the estate has previously been made or is made at the same time.

Effect of this Act on section 46(1)(vi) of Administration of Estates Act 1925
24. Section 46(1)(vi) of the Administration of Estates Act 1925, in so far as it provides for the devolution of property on the Crown, the Duchy of Lancaster or the Duke of Cornwall as bona vacantia, shall have effect subject to the provisions of this Act.

Interpretation
25.–(1) In this Act–
"beneficiary", in relation to the estate of a deceased person, means–
- (a) a person who under the will of the deceased or under the law relating to intestacy is beneficially interested in the estate or would be so interested if an order had not been made under this Act, and
- (b) a person who has received any sum of money or other property which by virtue of section 8(1) or 8(2) of this Act is treated as part of the net estate of the deceased or would have received that sum or other property if an order had not been made under this Act;

"child" includes an illegitimate child and a child en ventre sa mere at the death of the deceased;

"the court" unless the context otherwise requires means the High Court, or where a county court has jurisdiction by virtue of section 22 of this Act, a county court;

"former wife" or "former husband" means a person whose marriage with the deceased was during the lifetime of the deceased either–
- (a) dissolved or annulled by a decree of divorce or a decree of nullity of marriage granted under the law of any part of the British Islands, or
- (b) dissolved or annulled in any country or territory outside the British Islands by a divorce or annulment which is entitled to be recognised as valid by the law of England and Wales;

"net estate", in relation to a deceased person, means–

(a) all property of which the deceased had power to dispose by his will (otherwise than by virtue of a special power of appointment) less the amount of his funeral, testamentary and administration expenses, debts and liabilities, including any inheritance tax payable out of his estate on his death;
(b) any property in respect of which the deceased held a general power of appointment (not being a power exercisable by will) which has not been exercised;
(c) any sum of money or other property which is treated for the purposes of this Act as part of the net estate of the deceased by virtue of section 8(1) or (2) of this Act;
(d) any property which is treated for the purposes of this Act as part of the net estate of the deceased by virtue of an order made under section 9 of the Act;
(e) any sum of money or other property which is, by reason of a disposition or contract made by the deceased, ordered under section 10 or 11 of this Act to be provided for the purpose of the making of financial provisions under this Act;

"property" includes any chose in action;
"reasonable financial provision" has the meaning assigned to it by section 1 of this Act;
"valuable consideration" does not include marriage or a promise of marriage;
"will" includes codicil.

(2) For the purposes of paragraph (a) of the definition of "net estate" in subsection (1) above a person who is not of full age and capacity shall be treated as having power to dispose by will of all property of which he would have had power to dispose by will if he had been of full age and capacity.

(3) Any reference in this Act to provision out of the net estate of a deceased person includes a reference to provision extending to the whole of that estate.

(4) For the purposes of this Act any reference to a wife or husband shall be treated as including a reference to a person who in good faith entered into a void marriage with the deceased unless either–

(a) the marriage of the deceased and that person was dissolved or annulled during the lifetime of the deceased and the dissolution or annulment is recognised by the law of England and Wales, or
(b) that person has during the lifetime of the deceased entered into a later marriage.

(5) Any reference in this Act to remarriage or to a person who has remarried includes a reference to a marriage which is by law void or voidable or to a person who has entered into such a marriage, as the case may be, and a marriage shall be treated for the purposes of this Act as a remarriage, in relation to any party thereto, notwithstanding that the previous marriage of that party was void or voidable.

(6) Any reference in this Act to an order or decree made under the Matrimonial Causes Act 1973 or under any section of that Act shall be construed as including a reference to an order or decree which is deemed to have been made under that Act or under that section thereof, as the case may be.

(7) Any reference in this Act to any enactment is a reference to that enactment as amended by or under any subsequent enactment.

Consequential amendments, repeals and transitional provisions
[Section 26 not reproduced.]

Short title, commencement and extent
27.–(1) This Act may be cited as the Inheritance (Provision for Family and Dependants) Act 1975.

(2) This Act does not extend to Scotland or Northern Ireland.

(3) This Act shall come into force on 1st April 1976.

[Schedule of enactments repealed not reproduced.]

Appendix C

The Wills Act 1837

The text of the Act, as amended, most significantly recently, by the Administration of Justice Act 1982, the Family Law Act 1986, and the Law Reform (Succession) Act 1995, is set out below.

Wills Act 1837

An Act for the amendment of the Laws with respect to Wills

[3rd July 1837]

1.– ... the words and expressions hereinafter mentioned, which in their ordinary signification have a more confined or a different meaning, shall in this Act, except where the nature of the provisions or the context of the Act shall exclude such construction, be interpreted as follows; (that is to say,) the word "will" shall extend to a testament, and to a codicil, and to an appointment by will or by writing in the nature of a will in exercise of a power, and also to an appointment by will of a guardian of a child, ... and to any other testamentary disposition; and the words "real estate" shall extend to manors, advowsons, messuages, lands, tithes, rents, and hereditaments, ... whether corporeal, incorporeal, or personal, ... and to any estate, right, or interest (other than a chattel interest) therein; and the words "personal estate" shall extend to leasehold estates and other chattels real, and also to monies, shares of government and other funds, securities for money (not being real estates), debts, choses in action, rights, credits, goods, and all other property whatsoever which by law devolves upon the executor or administrator, and to any share or interest therein; and every word importing the singular number only shall extend and be applied to several persons or things as well as one person or thing; and every word importing the masculine gender only shall extend and be applied to a female as well as a male.

[Section 2 has been repealed.]

3.– ... it shall be lawful for every person to devise, bequeath, or dispose of, by his will executed in manner hereinafter required, all real estate and all personal estate which he shall be entitled to, either at law or in equity, at the time of his death, and which, if not so devised, bequeathed, and disposed of, would devolve ... upon his executor or administrator; and ... the power hereby given shall extend ... to all contingent, executory or other future interests in any real or personal estate, whether the testator may or may not be ascertained as the person or one of the persons in whom the same respectively may become vested, and whether he may be entitled thereto under the instrument by which the same respectively were created, or under any disposition thereof by deed or will; and also to all rights of entry for conditions broken, and other rights of entry; and also to such of the same estates, interests, and rights respectively, and other real and personal estate, as the testator may be entitled to at the time of his death, notwithstanding that he may become entitled to the same subsequently to the execution of his will.

[Sections 4 to 6 have been repealed.]

7.– … no will made by any person under the age of eighteen years shall be valid.

[Section 8 has been repealed.]

9.– No will shall be valid unless–

(a) it is in writing, and signed by the testator, or by some other person in his presence and by his direction; and

(b) it appears that the testator intended by his signature to give effect to the will; and

(c) the signature is made or acknowledged by the testator in the presence of two or more witnesses present at the same time; and

(d) each witness either–

(i) attests and signs the will; or

(ii) acknowledges his signature,

in the presence of the testator (but not necessarily in the presence of any other witness),

but no form of attestation shall be necessary.

10. ... no appointment made by will, in exercise of any power, shall be valid, unless the same be executed in manner herein-before required; and every will executed in manner herein-before required shall, so far as respects the execution and attestation thereof be a valid execution of a power of appointment by will, notwithstanding it shall have been expressly required that a will made in exercise of such power should be executed with some additional or other form of execution or solemnity.

11.– Provided always, … that any soldier being in actual military service, or any mariner or seaman being at sea, may dispose of his personal estate as he might have done before the making of this Act.

[Section 12 has been repealed.]

13.– ... every will executed in manner herein-before required shall be valid without any other publication thereof.

14.– ... if any person who shall attest the execution of a will shall at the time of the execution thereof or at any time afterwards be incompetent to be admitted a witness to prove the execution thereof, such will shall not on that account be invalid.

15.– ... if any person shall attest the execution of any will to whom or to whose wife or husband any beneficial devise, legacy, estate, interest, gift, or appointment, of or affecting any real or personal estate (other than and except charges and directions for the payment of any debt or debts), shall be thereby given or made, such devise, legacy, estate, interest, gift, or appointment shall, so far only as concerns such person attesting the execution of such will, or the wife or husband of such person, or any person claiming under such person or wife or husband, be utterly null and void, and such person so attesting shall be admitted as a witness to prove the execution of such will, or to prove the validity or invalidity thereof, notwithstanding such devise, legacy, estate, interest, gift, or appointment mentioned in such will.

16.– ... in case by any will any real or personal estate shall be charged with any debt or debts, and any creditor, or the wife or husband of any creditor, whose debt is so charged, shall attest the execution of such will, such creditor notwithstanding such charge shall be admitted a witness to prove the execution of such will, or to prove the validity or invalidity thereof.

17.– ... no person shall, on account of his being an executor of a will, be incompetent to be admitted a witness to prove the execution of such will, or a witness to prove the validity or invalidity thereof.

18.–(1) Subject to subsections (2) to (4) below, a will shall be revoked by the testator's marriage.

(2) A disposition in a will in exercise of a power of appointment shall take effect notwithstanding the testator's subsequent marriage unless the property so appointed would in default of appointment pass to his personal representatives.

(3) Where it appears from a will that at the time it was made the testator was expecting to be married to a particular person and that he intended that the will should not be revoked by the marriage, the will shall not be revoked by his marriage to that person.

(4) Where it appears from a will that at the time it was made the testator was expecting to be married to a particular person and that he intended that a disposition in the will should not be revoked by his marriage to that person,–

(a) that disposition shall take effect notwithstanding the marriage; and

(b) any other disposition in the will shall take effect also, unless it appears from the will that the testator intended the disposition to be revoked by the marriage.

18A.–(1) Where, after a testator has made a will, a decree of a court of civil jurisdiction in England and Wales dissolves or annuls his marriages or his marriage is dissolved or annulled and the divorce or annulment is entitled to recognition in England and Wales by virtue of Part II of the Family Law Act 1986,–

(a) provisions of the will appointing executors or trustees or conferring a power of appointment, if they appoint or confer the power on the former spouse, shall take effect as if the former spouse had died on the date on which the marriage is dissolved or annulled, and

(b) any property which, or an interest in which, is devised or bequeathed to the former spouse shall pass as if the former spouse had died on that date,

except in so far as a contrary intention appears by the will.

(2) Subsection (1)(b) above is without prejudice to any right of the former spouse to apply for financial provision under the Inheritance (Provision for Family and Dependants) Act 1975.

19.– ... no will shall be revoked by any presumption of an intention on the ground of an alteration in circumstances.

20.–. .. no will or codicil, or any part thereof, shall be revoked otherwise than as aforesaid, or by another will or codicil executed in manner herein-before required, or by some writing declaring an intention to revoke the same and executed in the manner in which a will is herein-before required to be executed, or by the burning, tearing, or otherwise destroying the same by the testator, or by some person in his presence and by his direction, with the intention of revoking the same.

21.– ... no obliteration, interlineation, or other alteration made in any will after the execution thereof shall be valid or have any effect, except so far as the words or effect of the will before such alteration shall not be apparent, unless such alteration shall be executed in like manner as herein-before is required for the execution of the will; but the will, with such alteration as part thereof, shall be deemed to be duly executed if the signature of the testator and the subscription of the witnesses be made in the margin or on some other part of the will opposite or near to such alteration, or at the foot or end of or opposite to a memorandum referring to such alteration, and written at the end of some other part of the will.

22.– ... no will or codicil, or any part thereof, which shall be in any manner revoked, shall be revived otherwise than by the re-execution thereof or by a codicil executed in manner herein-before required and showing an intention to revive the same; and when any will or codicil which shall be partly revoked, and afterwards wholly revoked, shall be revived, such revival shall not extend to so much thereof as shall have been revoked before the revocation of the whole thereof, unless an intention to the contrary shall be shown.

23.– … no conveyance or other act made or done subsequently to the execution of a will of or relating to any real or personal estate therein comprised, except an act by which such will shall be revoked as aforesaid, shall prevent the operation of the will with respect to such estate or interest in such real or personal estate as the testator shall have power to dispose of by will at the time of his death.

24.– … every will shall be construed, with reference to the real estate and personal estate comprised in it, to speak and take effect as if it has been executed immediately before the death of the testator, unless a contrary intention shall appear by the will.

25.– … unless a contrary intention shall appear by the will, such real estate or interest therein as shall be comprised or intended to be comprised in any devise in such will contained, which shall fail or be void by reason of the death of the devisee in the lifetime of the testator, or by reason of such devise being contrary to law or otherwise incapable of taking effect shall be included in the residuary devise (if any) contained in such will.

26.– ... a devise of the land of the testator, or of the land of the testator in any place or in the occupation of any person mentioned in his will, or otherwise described in a general manner, and any other general devise which would describe a ... leasehold estate if the testator had no freehold estate which could be described by it, shall be construed to include the ... leasehold estates of the testator, or his ... leasehold estates, or any of them, to which such description shall extend, as the case may be, as well as freehold estates, unless a contrary intention shall appear by the will.

27.– ... a general devise of the real estate of the testator, or of the real estate of the testator in any place or in the occupation of any person mentioned in his will, or otherwise described in a general manner, shall be construed to include any real estate, or any real estate to which such description shall extend (as the case may be), which he may have power to appoint in any manner he may think proper, and shall operate as an execution of such power, unless a contrary intention shall appear by the will; and in like manner a bequest of the personal estate of the testator, or any bequest of personal property described in a general manner, shall be construed to include any personal estate, or any personal estate to which such description shall extend (as the case may be), which he may have power to appoint in any manner he may think proper, and shall operate as an execution of such power, unless a contrary intention shall appear by the will.

28.– … where any real estate shall be devised to any person without any words of limitation, such devise shall be construed to pass the fee simple, or other the whole estate or interest which the testator had power to dispose of by will in such real estate, unless a contrary intention shall appear by the will.

29.– … in any devise or bequest of real or personal estate the words "die without issue," or "die without leaving issue," or "have no issue," or any other words which may import either a want or failure of issue of any person in his lifetime or at the time of his death, or an indefinite failure of his issue, shall be construed to mean a want or failure of issue in the lifetime or at the time of the death of such person, and not an indefinite failure of his issue, unless a contrary intention shall appear by the will, by reason of such person having a prior estate tail, or of a preceding gift, being, without any implication arising from such words, a limitation of an estate tail to such person or issue, or otherwise: Provided, that this Act shall not extend to cases where such words as aforesaid import if no issue described in a preceding gift shall be born, or if there shall be no issue who shall live to attain the age or otherwise answer the description required for obtaining a vested estate by a preceding gift to such issue.

30.– ... where any real estate (other than or not being a presentation to a church) shall be devised to any trustee or executor, such devise shall be construed to pass the fee simple or other the whole estate or interest which the testator had power to dispose of by will in such real estate, unless a definite term of years, absolute or determinable, or an estate of freehold, shall thereby be given to him expressly or by implication.

31.– ... where any real estate shall be devised to a trustee, without any express limitation of the estate to be taken by such trustee, and the beneficial interest in such real estate, or in the surplus rents and profits thereof shall not be given to any person for life, or such beneficial interest shall be given to any person for life, but the purposes of the trust may continue beyond the life of such person, such devise shall be construed to vest in such trustee the fee simple, or other the whole legal estate which the testator had power to dispose of by will in such real estate, and not an estate determinable when the purposes of the trust shall be satisfied.

[Section 32 has been repealed.]

33.–(1). Where–

(a) a will contains a devise or bequest to a child or remoter descendant of the testator; and

(b) the intended beneficiary dies before the testator, leaving issue; and

(c) issue of the intended beneficiary are living at the testator's death,

then, unless a contrary intention appears by the will, the devise or bequest shall take effect as a devise or bequest to the issue living at the testator's death.

(2) Where–

(a) a will contains a devise or bequest to a class of person consisting of children or remoter descendants of the testator; and

(b) a member of the class dies before the testator, leaving issue, and

(c) issue of that member are living at the testator's death,

then, unless a contrary intention appears by the will, the devise or bequest shall take effect as if the class included the issue of its deceased member living at the testator's death.

(3) Issue shall take under this section through all degrees, according to their stock, in equal shares if more than one, any gift or share which their parent would have taken and so that no issue shall take whose parent is living at the testator's death and that no issue shall take whose parent is living at the testator's death and so capable of taking.

(4) For the purposes of this section–

(a) the illegitimacy of any person is to be disregarded; and

(b) a person conceived before the testator's death and born living thereafter is to be taken to have been living at the testator's death.

34.– … this Act shall not extend to any will made before the first day of January 1838; and every will re-executed or republished, or revived by any codicil, shall for the purposes of this Act be deemed to have been made at the time at which the same shall be so re-executed, republished or revived; and this Act shall not extend to any estate pur autre vie of any person who shall die before the first day of January 1838.

35.– … this Act shall not extend to Scotland.

[Section 36 has been repealed.]

Appendix D

The Chancery Guide

Chapter 24: Probate and Inheritance Claims

Key Rules and PD: CPR Part 57 and PD 57

Probate

24.1 In general, contentious probate proceedings follow the same pattern as an ordinary claim but there are important differences and Part 57 and PD 57 should be carefully studied. Particular regard should be had to the following:

(1) A defendant must file an acknowledgement of service. An additional 14 days is provided for doing so.

(2) Save where the court orders otherwise, the parties must at the outset of proceedings lodge all testamentary documents in their possession and control with the court. At the same time parties must file written evidence describing any testamentary document of the deceased of which they have knowledge, stating, if any such document is not in the party's possession or control, the name and address, if known, of the person in whose possession or under whose control the document is. In the case of a claimant, these materials must be lodged at the time when the Claim Form is issued. In the case of a defendant, these materials must be lodged when service is acknowledged. If these requirements are not complied with it is likely that the claim will not be issued and, correspondingly, that the acknowledgment of service will not be permitted to be lodged.

(3) The court will generally ensure that all persons with any potential interest in the proceedings are joined as parties or served with notice under Part 19.8A.

(4) A default judgment cannot be obtained in a probate claim. Where, however, no defendant acknowledges service or files a defence, the claimant may apply for an order that the claim proceed to trial and seek a direction that the claim be tried on written evidence.

(5) If an order pronouncing for a will in solemn form is sought under Part 24, the evidence in support must include written evidence proving due execution of the will. In such a case, if a defendant has given notice under rule 57.11 that he raises no positive case but requires that the will be proved in solemn form and that, to that end, he wishes to cross examine the attesting witnesses, then the Claimant's application for summary judgment is subject to the right of such a defendant to require the attesting witnesses to attend for cross examination.

(6) A defendant who wishes to do more than test the validity of the will by cross examining the attesting witnesses must set up by Counterclaim his positive

case in order to enable the court to make an appropriate finding or declaration as to which is the valid will, or whether a person died intestate or as the case may be.

(7) The proceedings may not be discontinued without permission. Even if they are compromised, it will usually be necessary to have an order stating to whom the grant is to be made, either under rule 57.11 (leading to a grant in common form), or after a trial on written evidence under paragraph 6.1(1) of PD 57 (leading to a grant in solemn form) or under section 49 of the Administration of Justice Act 1985 and paragraph 6.1(3) of PD 57 (again leading to a grant in solemn form).

24.2 When the court orders trial of a contentious probate claim on written evidence, or where the court is asked to pronounce in solemn form under Part 24, it is normally necessary for an attesting witness to sign a witness statement or swear an affidavit of due execution of any will or codicil sought to be admitted to probate. The will or codicil is at that stage in the court's possession and cannot be handed out of court for use as an exhibit to the witness statement or affidavit, so that the attesting witness has to attend at the Royal Courts of Justice.

24.3 Where an attesting witness is unable to attend the Royal Courts of Justice in order to sign his or her witness statement or swear his or her affidavit in the presence of an officer of the court, the solicitor concerned may request from Room TM7.09, Thomas More Building, a photographic copy of the will or codicil in question. This will be certified as authentic by the court and may be exhibited to the witness statement or affidavit of due execution in lieu of the original. The witness statement or affidavit must in that case state that the exhibited document is an authenticated copy of the document signed in the witness's presence.

24.4 When a probate claim is listed for trial outside London, the solicitor for the party responsible for preparing the court bundle must write to Room TM7.09 and request that the testamentary documents be forwarded to the appropriate District Registry.

Inheritance (Provision for Family and Dependants) Act 1975

24.5 Claims under the Inheritance (Provision for Family and Dependants) Act 1975 in the Chancery Division are issued by way of a Part 8 claim. Ordinarily they will be heard by the Master. [At present they are governed by RSC Order 99, but this is to be replaced by additions to Part 57 and PD 57 before the end of 2002. The following paragraphs describe the procedure as it will be under the new rules.]

24.6 The written evidence filed with such a claim must exhibit an official copy of the grant of probate or letters of administration together with every testamentary document in respect of which probate or letters of administration was granted.

24.7 A defendant must file and serve acknowledgment of service not later than 21 days after service of the Part 8 claim form. Any written evidence (subject to any extension agreed or directed) must likewise be served and filed no later than 21 days after service.

24.8 The personal representatives of the deceased are necessary defendants to a claim under the 1975 Act and the written evidence filed by a defendant who is a personal representative must comply with paragraph 15 of PD 57.

24. 9 On the hearing of a claim under the 1975 Act, the personal representatives must produce the original grant of representation to the deceased's estate. If the court makes an order under the Act, the original grant together with a sealed copy of the order must be sent to the Principal Registry of the Family Division for a memorandum of the order to be endorsed on or permanently annexed to the grant.

24.10 Where claims under the 1975 Act are compromised the consent order lodged must comply with paragraph 9.14 of this Guide.

Index